Amazing
North Carolina

***

Fascinating Facts, Entertaining Tales,
Bizarre Happenings, and
Historical Oddities from the Tar Heel State

T. Jensen Lacey

T. Jensen Lacey

ISBN: 978-1-7342111-0-8
Cover by Michael Ilaqua
www.Cyber-Theorist.com
ANC – 13
Printed in the United States

WWW.MOONHOWLERPUBLISHING.COM
PO BOX 1175, FAIRHOPE, AL 36533

MOON HOWLER PUBLISHING, LLC
P. O. Box 1175
Fairhope, AL 36533

TABLE OF CONTENTS

T. Jensen Lacey

FROM THE GOVERNOR

From the magnificent Blue Ridge mountains to the pristine beaches of the east, North Carolina is full of beauty in its land and in its people. The Tar Heel State boasts some of history's most fascinating and determined individuals and was the birthplace of some of mankind's greatest achievements. It was this determination that first powered flight on the shores of Kitty Hawk.

In *Amazing North Carolina,* author T. Jensen Lacey captures stories and facts that help paint a colorful picture of life in the Old North State.

Governor Roy Cooper

T. Jensen Lacey

PREFACE

After writing this latest edition in what I call my "Amazing America" series, I have to admit I've once again fallen in love with yet another state. That place is called North Carolina. From her breathtaking mountains to her crystalline shores and all places in between, the Tar Heel State is full of wonders. In researching this, the latest edition of the book, I discovered fascinating stories and incredible tales, and also had the great fortune of meeting some of the friendliest people on earth.

Whether they were famous, infamous, or just regular folks, the people of North Carolina that I met caused me to realize that they are what makes the state great. If you live within its borders, you're lucky. If you haven't visited yet, you're missing out on experiencing a state that makes this entire country a wonderful place.

Even if you are a long-time resident of North Carolina, you are sure to read some tale within these pages that will reveal a fascinating tidbit you didn't know before. Read on and discover why North Carolina is a state of endless mystery, beauty, and charm.

T. Jensen Lacey

ACKNOWLEDGMENTS

No project is ever completed by one single individual; the same goes for *Amazing North Carolina*. Here are just some of the "amazing" people I would like to thank for their contributions, patience with my questions, photographs, or expertise, or for just putting me in touch with the right person.

Besides the hundred or so people who were helpful in a myriad of ways, special thanks go to the following: Governor Roy Cooper, for writing the Foreword for this edition; R. J. Grady of Sapphire who looked over the story on the "Outhouse Races," and for sending me those great photos; Greer Beaty and Bill Teague of the North Carolina Department of Commerce for all their help; James Villas and his late mother, Martha Pearl Villas, cookbook authors and North Carolina Personalities, for their "bereavement" recipes; Lee Ann Donnelly and Marissa Jamison for the Biltmore House story.

Thanks to Guy Gaster, Director of the North Carolina Film Commission, for the update on the film industry; Albemarle's Christine Dwyer for the many interesting tidbits and photographs; Rodney Butler with the North Carolina Natural Heritage Program, for information on the Venus flytrap; Jo Langone for the information on the Corolla wild horses; Susan Hartley of the tourism office, Visit Elizabeth City, for the updates on their Ghost Walk tours and the "Rose Buddies"; Rebecca Stiles of The Museum of the Albemarle for help with information about Elizabeth City history; Margaret Martine and Sharon Underwood of Whippoorwill Academy & Village for their help with the Tom Dooley and the Daniel Boone stories (also a big thanks goes to Eden Hamby of the Wilkes Heritage Museum for her additions to the Dooley story). Thanks to Polk State Historic Site Director Scott Warren and Assistant Site Manager Kyle Booker for the update and photos of Pineville-born President James K. Polk.

Keith Price and Betsy Woolridge, docents at the Bostic Lincoln Center, were very helpful with information and insight as to the *real* place of Abraham Lincoln's birth. Lynell Seabold, Director of the Ava Gardner Museum in Smithfield, was helpful with my story on the life of the famous Tar Heel actress. To Erienne Dickman and Alexis Tobias-Jacavone of Edenton, thanks for helping me out with the story on the Roanoke River Lighthouse.

Meghan Minton was a big help in the update on the story of Tweetsie Railroad. James Hickey with the Hot Springs Welcome Center, thanks for your kindness and willingness to help with the update on that story. A big thanks goes to Cathy Steever with the Fort Raleigh National Historic Site for help with the story on the First Freedmen's Colony of Roanoke Island. Sarah Wheat and Elliot Provance of Discovery Place, y'all were awesome to work with.

Calvin Reyes of Henry River Mill Village, you were a delight! Tom Harrison of Plymouth's Bear Fest, you and your staff were amazing and most helpful. Suzanne Brown at VisitNC.com, your help was invaluable. Cynthia Crane, Director of the Fossil Museum in Aurora, I appreciate your help. A special thanks goes to Kathy Prickett, Tourism Specialist, Visit North Carolina, for helping me fill in the proverbial blanks.

For the other hundred or so people who were friendly faces or helpful voices over the phone, thank you all.

Amazing
North Carolina

✳✳✳

Fascinating Facts, Entertaining Tales,
Bizarre Happenings, and
Historical Oddities from the Tar Heel State

T. Jensen Lacey

CHAPTER 1.

Truly Bizarre Events and Notorious North Carolinians

These Brothers Were Really Close!

Born in 1811 to a poor couple in Bangkok, Thailand (then Siam), twin brothers Chang and Eng shared everything. When one got sick, so usually did the other. When one laid down for a nap, his brother followed. When one went for a walk, his brother joined him. The brothers had no choice: Chang and Eng were the original Siamese twins, joined at the chest.

When they were fourteen years old and working as peddlers on the streets of Bangkok, they met a Scottish trader named Robert Hunter, who introduced them to American ship captain Abel Coffin. Coffin saw the marketable possibilities in the pair right away, and smelled money.

Coffin brought Chang and Eng first to Boston, where they were a hit; from there, he exhibited them in New York, then

3

London, where they were invited to tea with the Royal College of Surgeons. For a time, they were part of Phineas T. Barnum's circus.

When they were twenty-one, Chang and Eng parted ways with Coffin and Barnum and decided to tour America on their own, exhibiting themselves for fifty cents. They became U.S. citizens, and took the last name Bunker from a Fred Bunker they had met by chance in the New York Naturalization Office. In 1837 Chang and Eng Bunker's two-man show took them to Wilkesboro.

The twins fell in love with the beauty of the mountains and decided to make their home there. They also met and fell in love with Sarah and Adelaide Yates, the daughters of a Wilkes County farmer. Although it seems the father initially opposed the marriage, finally the four married in the local Baptist Church. Chang married Adelaide, nineteen; Eng married Sarah, who was one year older. The twins' twenty-second birthday was the next month.

They built their homes one mile apart near Mount Airy. When they weren't touring, the brothers had a visitation pattern from which they never varied: they spent three days at Sarah's house, then three days at Adelaide's. The first child—a beautiful boy—was born to Adelaide and Chang. Eng fathered twelve children, and Chang ten.

The twins were not alike in their personalities. Chang enjoyed his drinking, while Eng abhorred the stuff. Chang liked to stay up late, while Eng was more of what we call a "morning person."

Chang's health began to deteriorate following a stroke, after which he began to drink even more heavily, despite his brother's pleas to stop. Finally, in January 1874, Chang's health took a turn for the worse. He came down with bronchitis and although physicians told him to stay in bed, it was time for the brothers to go to Eng and Sarah's home. Eng was reluctant to move Chang (and thereby himself), but Chang insisted.

During the night, Chang's breathing became labored and then his heart stopped beating. When Eng awoke and found his brother dead, he also passed away—some say of fright.

You can see their tombstone where the brothers are buried

When Chang and Eng Bunker's two man show took them to Mt. Airy, they fell in live with the scenery and decided to make it their home.

in the old White Plains Baptist Church, two miles west of Mount Airy, on old U.S. 601. They were joined later by their wives, Sarah and Adelaide. You can learn more about these intriguing twins' lives by visiting the Andy Griffith Museum. Located in the famous actor's hometown of Mt. Airy, the museum, which opened in 2009 and was founded by Emmett Forrest, houses an exhibit showcasing the lives of Chang and Eng Bunker (see "Virtual North Carolina" for websites).

An interesting update to this story is that the Bunker family continues to hold their family reunions in Mt. Airy. I was invited to one a few summers ago when I was in town on a book-signing tour, and never was I treated more warmly. Their family get-togethers have become so well-known, they were featured in *National Geographic* magazine in 2007.

The Unsolved Murder of Beautiful Nell Cropsey

In 2001, Elizabeth City marked the hundredth anniversary of the mysterious death of one of its own southern belles, Nell Cropsey. The story continues to intrigue and confound even the most persistent sleuths—and the home from which she disappeared is reported to be haunted by her spirit.

Elizabeth City is a lovely town in the northeast part of the state, on the banks of Pasquotank River near the Albemarle Sound. Ella Maud Cropsey, known as Nell, was one of the more celebrated beauties of the town, with light brown hair and piercing blue eyes.

She attracted many admirers, and by the time she was eighteen all expected her to make a brilliant marriage and settle down as one of the town's matrons. But this was not to be. Nell had a steady admirer, Jim Wilcox, but as time went on with no marriage proposal, the couple began to have disagreements.

On the night of November 20, 1901, a young man named Roy Crawford called on Nell's sister, Ollie, at the same time Jim called on Nell. Jim and Nell were the first to go to the front porch to say their goodbyes, and when Ollie and Roy came outside to do the same and saw neither of them, Ollie assumed Jim had left and Nell had slipped upstairs to the bedroom the two girls shared. But when Ollie went to their room, Nell wasn't there.

Legend has it that Nell's father, William Cropsey, sat in the back of the house near the kitchen, and so was unaware of these goings-on. When Ollie awoke some time later and reported her sister still absent, neighbors and family set out to search for her. Thirty-seven days later, Nell's body was found in nearly perfect condition floating in the Pasquotank River.

She was carried home and an autopsy conducted in the summer kitchen revealed that Nell had been killed by head trauma. Then the speculations began.

Jim Wilcox said that he and Nell had had a disagreement the last night she was seen alive—as a matter of fact, he said he had broken off the relationship, leaving the young beauty weeping forlornly on the front porch.

The young man denied having seen Nell since he had left her on the porch. The father said he saw and heard nothing that night. Wilcox was jailed under suspicion of murder and guarded by reserves called out by the governor.

A lynch mob came to the jail but was dispersed by Nell's father. Wilcox was tried for the murder in 1902 and sentenced to hang. A mistrial was declared because of public disturbances during the trial; at retrial Wilcox was again convicted and sentenced to thirty years in prison. The Cropsey family left the area, and Nell's sister Ollie went into seclusion.

Tragedy after tragedy hounded the people surrounding Nell and her disappearance. In 1908 Ollie's old beau Roy Crawford shot himself to death. In 1913 Nell's younger brother, Will, ingested poison and died in Norfolk, Virginia.

In 1918, Governor T. Walter Bickett pardoned Wilcox, and although Wilcox and W. O. Saunders (the editor of the Elizabeth City newspaper, the *Independent*) planned to collaborate on a book about the mysterious disappearance and death of Nell, Wilcox kept backing out. In 1934, also for reasons unknown, he committed suicide.

There is still much speculation about the nationally infamous unsolved murder, but Robin Caruso, the current owner of the house, believes the father killed his daughter accidentally.

"The night Nell disappeared and shortly after the suitor had left, her father heard their pigs squealing in the backyard," Caruso told me. "Seeing a figure running in the yard, and thinking it was a pig thief, he shot at the person, striking them in the head. Then, I believe, Nell's father and sister realized it was Nell the father had shot. They brought the stricken girl back in the house, to try to secretly nurse her back to life and health. When they failed and she died, they put her in the river so no one would suspect the father. That explains the nearly perfect condition of the body. In other words, although she had been missing for thirty-seven days, she had only just recently died when her body was discovered in the river."

Today, the house seems to be haunted by the spirit of one whose murder will never be solved. The son of the owner, near in age to Nell at the time of her death, says he has seen her, and others have heard noises and seen objects move in the house.

If you go to Elizabeth City, be sure to see the beautiful homes, walk by the piers and shoreline of Pasquotank River, and enjoy the friendliness of the people and the great seafood.

You cannot tour the home of Nell Cropsey (although it has been open for tours on occasion), but you can drive down Riverside Avenue and see it for yourself. Maybe you'll see Nell's face in a window, perhaps waiting for the suitor who will never come back or for her own murder to be solved, once and for all. Read more about Nell Cropsey in Chapter 16 (Unusual Grave, Ghost and Burial-Site Tales).

"Just Hanging Around" in Caswell County

In the town of Yanceyville you can tour the Old Jail, which has a curious history.

Built in 1906, the Old Jail contains the only remaining hanging cell in the state. When docents open the great iron door to the cell, you can see a hangman's noose and a trapdoor beneath it. That trapdoor is controlled by an iron handle next to the stairs that mount to the floor where the inmates lived. There you'll get chills as you view the bare springs of the iron bunkbeds, the ancient plumbing fixtures, and the stark metal walls displaying graffiti left by prisoners of long ago.

The ironic part is that the hanging cell was never used, as the last public hanging in Caswell County was in 1902 and hanging cells were outlawed while the Old Jail was still under construction. The last ne'er-do-wells inhabited the Old Jail until 1977.

Besides being entertaining, the hanging cell may offer another, more pragmatic value. Parents can show their unruly children the Old Jail, and the sight of the hanging cell with its trapdoor can work wonders on the kids' attitudes.

The "Devil's Tramping Ground"

Ten miles from Siler City in western Chatham County off North Carolina 902 is a strange, uninhabited spot surrounded by trees. It's almost a perfect circle, about forty-four feet in diameter, and barren of vegetation. Siler City residents say that even the birds won't make nests in the trees near the strange circle. It's been like this for more than two hundred years, long enough to become a place of legend. Locals know this privately owned land as the Devil's Tramping Ground.

Some say that nothing grows in this area because Old Beelzebub paces here, night after night, as he plans his mischief for the souls he desires. Others say the place remains bare because it is a sacred place: Native American people are said to have celebrated victories in war or hunting here.

A related story holds that two warring Native American tribes battled here and Chief Croatoan, the leader of one of the tribes, was killed in the fray. The legend further states that he was buried in this circle before his people fled to the coast. There they met with the surviving members of the Lost Colony, and agreed to join forces with them, explaining why the word "Croatoan" was carved on that famous tree in Roanoke (see "The Enduring Mystery and Legacy of Roanoke," in Chapter 7).

A more scientific explanation is that the high salt content of the area has rendered the soil sterile, and a number of soil samples have borne this out. This doesn't explain, however, why sticks placed within the circle are found moved the next day or why hunters' hounds on nighttime forays refuse to go near the area.

Whatever the reason, the circle remains bare, and the cause of this bizarre barrenness remains open to speculation. While the residents of Siler City have told me they would prefer to be famous for something besides being home to the Devil's Tramping Ground, they are friendly people and would welcome you coming to spend your money in town before going out to check the place out for yourself. As of press time, the site is still open to the public, and there is a sign marking the spot. See "Virtual North Carolina" for website information.

The Mysterious Origins of Judaculla Rock

In the town of Cullowhee is a sandstone boulder covered with pictures and prehistoric messages. They have never been deciphered, and although the Cherokee discovered it on their land, the pictographs have never been attributed to any specific tribe or time in history.

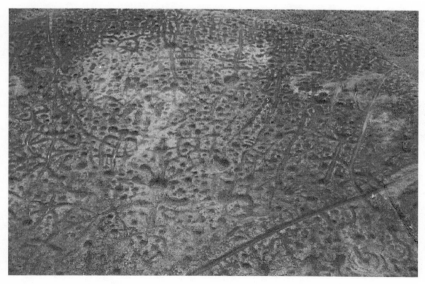

Judaculla Rock

Legend says that the pictographs are actually the footprints of a giant. The Cherokee call him "Tsul'kula," and say that he lived in a mountaintop home here.

There is a newer explanation, however: In August 2002, a group of paranormal researchers based in Asheville (L.E.M.U.R Paranormal Investigations) visited the rock, and have connected the images to, of all things, microbiology and alien life.

The group has ventured a guess that, since the first known viewing of microscopic creatures was in 1674 by a scientist named Anton Van Leeuwenhoek, the symbols in the rocks that eerily resemble amoebas, diatoms, bacteria and other microscopic life forms had to either have been placed there by an earlier, educated civilization...or by alien visitors.

You can go see the footprints—or pictographs, or images resembling microscopic life—for yourself. The mysteriously marked outcropping now known as Judaculla Rock is six miles past the town of Cullowhee, near the intersection of U.S. 441 and Caney Fork Road.

Bath and the Mysterious Hoof prints

About a mile outside the small town of Bath in Beaufort County is one of the greatest unsolved mysteries of North Carolina. If you drive along the Goose Creek State Park Road just off U.S. 264 and wander about two hundred and fifty yards into the forest, you'll find a trail. Near this trail is a series of round, shallow depressions, ranging in size from large saucers to plates. Nothing grows in these strange, barren shapes, which (according to the TV news show, *Tar Heel Traveler*) have been here for roughly 200 years. If the depressions are filled or if things are placed or planted in the holes, the next day they are just as empty and barren as before. A number of possible explanations exist for this strange phenomenon.

The most popular legend holds that one gentleman of Bath was so obsessed with horse racing that he defiantly did so on a Sabbath, saying to his horse as he took off, "Take me in a winner or take me to hell!" The reckless man, Jesse Elliott, was said to be racing the devil himself. Legend further says that, when Elliott looked back to see how far behind the devil was, Elliott's mare was spooked so much that she dug her hooves into the ground. Elliott, however, kept going and was killed instantly when he violently landed against a tree.

Today, visitors by the hundreds go see these mysterious hoof prints. Some locals say the marks are Elliott's horse's hoof prints, made by a horse delivering a "man on his way to hell." The depressions are, indeed, in the pattern that a horse might make.

Whatever the reason for their existence, the mysterious hoof prints of Bath remain, along with the legend handed down by each generation.

Pardoning a Legend

On May 1, 1868, a young man named Tom Dula was hung in Statesville for murder.

To tell the story, we have to go back to just before the Civil War. Young Tom and a girl named Anne Foster were childhood sweethearts. Dula had a reputation for being lively at social gatherings, playing the fiddle, and flirting with the girls. Tall and good-looking, with dark curly hair, he must have stolen many a heart before he became a soldier in the Civil War.

The war separated him from Anne. While scores of women waited for their husbands and beaus to return, Dula came home to find Anne married to a man named James Melton. Then Dula began courting Anne's cousin, Laura Foster.

As time went on, although he and Laura were regarded as a couple, Dula couldn't deny the love he and Anne still felt for each other. He began visiting another cousin of Anne's, Pauline Foster, who was their accomplice in helping Anne and Tom see each other. The plot thickened when Laura realized she was expecting Tom's child.

The Gravestone of Laura Foster, murdered in 1865

In May 1866 neighbors saw Laura riding her father's horse toward the ridge (now called Laura's Ridge) where she and Tom often met—and it was the last time anyone saw her alive. When the riderless horse returned home, Laura's father and others began searching for her.

Laura's body was found; it was determined she had been stabbed to death. Hearing the news and realizing he was the prime suspect, Dula fled to Trade, Tennessee, where he stayed with a man named Colonel James W. M. Grayson under the assumed name of Hall. Meanwhile, Pauline blurted out her role in the affair. Anne was also implicated.

Officials found Tom through Grayson; the young man was then extradited to Wilkes and tried for Laura's murder. He was convicted and again found guilty after his appeal resulted in another trial.

At age twenty-two, Tom was sentenced to hang in Statesville. The night before his hanging, he scrawled in pencil a single sentence to save Anne from sharing his fate: "I declare that I am the only person that had any hand in the murder of Laura Foster." Next morning, as he stood by the

Tom Dula's Grave Marker

gallows, Dula declared his innocence in the murder. Legend says his famous last words were, "I am only guilty of loving two women."

The sentence was carried out in front of three thousand witnesses on May 1, 1868. Tom's sister, Anna, brought the body to the family homestead in Elkville (now Ferguson), and buried him in a coffin made by her husband. Tom rests near a bend in the Yadkin River close to the intersection of North Carolina 1134 and 268 West, near the Caldwell County line. A historical marker is near the spot where he is laid in his final resting place. And, in case you were wondering, Tom's sweetheart, Anne Foster, lived to a ripe old age. But that's not the end of the story.

In North Wilkesboro, a playwright named Karen Wheeling Reynolds began writing about the legend of Tom Dula. As she continued her research, Reynolds became intrigued about the trial and the lack of evidence against Tom, and the fact that Dula professed his innocence even up to the moment of his hanging. The playwright spoke with other townspeople about her increasing conviction that Dula was innocent. When she was finished, the play she wrote, *Tom Dooley: A Wilkes County Legend*, had picked up so much interest and momentum in the community that it sold out twelve performances before it opened in July 2001. ("Dooley" is the local pronunciation of the name "Dula.")

Locals began to think it was time to reconsider the case and have Dula pardoned. Ken Welborn, publisher of the local newspaper, *The Record*, went so far as to secure the services of a local law firm to start the paper trail. McElwee Law Firm wrote a petition asking for Dula's posthumous pardon from then-Governor Mike Easley.

The town's mayor, Conley Call, issued a proclamation in July 2001 asking people to sign the petition, which was forwarded to the governor's office in Raleigh. Wilkesboro residents held a month-long celebration of their history and heritage in July 2002, calling it "Dooley Days." This event, which includes the performance of the play, is now an annual occurrence.

Reynolds believes Laura's murder will remain a mystery. "I believe people are not comfortable with what happened, and that's why even after all this time, there is still this interest in getting him pardoned," she says. "I don't think he'd write a confession one night, then tell a lie at the gallows. And Pauline wasn't a credible witness and didn't have to back up what she told the authorities."

The tragic story of Tom Dula was retold in quite a few songs. One, recorded by the Kingston Trio in 1958, includes the lyrics "hang down your head, Tom Dooley," and caused a surge of interest in folk music. As of press time (2022), there was no pardon forthcoming from the governor's office, but if Dula ever is pardoned, then maybe the Kingston Trio will sing a slightly different song about Tom.

The story of Tom Dula continues to intrigue the citizens of Wilkes County. Wilkesboro resident Seth Cohn went so far as to open a restaurant capitalizing on the tale of Tom Dula. When it opened in 2014, Dooley's Tavern & Grill was an instant success. General Manager Sheila Sisneros told me, "Virtually every item on our menu is named for one of the characters in the tragic tale. For example, we have a sandwich called 'Laura Foster's French Dip', which is a big seller. And both our graphic design of our t-shirts and the icon on our menu has an image of a hanging tree complete with a noose hanging from a branch." Wilkesboro celebrates and remembers Tom Dula at two other places: Whippoorwill Academy and Village, a living history museum, has their own Tom Dooley Museum on the grounds and celebrates "Tom Dooley Days" every other year (the opposite year finds them celebrating the Daniel Boone Festival); and the Wilkes Heritage Museum is home to the actual jail cell which housed the luckless man before his hanging (they also offer Candlelight Ghost Tours from time to time, and visitors swear they can hear the clanking of Dooley's chains in the cell). The

Wilkes Playmakers now have their performances of the play every year, beginning in June (see "Virtual North Carolina" for websites).

Yet another "strange but true" footnote to this story is about a friend of Tom's who served with Dula during the Civil War. Named Joseph Blevins, after the war was over, he became a journalist for the *New York Herald*. Strangely enough, one of his first assignments was to cover Dula's trial and hanging!

Before Viagra, There Was "Goat Gland" Brinkley

John Romulus Brinkley was a native of Jackson County, born near the end of the 1800s. Always believing he was destined for greatness, he set his sights on making a name for himself in the world of medicine and undertook the study of the healing arts—by mail. In 1911 he was granted the title of "undergraduate doctor" by the North Carolina Board of Medical Examiners and went on to earn his medical degree by mail from the Eclectic Medical University of Kansas City.

Most medical boards were loath to grant Brinkley a medical license with such a dubiously earned degree, but Brinkley finally found that the state of Arkansas would honor a medical diploma from Eclectic. Once Arkansas granted him a license, other states followed suit, and he gathered licenses to practice medicine in Texas, Connecticut, and Kansas. By 1917 Brinkley was practicing medicine in Milford, Kansas.

Still searching for a way to make his name a household word, Brinkley began reading about how ancient peoples revered the goat as the most sexually potent of all animals, and also of old legends in which goat-like men mated with human women.

He announced to the world that he had discovered a way to transplant goat testicles to men, thereby increasing men's virility and potency. After a childless man from Wakefield impregnated his wife following the procedure, Brinkley's bizarre operation became his own pot of gold.

Patients lined up for the surgical procedure, each paying the required $200, and Brinkley was obliged to build a fifty-bed hospital on borrowed funds. The price of goat testicles rose to $1,500 a pair; still more patients filled the hospital beds, awaiting their own miracles. Shortly after 1921, however, the American Medical Association stepped in and charged Brinkley with fraud and "gross immorality." They took away his Arkansas license, but Brinkley quickly moved to Mexico, where he established a radio station, WXER. He used the station to garner even more fans (and funds), answering medical questions on the air for a small fee. Those "small fees" poured in, making Brinkley even wealthier. By the time the inevitable lawsuits occurred, Brinkley had amassed a fortune of more than $10 million.

Before the U.S. courts in San Antonio could take action against Brinkley for medical fraud, he ran for the U.S. Senate. Although Brinkley's name has all but disappeared from historical annals, this story has one more strange twist. In this particular Senate race, Brinkley was beaten by a man whose name later became synonymous with Texas history: Lyndon B. Johnson.

By the way, if you'd like to see what the *legal* practice of medicine was like way back in the day, look no further than The Country Doctor Museum in Bailey (roughly 45 minutes from Raleigh). Established in 1967, the museum takes visitors back in time to more than 100 years ago. Visitors can take docent-led tours, and see how doctors performed bloodletting, amputations, dental and other medical procedures. Just seeing the dentistry tools can give you the creeps! Curator Matthew Bisette can happily describe how doctors used leeches to "cure" a variety of blood-borne illnesses. It's worth the trip—and will make you more than appreciative of how far medicine has come! See "Virtual North Carolina" for website information.

The Haunting of the Double-wides

You can hear many stories about beautiful mansions haunted because they were built over Native American burial grounds, or because someone died under tragic circumstances there before the new and naive owners bought it. But what about the poltergeists of the trailer parks?

Comedian and musician Larry Weaver of Chapel Hill claims that, yes, ghosts do indeed haunt mobile homes and trailer parks. Weaver's album, *Looking for Fun,* features the song "Ghost in the Trailer" about a family terrorized by a "redneck ghost." His website, www.larryweaver.com, includes warning signs to look for, such as moving eyes in the velvet Elvis painting or the trailer shaking with no tornado in sight. On the job, if Nehi strawberry soda comes out of the coffee machine, you can assume your trailer ghost has accompanied you to work! If you think you may be haunted by a redneck ghost, don't worry—Weaver offers trailer-ghost-busting kits via his website.

Fascinated with the Unexplained? Check Out This Museum

The town of Littleton has a museum that is sure to fascinate you. Known as "The Cryptozoology & Paranormal Museum," the owner, Stephen Barcelo, says he bought the property because he was warned that it was haunted.

The Cryptozoology & Paranormal Museum

For those of you who need a refresher, a cryptozoologist is anyone interested in legendary creatures, such as Sasquatch. There are plenty of "Bigfoot" foot imprints to be found in this museum, along with haunted dolls, Bigfoot statues and many artifacts relating to the paranormal. The museum is host to "Bigfoot in the Park," whereby visitors to Hollister's Medoc Mountain State Park may catch a glimpse of Bigfoot (there are said to be numerous such sightings in this park). In addition to hosting ghost walks through Littleton's Historic District, every spring the museum also hosts the town's Crypto Paranormal Festival.

Barcelo said that since he opened his museum, it has been featured in such television shows as The Travel Channel and PBS specials. The town has embraced the museum, and its Bigfoot icon: one restaurant, Littleton Food & Spirits, has as one of its daily specials a Bigfoot Burger. See "Virtual North Carolina" for website information.

DID YOU KNOW?

According to the Bigfoot Field Researcher Organization based in California (that was founded in the early 1970s), North Carolina ranks 17th in the U.S. for Bigfoot sightings. Most of these sightings have occurred in the Uwharrie National Forest, Montgomery County. There are groups of Bigfoot seekers who go out on overnight excursions, hoping to catch a glimpse of the elusive creature!

"Normie," Lake Norman's Monster

About 13 miles from Huntersville lies Lake Norman, a manmade lake which has been a haven for swimmers, anglers, skiers and boaters. Created in 1963, the lake has also been home to a mysterious monster that locals have affectionately dubbed "Normie."

The creature, said to resemble anything from an overgrown alligator to a red-eyed catfish or even a huge salamander known as a "hellbender," has reportedly harassed boaters, scuba-divers and skiers. The monster has been investigated on such TV series as "Monster Fish" and "Boogeymen." What Normie really is remains a mystery.

When Blackbeard Terrorized the Coast

The most feared and notorious pirate ever to be seen off North Carolina's shoreline was the Bristol-born, bloodthirsty Blackbeard (his given name may have been Edward Teach or Edward Drummond). He and his crew stole a French merchant's ship, outfitted it for piracy (complete with forty cannons), and renamed it the *Queen Anne's Revenge*. This became his flagship and the beginning of his diabolical fleet. The sight of Blackbeard's ship and his countenance alone put many a captain and crew of a mind to give way, and with good reason.

Accounts agree that Blackbeard was a big man, with long black hair and a scraggly, ebony-colored beard. Blackbeard was perhaps one of the first to use psychological warfare in battle, and intimidation was a big part of his success. Before boarding another ship, he would light slow-burning artillery fuses, which he had braided into his beard. The sight of the tall, swarthy figure mounting their gunwales, his beard and grim countenance surrounded with smoke and sparks, filled many a crew member with dread. Often ships' crews surrendered without so much as a skirmish.

He was a ferocious fighter, once going up against a thirty-nine-gun British man o' war—a daring, reckless act, which few other pirates would attempt. By the early 1700s, Blackbeard and his fierce crew had acquired a squadron of vessels and continued to torment the merchants plying the waters of the Atlantic between Europe and the Carolinas. Blackbeard's favorite haunt was the area around Ocracoke Island, on the Outer Banks. It was within striking distance of the rich port of Charleston, which allowed Blackbeard to continue his friendship with Charles Eden, the governor of

North Carolina. Eden pardoned Blackbeard for extortion, after which the pirate wedded a sixteen-year-old girl (some say this was his eleventh wife, others say she was number thirteen) and temporarily settled down in the coastal town of Bath.

In Virginia, Governor Alexander Spotswood was angered at Blackbeard's coddling and decided to offer British sailors the chance to wreak revenge on the "Terror of the Black Flag." In November 1718 Spotswood sent Lieutenant Robert Maynard and a squadron of ships to sail to Ocracoke to attack the pirate. Blackbeard and his crew tried to flee, then fought. For many crew members, including the infamous pirate, it was a fight to the death. (Note: Blackbeard's famous ship, *Queen Anne's Revenge*, has been discovered and is being salvaged. You can read about in "Lost and Found: The *Queen Anne's Revenge*," which is in Chapter 11.)

Blackbeard received twenty-five wounds that day and literally lost his head. When Maynard sailed back to Virginia, he had the pirate's decapitated head on the ship's bowsprit. Although piracy continued along the Atlantic seaboard, the death of the most infamous pirate of all time was the beginning of the end of piracy.

You can learn more about Blackbeard and the life of pirates at several museums in the Tar Heel State. One in Beaufort is the North Carolina Maritime Museum; a second is the Graveyard of the Atlantic Museum on Hatteras Island; a third is the North Carolina Maritime Museum at Southport. But the one in Ocracoke may beat 'em all: it's Teach's Hole, which claims to have the largest collection of pirate paraphernalia of any other museum (more than 2,000 pieces when last I checked). See "Virtual North Carolina" for website information.

When You "Gotta Go," You Go to Sapphire

Every year in February, when snow-skiing is beginning to wind down a bit, the Sapphire Valley Ski Resort hosts a skiing race. It's not just any race: this race is one in which the participants ski down a snowy slope, wearing not just skis, but *inside* a homemade outhouse. The Great Outhouse Races,

Sapphire outhouse races.

as they are now called, gives everyone a fun break from the

usual winter entertainment, and the North Carolina Tour Guide says that participants are "flush" with excitement. It's all for a good cause: the proceeds from the race always go to a local charity. See "Virtual North Carolina" for website information.

The Mysterious Murder of a "Scalawag"

In the town of Yanceyville on May 21, 1870, John Walter "Chicken" Stephens was murdered in the backroom of the Caswell County Courthouse (he was previously given the derogatory nickname "chicken" because of an argument he'd had with a neighbor over a "trespassing chicken" he'd taken as his own). Referred to by his peers as "a notorious scalawag," he had a reputation for being politically manipulative and inflammatory and was hated by such a great number of Caswell County residents that the identity of the assailant was a mystery. At the time of the murder, many people were milling around at the courthouse, so more than two hundred people were held in the county jail that summer as suspects for the crime. (This may be the record for the greatest number of suspects ever held in jail for a single murder.) So many people were suspected of the murder that the town was in chaos.

When he became aware of this, then-governor William H. Holden declared martial law and sent Colonel George W. Kirk to the town to restore its usual ambience of civility (this is now recorded in the history books as the Kirk-Holden War). According to Yanceyville historian Sallie Anderson, although no one was ever definitely named as the killer, the murder was believed to have been the work of members of the Ku Klux Klan. Other sources such as one on the life of John

Stephens says that the leader of the Ku Klux Klan by the name of John G. Lea confessed (in a written statement) to the crime, but asked that the confession be sealed until his death. When he died in 1935, the confession was unsealed (you can read it on an official site of the North Carolina Historical Commission—see Virtual North Carolina at the back of the book).

Today, you can take a tour of the courthouse and see the room where the murder occurred. You can also see Chicken Stephens's pistol, taken from him at the time of the murder, on display at the Richmond-Miles Historical Museum, also in Yanceyville.

If You Still Want to See Something Bizarre…

There's a museum in Wilmington that you won't want to miss. The Museum of the Bizarre, owned and curated by Justin Lanosa, has a plethora of exhibits that will give you chills. He says after he got married, he began moving strange objects that he'd acquired over the years from his home to what is now his museum in downtown Wilmington. The exhibits range from the interesting (such as a Bigfoot imprint) to the creepy (such as the clown) to the ghastly (such as train engineer's Joe Baldwin's legendary lantern (see more about him in the Q&A below). Holding the lantern is a headless, bloody mannequin, wearing period clothes a train engineer might have worn. See "Virtual North Carolina" for website information.

Brown Mountain Lights: An Enduring Mystery

Brown Mountain lies within the Pisgah National Forest, and for more than a hundred years, has been the source of speculation and mystery. It is here that strange lights appear and disappear with irregularity and have never been satisfactorily explained.

The U.S. government has thrice investigated the cause of the strange lights, to no avail. Students at Appalachian University have researched the possible source of the lights. Researchers delved into the mystery of the lights and featured their investigation in an episode of *The X-Files* in 1999.

Some say that the lights are the ghosts of Indian maidens, who use torches to seek their loved ones who died in a battle on the mountain. Others say that they might be the lights of alien spaceships.

Along this theme, a movie, "Alien Abduction," was filmed in 2014 by Matty Beckerman, who learned of the lights when visiting his grandparents in Blowing Rock. The movie premiered in Morganton, and today a business in town is offering guided tours to try and see the lights.

If you want to try and see the lights for yourself, there are a number of venues. Milepost 310 (north of Linville Falls) on the Blue Ridge Parkway has a marked viewing place at the Lost Cove Overlook. About twelve miles north of Morganton, NC Highway 181 has a Brown Mountain overlook. Wisemans View is an overlook that also offers a wonderful view of Linville Gorge.

Q&A

Q. What world record is held by Hendersonville twins Billy and Benny McCrary?

A. They were the world's largest twins, one weighing 743 and the other weighing 723 pounds. Billy died from injuries during a mini-bike stunt in 1979; Benny, of heart failure, in 2001. Their tombstone is also the world's largest granite gravestone—you can see it in the cemetery at Crab Creek Baptist Church, Hendersonville.

Q. What curiosity in the Belhaven Memorial Museum must be viewed with a magnifying glass?

A. The "flea wedding," complete with a tiny church and dried-up fleas dressed in full wedding regalia.

Q. What town has a "ghost light," said to be the spirit of lantern-wielding Joe Baldwin, a train engineer who was beheaded in an accident in 1867?

A. Maco. The light is called Maco Railroad Light or simply Maco Light.

Q. What stuffed animal can you find in the Fireman's Museum in New Bern?

A. Fred the fire horse. When he died on the job (pulling a hose-wagon) in 1925, the firefighters decided to have him stuffed. Fred is now on display in the museum.

Q. Where was the world's first university-based parapsychology laboratory established?

A. At Duke University in 1927, by Dr. Joseph B. Rhine, who is now regarded as the "Father of Parapsychology."

Q. What small building in Salvo holds (nearly) a national record?

A. The post office. At 8 x 12 feet, it's the second smallest in America, beat only by the Ochopee, Florida post office, measuring 7 x 8 feet.

Q. What was the name of the "emergency hospital" hurriedly constructed in 1945 in Catawba County in response to a polio epidemic?

A. The "Miracle of Hickory."

CHAPTER 2

Politics, Transportation & Military Tales

Abraham Lincoln: Tar Heel by Birth?

Some people in Rutherford County insist that "Honest Abe" was *not* born in Kentucky but took his first breath in Bostic. Here's the story—honest!

In Rutherford County around the latter part of the eighteenth century, a woman named Lucy Hanks made her living by spinning for local families, and she bore two daughters, Mandy and Nancy. Unable to provide for them herself, Lucy Hanks put her daughters in the care of local families. Nancy was placed with a farmer-teacher named Abraham Enloe and his wife.

Tom Melton stands beside the historical marker in Bostic that states 'Honest Abe' was born not in Kentucky, but in Rutherford County, North Carolina. (Courtesy Mike Felton)

Not long after the turn of the century, Enloe and his family moved to a farm near the banks of the Oconaluftee River. At the time, unbeknownst to everyone, Nancy was in, as they say euphemistically, "the family way." When the situation became apparent, Abraham Enloe's wife was understandably upset.

Nancy disappeared for a few months and when she returned, she brought along her newborn baby boy. Enloe made an offer to an itinerant laborer, Tom Lincoln: take a team of horses with all the accoutrements, some money, Nancy and her son; marry her and move to Kentucky.

Apparently, this was an offer Tom couldn't refuse. The result? Although the history books claim that Abe Lincoln was born near Hodgenville, Kentucky, Rutherford Countians say Abe was born on *their* soil and that he was named after his biological father, Abraham Enloe.

People who lived in Rutherford County around 1809 (when Abraham Lincoln was born) swore that Nancy had returned to the old Enloe home place to give birth, and that they had seen her and her baby there. The story was further borne out by J. C. Coggins, a Rutherford County–based legislator and teacher, who in 1920 wrote a book entitled *Abraham Lincoln: A North Carolinian with Proof.*

Back in 2003, when I first was doing research for that edition of this book, I met a man named Tom Melton. Tom Melton, a resident of Bostic in Rutherford County, believed he had found the remains of the old Enloe place and the *true* site of Honest Abe's birth. Back then, for the price of lugging a stone to the site (to further mark the historic place), this former principal and teacher led me down a path through the woods along the banks of Puzzle Creek. There I could see the remains of an old stone cellar, all that is left of what locals, even today, claim to be Lincoln's true birthplace.

Today, the people of Bostic have bought into the idea that "honest Abe" was born a Tar Heel, and there are more places to go and learn about it. People still hike the trail to get to the remains of Lincoln's birthplace, which is now called "Lincoln Hill." If you don't have the time for a hike in the woods, you can more easily see the plaque commemorating what is said to be Lincoln's true birthplace. In 2000 the Historical Society of Rutherford County erected a granite plaque at the intersection of Walker Mill Road and Bostic "Sunshine" Highway (N.C. 106). The plaque reads:

Traditional Birthplace of Abraham Lincoln

The Sixteenth President of the United States

One Mile East

To further commemorate and promote the story of Lincoln's true birthplace, the citizens of Bostic began working on building The Bostic Lincoln Center. The Center was established to, in the words of their website, "...preserve, study, prepare and make visitor-friendly the traditional birthplace" of Honest Abe. Tom Melton (who passed away in

2008) was the visionary behind all this, and now the Bostic Lincoln Center is located at 112 Depot Street, and is open Thursday, Friday and Saturday (with donations gratefully accepted). Richard Eller and Jerry Goodnight, who co-authored the book, *The Tarheel Lincoln*, say that interest is growing by the day to prove that the 16th president was born in Bostic. Currently, there is a petition people are signing at the Center to try and have DNA testing done of the Lincoln cabin remains. "If DNA evidence proves this to be Lincoln's true birthplace," said Center docent Keith Price, "it will alter American history." DNA evidence or not, the citizens of Bostic celebrate Lincoln as one of their own: every April they hold their annual "Bostic Lincoln Spring Festival." See "Virtual North Carolina" for website information.

Why the Name "Tar Heel"?

Various reasons explain why the people of the Old North State are nicknamed "Tar Heels." Here are the two most persistent.

The principal products during the state's early days— turpentine, pitch, and tar—came from the great numbers of pine trees within its borders. As processors worked with these substances, they got them on the soles of their shoes.

The second story, however, is to me much more entertaining. Legend holds that during the Civil War the fiercest fighters hailed from North Carolina. In one battle, Union forces drove back the forces supporting the North Carolina troops, but the North Carolina soldiers stood their ground. When General Robert E. Lee heard of what had happened, and that the North Carolina soldiers had held fast as though they had "tar on their heels," Lee is said to have commented, "God bless the Tar Heel boys."

North Carolinians have proudly called themselves by that moniker ever since.

DID YOU KNOW?

Among the thirteen colonies, North Carolina was the first to vote for independence from England. North Carolina became the first colony to declare its complete independence from Britain in 1776 in the document entitled "The Halifax Resolves," drawn up after the Battle of Moore's Creek Bridge.

Official State Symbols

Here are some of the state symbols of North Carolina, and the year the General Assembly made them official:

State Symbol   Year

Flower: Dogwood   1941

Bird: Cardinal (or Winter Redbird)   1943

Toast: "The Old North State"   1957

Tree: Pine   1963

Shell: Scotch Bonnet (bo-NAY)   1965

Mammal: Gray Squirrel   1969

Fish: Channel Bass   1971

Precious Stone: Emerald   1973

Insect: Honeybee   1973

Reptile: Turtle   1979

Rock: Granite   1979

Historic Boat: Shad Boat   1987

Beverage: Milk   1987

Dog: Plott Hound   1989

Vegetable: Sweet Potato   1995

Fruit: Scuppernong Grape   2001

Berries: Strawberry and Blueberry   2001

Carnivorous Plant: Venus Flytrap   2005

Christmas Tree: Fraser Fir   2005

State Dance: Clogging   2005

(Freshwater) Trout: Southern

   Appalachian Brook Trout   2005

State Birthplace of Traditional Pottery:

   Seagrove   2005

Wildflower: Carolina Lily   2003

Hail To The "Vertically Challenged" Chief!

The tune "Hail to the Chief" was first played at the inauguration ceremony of Martin Van Buren in 1837. Sarah Childress Polk, however, is said to be the person responsible for the tune being played every time the president enters a room. She started this during the presidency of her husband, Pineville-born James K. Polk, who took office in 1844.

President Polk was five feet, six inches, not particularly tall for a man. As a result, his entry often went unnoticed, and this annoyed Sarah. She had the White House band play "Hail to the Chief" so everyone in the room would take note of her husband's entry.

Every president since then (vertically challenged or not) has continued with this musical tradition.

During the Presidency of James K. Polk, Sarah Polk is said to have initiated the playing of 'Hail to the Chief' every time the President entered the room. (Library of Congress)

Here are the words, so now you can sing along.

Hail to the Chief

Hail to the Chief we have chosen for the nation,

Hail to the Chief! We salute him, one and all.

Hail to the Chief, as we pledge cooperation

In proud fulfillment of a great, noble call.

38

Yours is the aim to make this country grander,

This you will do, that's our strong, firm belief.

Hail to the one we selected as commander,

Hail to the President! Hail to the Chief!

—Words by Albert Gamse; music by James Sanders

Incidentally, you can tour the President James K. Polk Historic Site near Pineville (Mecklenburg County) if you want to get a feel of his early days. Hum the tune as you stroll the grounds; Polk would've liked that.

GUESS WHO?

In 1824, four men ran for the office of President of the United States: William Crawford of Georgia, John Quincy Adams of Massachusetts, Henry Clay of Kentucky, and a North Carolinian. The Tar Heel candidate won the most popular and electoral votes but lacked the majority of electoral votes mandated by the Constitution. So, the decision went to the House of Representatives, who chose Adams. When Adams appointed Clay as the new Secretary of State, the Tar Heel candidate suspected the two had "rigged" the election. Four years of bitter accusations of corruption followed, but in 1828 the North Carolina man did become president.

This man was Andrew Jackson. Incidentally, this rift helped lead to the dual-party system, with Jackson, John C. Calhoun, and Martin Van Buren forming the Democratic Party, and Adams and Clay referred to as National Republicans.

Andrew Jackson

You can learn more about the 7th President of the United States at the Museum of the Waxhaws and Andrew Jackson Memorial in Waxhaw, NC., located near the North Carolina-South Carolina border. See "Virtual North Carolina" for website information.

Power of the Written (and Read) Word

The little boy had nearly always felt inferior to kids his own age because of his secret. He dreaded anyone ever calling upon him to read, much less write, because both were nearly impossible for him. Born in Raleigh in 1808 to impoverished parents, Jacob and Mary McDonough Johnson, his life took a turn for the worse when his father died. Although his mother remarried, the family remained poor, and at the age of ten, he was apprenticed to work in a tailor shop.

He was seventeen years old and well accomplished with needle and thread when the family moved to Greeneville, Tennessee. There he eventually set up his own tailor shop, but he remained illiterate.

Then the young man met a sixteen-year-old girl, Eliza McCardle. She fired his imagination with not only love but ambition. Eliza was well read, and after the two married in 1827, she began teaching her husband to read. Night after night, when the tailor shop was closed and the chores were done, he labored over book and paper, learning to read and write.

Eliza taught her husband well, and he embarked on a political career that took him from mayor of the town to governor of Tennessee, then vice president to Abraham Lincoln. After Lincoln's assassination, he became the seventeenth president of the United States—Andrew Johnson.

You can visit Johnson's birthplace located at Mordecai Historic Park in Raleigh. The home—which is actually part of a complex, which includes a law office, a chapel, a kitchen garden and more—is open for tours. See "Virtual North Carolina" for website information.

The Infamous Misadventures of Nolichucky Jack

In the formative years of the United States, there were thirteen original states. But there was a fourteenth that no one would accept into the Union. This state went by the name Free Republic of Franklin, and its governor was a notorious politician—John Sevier, a man everyone knew as Nolichucky Jack because his home was near the Nolichucky River.

The Free Republic of Franklin existed for four short years (1784–1788), but during that time its existence and its governor's antics caused a great deal of political controversy and intrigue. Nolichucky Jack was for a time tempted to sign a treaty with Spain, a move that would have been disastrous for the still-emerging United States, and came close to declaring war against North Carolina—but that's getting ahead of the story.

The land in question was once a part of North Carolina. In the early 1780s, North Carolina's borders extended clear to the

Mississippi River, but this didn't last long. After the Revolutionary War, many North Carolinians settled in the western boundaries of the then-wilderness lands of the Tar Heel State. Many of those settlers then demanded that the government of North Carolina defend them from hostile natives and roving outlaws. Others in the state, however, were of the mind that those settlers were little better than the outlaws from which they demanded protection. Something had to be done, and Governor Alexander Martin was just the one to do it.

At Martin's urging, the North Carolina Assembly ceded the western lands back to the Continental Congress, for them to take care of the problems. This raised the ire of Nolichucky Jack. Already known as a fighting man who had made a name for himself in the Battle of Kings Mountain during the War for Independence, he rounded up a few like-minded independent types and in 1784 they held a secession convention. They declared three of North Carolina's counties—Greene, Sullivan, and Washington—to be independent. They held a constitutional convention and named the newly seceded counties the Free Republic of Franklin, after Benjamin Franklin. Nolichucky Jack was elected governor.

Nolichucky Jack (Wikipedia)

Martin was infuriated at this political and geographical impertinence. He said this was akin to treason and sent word to Jack that he would send troops to reclaim the counties as North Carolina's own. Jack responded in kind, saying he would (and could) quickly raise an army to defend this new republic.

To add to the chaos, a representative of the new republic, William Cooke, arrived at the 1785 meeting of the Continental Congress, presenting Franklin's petition for statehood. After the North Carolina delegation caught its collective breath, it hotly debated such insurrection. A vote was taken, which fell short by two for the republic to become admitted to the Union.

The unendorsed and unofficial Free Republic of Franklin endured an increasing amount of chaos. For one thing, there was nothing to back Franklin's currency and the settlers were obliged to barter for what they needed. Meanwhile, the North Carolina Assembly tried to entice the people to return to the geographic fold by offering to waive all back taxes owed. Then Spain tried to get Jack to cooperate in forming colonies in America (he declined).

Written records were confusing if not worthless. Marriage licenses, land transactions, judicial decisions, and more were duplicated or reversed, because North Carolina officials continued in these capacities even as the Franklinite officials issued their own documents.

Finally, in November 1787, Congress handed down a decision that the original claimant to a territory (in this case, North Carolina) could grant or deny statehood to a territory within it that was petitioning for admission to the Union. Naturally, North Carolina chose not to grant statehood to

Franklin, and the military of North Carolina seemed ready to swarm down on the Franklinites. Jack petitioned Spain for help, but before Spain could respond, a Tar Heel named John Tipton and a group of law enforcement men invaded Franklin, arrested Jack, and put him in jail. No sooner was he in jail than some of Jack's buddies from Franklin "busted him out" again and took him back home.

Finally Jack and his Franklinites saw the futility in continuing with such a political tug-of-war. They surrendered and stood trial. Their punishment? They all had to take the Oath of Allegiance to the State of North Carolina.

When everything was calm again, the land that had been the Free Republic of Franklin was renamed the "Territory of the United States of America South of the Ohio River." From this came a new state, which we know today as Tennessee.

Its first governor? John Sevier, or Nolichucky Jack. I'd say he got what he wanted in the end. Incidentally, you can explore and learn more about North Carolina's early days at the North Carolina Museum of History in downtown Raleigh, which has also earned the distinctive honor of becoming a Smithsonian Affiliate. See "Virtual North Carolina" for website information.

Two "Rights" and a Wrong Choice

During the election year of 1844, Henry Clay came to Raleigh, campaigning for the office of president. As a candidate, he was very popular; thousands came to hear him give a speech at the state capitol. At the time, Texas was being considered for statehood, which Clay vehemently opposed.

Under the shade of an oak tree, Clay wrote what Raleigh historians refer to as "Clay's famous Texas letter." His letter warned that if the United States admitted Texas into the Union, the country would end up at war with Mexico. His advisors told him not to send the letter to the media, saying it would cost him the presidency. He is said to have retorted, "I would rather be right than president!" and mailed the letter.

He and his advisors both were right. The United States annexed Texas in 1845, went to war with Mexico the following year—and Clay lost the presidential race to James K. Polk, a North Carolinian.

The oak tree, dubbed "Henry Clay's oak," was later lost to disease, but the spot in downtown Raleigh where Clay wrote the famous letter is marked with a stone plaque.

Senator Jesse Helms's Secret for Longevity?

Forget health food stores when you're thinking about ways to live longer and better. The late Senator Jesse Helms claimed to be long-lived (he died in 2008 just before his 87th birthday) because of what was served in the Senate Cafeteria. *Slate* magazine attributed Helms's energy and longevity to this "famous Senate Bean Soup."

Senate Bean Soup

2 pounds dried navy beans (pea beans)
4 quarts hot water
1 ½ pounds smoked ham hocks
1 onion, chopped
2 tablespoons butter
Salt and pepper to taste

Wash and run hot water through the beans until they are slightly whitened. Place the beans in a large pot with the hot water. Add ham hocks and boil for 3 hours. Set aside to cool. Dice the ham and return to the soup. Lightly brown the chopped onion in butter and add to the soup. Before serving, bring to a boil, then season with salt and pepper. Serves 8.

STRANGE BUT TRUE! THE GUBERNATORIAL GHOST

North Carolina is chock-full of ghosts and their stories; that even goes for the governor's mansion. When I was writing the first edition for this book in 2002, Raleigh historian Parker Call told me the ghost is believed to be the spirit of Governor Daniel Fowle, the first governor to live in the mansion. When he moved into the mansion, Fowle brought his own furniture into it, including his bed.

"Unfortunately," Parker Call told me back then, "he only lived in the mansion three months before he died, but his bed remained in the house. In the 1960s, when Bob Scott became governor, he was a large man and couldn't sleep in that bed. He had it moved to another bedroom in the mansion and replaced it with a larger bed to accommodate his size." Call told me that it was after Fowle's bed was moved that the mansion began to be disturbed with mysterious, knocking sounds. "People think it is the spirit of Daniel Fowle, because he probably doesn't appreciate his bed being moved from the executive sleeping chambers," Call said. The Executive Mansion has been proclaimed to be (by such notables as FDR himself) as "the most beautiful in America." For a while, due to the COVID pandemic, it was closed to tours, but reopened in the Fall of 2021. Today, you can get a free tour of the

Executive Mansion if you contact them at least two weeks in advance; virtual tours are also available through such internet outlets as YouTube.

Some say the Gubernatorial Mansion in Raleigh is haunted by the first Governor who lived and died there, Daniel Fowle. (Photo by the author)

Q&A

Q. Who came as a surveyor to Gates County, surveyed the area, formed a company to drain part of the Dismal Swamp, and bought a tract of land in the county?

A. George Washington.

Q. Who was the first woman in the nation to be appointed to the position of postmistress?

A. Sarah DeCrow was appointed on September 27, 1792, in Hertford.

Q. What was the name detractors gave the Safe Storage of Firearms bill, introduced into the House of Representatives in April 2001?

A. Home Invaders Protection Act.

Q. Until October 2001, at what age could a girl get married in North Carolina without parental or guardian consent?

A. On October 1, the minimum marriage age was raised from twelve to fourteen.

Q. In 1866 a law was passed prohibiting what activity in the halls of the Davie County Courthouse?

A. Horseback riding in the hallways.

Q. How many representatives are there in the North Carolina State Legislature?

A. 120.

Q. What president established the Appalachian Regional Commission to improve the lives and prospects of the people in this area?

A. President John F. Kennedy.

Q. What thirteen states are now part of this commission?

A. North Carolina, South Carolina, Tennessee, Georgia, Alabama, Kentucky, Maryland, Pennsylvania, Virginia, West Virginia, New York, Mississippi, and Ohio.

Q. What is the "youngest" county in North Carolina, created in 1911?

A. Avery County.

Q. How many counties are in North Carolina?

A. Exactly 100.

Q. Who was the first woman to be named to a post by the Reagan administration of 1980?

A. Elizabeth Hanford Dole, born in Salisbury, became assistant to the president for public liaison.

CHAPTER 3

Planes, Trains and Automobiles

Warping, Rudders, and Mosquitoes

The two men were drawn to this Outer Banks village. Despite the mosquitoes that one described as coming "in a mighty cloud...darkening the sun," and causing "extreme misery," the two were determined to spend time here. It was, they agreed, the perfect place for what they had in mind. It was extremely isolated. It had fair breezes. The uncluttered beaches stretched for miles and were at least one mile wide. And the people of the town, although somewhat suspicious of their motives, at least put up with what was considered eccentric, somewhat bizarre behavior.

What surprised the two were the unexpected squalls that came up several times weekly, forcing them to hold their tent down in the night to keep it from blowing away. Between the squalls and "bone-chilling cold" temperatures at night, it was a wonder either of them wanted to ever return to this exotic but forbidding place.

But return they did, determined to work with the elements and each other. Engineers primarily, the two had chosen a place near Kitty Hawk as the place to solve the mystery of flight and prove, once and for all, that heavier-than-air transportation was possible.

For several years the problem of balance had stumped brothers Orville and Wilbur Wright. Then they added a warp—a helical twist applied across the entire wing of the plane— that would control balance in flight. This problem had hindered the efforts of Germany's Otto Lilienthal

and other aeronautical pioneers. Modifying the rudder helped with control and added lift.

Finally, in twelve seconds and with Orville at the controls of the machine named the *Flyer*, the possibility of manned flight was proven, and history was changed. It had taken years of struggles with squalls, mosquitoes, and engineering frustrations, but because of the determination of two brothers from Dayton, Ohio, the first airplane flew 120 feet in the air above the sand dunes near Kill Devil Hills, on December 17, 1903. The jubilant brothers made three more attempts at flight on that historic day, with the longest flight lasting fifty-nine seconds and covering 852 feet (further flights were not possible because the plane was damaged by a sudden gust).

The *Flyer* that became airborne on that historic day is now on display at the Smithsonian in Washington, D.C. In 2003, the Centennial Celebration of the historic "First Flight" was held at Kitty Hawk, with exhibits, speakers, visitors from around the globe, and a re-creation of the Wright brothers' accomplishment.

STRANGE... but True

How Technology Changed the History Records

Most people believe that the historic first flight took place in Kitty Hawk. This is not exactly true, despite what the history books say.

The day the brothers made their historic flight at Kill Devil Hills, five miles south of Kitty Hawk, they were justifiably euphoric and wanted to share the news with their father. The only way to get word to him was by telegraph, and the nearest telegraph station was in Kitty Hawk.

Thus, with a telegraphed message datelined Kitty Hawk and *not* Kill Devil Hills, technology changed the way this historical event was recorded for posterity. Incidentally, you can find the Wright Brothers National Memorial (which was established in Kill Devil Hills in 1927) and pay your respects.

It is under the auspices of the National Park Service.

In December 2003, to celebrate the 100th anniversary of the Wright brothers' historic flight, engineers and aviation mechanics introduced a reproduction airplane they had created, made as historically accurate as the first one. The repeat-flight was attempted with this vintage reproduction plane, and the event was attended by half of Congress, foreign dignitaries, and President George W. Bush and others, again at the Outer Banks. The flight failed, and members of the MWNF Society were jubilant.

Annually, the Society presents two anti-aviation awards for those who have done the least to further the cause of the society. The last four such awards were given to U.S. Presidents, but not a single one has acknowledged receipt.

DID YOU KNOW?

Since December 16, 1959, and for every year since, the Man Will Never Fly Memorial Society has met in Kitty Hawk. It's no coincidence that they meet on the night previous to the anniversary of the first manned flight of Orville and Wilbur Wright. Saying that the Wright brothers faked that flight by using a bicycle to pull the airplane, the primary agenda of this society is just having a good time on the ground (one indicator of this might be their motto, "Birds Fly, Men Drink"). Al Jones, spokesperson for the society, admits that some of the members arrive by airplane for the convention.

America's "First Airplane"

In 2002 students in the carpentry class at the Roanoke-Chowan Community College in Ahoskie were busy working on an airplane. Not just any airplane—a replica of what they say is America's first airplane, built by James Henry Gatling in 1873 (you can read about his brother, Richard Gatling, in Chapter 9).

Students at the Roanoke-Chowan Community College built a replica of the 1873 James Henry Gatling Airplane, which they claim is America's first airplane. (Courtesy Murfreesboro Historical Association)

Thomas C. Parramore, Ph.D., a North Carolina aviation historian, says that although the original Gatling airplane failed to fly, some features of it were embodied in the Wright airplane that successfully flew in 1903. Completed for the hundredth anniversary celebration of the Wright brothers' first flight, the replica is permanently located in Murfreesboro's Historic District at the Agriculture and Transportation Museum.

The Bumblebee That Didn't Quite Fly

Born in 1869 and growing up in Core Sound, William Luther Paul was fascinated with how things worked, and as a teenager was known as "Mr. Fix It."

Paul was fascinated with flight and the strides made to achieve manned flight. In 1903 he built his own flying machine, an experimental helicopter he named *The Bumble Bee*. He tested it in a makeshift wind tunnel, an open-ended barn, and found that *The Bumble Bee* could achieve lift as high as five feet carrying sixty pounds of ballast.

Of course, later that same year, the Wright brothers made their historic first flights. This, combined with Paul's wife's concern for his safety and a lack of funds, prompted him to abandon his work on *The Bumble Bee*.

He and his family moved to Beaufort in 1911 and Luther continued to work on his inventions (he is credited with building one of Carteret County's first automobiles). He was also involved in making motion pictures, and when in the 1920s he wrote Thomas Edison about collaborating on a "talking-motion picture" project, Edison responded, saying he was too busy.

Paul died in 1946, but a model of the original experimental helicopter is on display at the North Carolina Maritime Museum. It was built by Luther Paul's grandson, Grayden Paul Jr.

Operation Bumble Bee

In the post–World War II years of 1946 to 1948, the U.S. government chose Topsail Island as a site to test secret missiles. Termed Operation Bumble Bee, the goal of the project was to develop a supersonic missile that could reach an air target at a range of ten to twenty miles.

The project, one of the earliest developments of the U.S. missile program, used facilities at nearby Camp Davis in

Holly Ridge to accommodate five hundred personnel. The missile test range was built in a year and was one of the best-equipped facilities in the country.

From the research conducted during Operation Bumble Bee, more than one triumphant development emerged. Operation Bumble Bee provided technology that allowed U.S. warships to carry onboard missiles with enhanced ability to destroy enemy aircraft. In addition, the Ramjet Engine was developed, which is now the basis for all jet aircraft.

Buildings that remain from Operation Bumble Bee have been designated as historical sites in the National Register of Historic Places, and now the formerly top-secret area is open to the public. This museum is known now as "Missiles and More Museum," and is located at 720 Channel Blvd., Topsail Island.

The Comeback Train

When the logging industry became a major source of income for the people of western North Carolina in the 1890s, transporting men, tools, and logs was a problem. Most locomotives of the day couldn't climb the steep grades of the area. To hold traction on the rails placed so hastily in the region, two types of locomotives, the Shay and the Clima, were used. The Shay had increased traction because of its vertical cylinders, placed to the right of an offset boiler, and the Clima also had a vertical drive gear. These trains ran between Dillsboro and Murphy on a rail line owned by the Norfolk Southern Railroad.

Until the Great Smoky Mountains National Park was established in 1934, the Shay and the Clima ruled the land, as

Once an abandoned logging rail line, the Great Smokey Mountains Railroad is now one of the main attractions of western North Carolina. (Courtesy N.C. Division of Tourism, Film and Sports Division)

did the logger. Once the park was established and set aside as a wilderness area and people began to travel primarily by highways, the railroad lost its usefulness. In 1988 increasing maintenance costs and decreasing traffic obliged the Norfolk Southern to abandon the Dillsboro-Murphy line.

The line was saved from possible destruction by the quick action of the state of North Carolina. It purchased the line and leased it to a group of shippers and investors, incorporated as the Great Smoky Mountains Railroad and based in Dillsboro.

Now the locomotives, with an additional locomotive, a Baldwin, give passengers entertaining rides on a fifty-three-mile route from Dillsboro to Andrews and Murphy. The Baldwin has a history of its own—it was a World War II locomotive and "starred" in the movie *This Property Is*

Condemned, with Charles Bronson, Robert Redford, and Natalie Wood. The cars the locomotives pull have been used on various other lines and have poetic names such as the Silver Meteor and Dixie Flyer. They've added other excursions to their repertoire, including one 44-mile route through Nantahala Gorge and a 32-mile round trip, called the Tuskasegee River Excursion (and they offer special wine-and-cheese sightseeing trips for adults, called "Uncorked Train Rides"). Besides having entertainment value, the line services the agricultural, business, and industrial needs of the three cities.

The abandoned logging rail line nobody wanted has become one of the main attractions of western North Carolina. See "Virtual North Carolina" for website information.

DID YOU KNOW?

One of the most photographed railroad stations in the United States is in the tiny town of Hamlet. It's the circa-1900 depot originally belonging to the old Seaboard Air Line Railway now used as the National Railroad Museum and Hall of Fame. It's open for tours on Saturday and Sunday afternoons.

Along This "Train" of Thought

In 1866 the East Tennessee and Western North Carolina Railroad Company built a railroad that ran from Johnson City, Tennessee, to iron mines in Cranberry, North Carolina. The narrow-gauge line began running in 1881, and in 1916 it was extended to Boone and transported lumber and passengers between the cities. The train, dubbed "Tweetsie" by the locals for its shrill whistle, became a part of mountain life.

Like trains elsewhere, Tweetsie's livelihood was adversely affected by the construction of highways, and in 1950 the railroad company met its demise. Some railroad enthusiasts purchased Tweetsie Locomotive Number 12 and moved her to Virginia, where they planned to put her back on track. Hurricane Hazel destroyed the railroad tracks, however, so the discouraged rail buffs had to sell the locomotive.

Famous singing cowboy Gene Autry bought her from the Virginians, supposedly to feature her in Western films. Somehow, a North Carolina native named Grover Robbins Jr. talked the movie legend into selling him Tweetsie Number 12 for the sum of one dollar—so she could come back home to the mountains. Robbins brought Tweetsie to his hometown of Blowing Rock and had her restored by expert train-repair folks in Hickory.

Tweetsie made her tourist debut just a few miles away from the old railroad depot in Boone, along with some of the original rail cars, also restored in Hickory. Now the legend of the coal-fired steam train lives on as Tweetsie transports delighted families, once again sounding her shrill, cheerful whistle through the hills and valleys of the Blue Ridge Mountains. Now known as "Tweetsie Railroad Wild West Theme Park," the family-friendly tourist spot hosts all kinds of annual events such as "Railroad Heritage Weekend," a "Ghost Train" during Halloween, and more.

Once in danger of the scrap heap, Tweetsie enjoys life anew and is listed on the National Register of Historic Places.

The Man Who Transformed Commercial Transportation

Born in Maxton, trucker Malcolm P. McLean got his start hauling barrels of tobacco. He must have been an extraordinarily observant man, for he noted the problems inherent with the way goods were shipped. As late as the early 1950s, goods were transferred using cargo nets, but loose cargoes often suffered damage in transit and pilferage occurred, causing insurance rates for cargo carriers to skyrocket. McLean also noticed that it took truckers and dock workers far too long to load and offload cargo.

Malcolm P. McLean (Wikipedia)

Then McLean had an idea: get rid of cargo nets and pack the goods into boxes. He experimented with large boxes he called containers and in 1956 converted an old World War II tanker, *The Ideal X*, into the first container ship. On its maiden voyage, the old tanker successfully transported fifty-eight containers from Port Newark, New Jersey, to Houston, Texas. The shipping world took note and realized McLean's "boxes" would decrease insurance rates and increase the speed and safety of shipments. Observers also noted the speed with which McLean's company offloaded cargo, using Gantry cranes instead of the hands (and backs) of longshoremen.

The trucker-turned-shipping-magnate named his infant company Sea-Land Service. McLean's company became the world's largest container shipping service, and at least 90 percent of today's cargo is shipped in containers. Malcolm P. McLean died in May 2001 but will always be remembered as the "Father of Containerization."

DID YOU KNOW?

The world's most complicated bridge is the Linn Cove Viaduct around the base of Grandfather Mountain, on the Blue Ridge Parkway near Linville. It's internationally famous because it is an engineering marvel, with so many curves that each 50-ton segment was constructed one at a time. Each segment is unlike any other piece on the bridge, and the entire bridge has only one straight segment. You'll have to drive it to truly appreciate it!

The Linn Cove Viaduct around the base of Grandfather mountain is the world's most complicated bridge.. (Courtesy N.C. Division of Tourism, Film and Sports division)

Wagons, Ho!

A two-hour drive along the crest of the Unicoi Mountains takes you over the Cherohala Skyway, a lovely, winding two-lane road that connects western North Carolina to eastern Tennessee. The road, completed in 1996, carries travelers past cascading waterfalls, wilderness areas, and hiking trails. It also boasts, among other natural attractions, Joyce Kilmer Memorial Forest. It took the vision of a local Kiwanis Club group to foster sufficient interest for this road to see completion.

It all started in the 1950s in nearby Tellico Plains, Tennessee, where some residents complained that the roads to North Carolina were so bad, they might as well be traveling by wagon train. The comments sparked the local Kiwanis Club members, led by local historian Charles Hall, to organize a wagon train to generate media attention (and thereby funds) to build a sure-enough highway from Tellico Plains to Robbinsville. The first wagon trains left Tellico Plains for North Carolina in June 1958 with nearly seventy wagons and more than three hundred riders on horseback. The event gained media attention and did, indeed, generate funds for a highway.

The Kiwanis Club members and others decided not to stop with one wagon train; it became an almost annual event until the highway was nearly completed. Even though the opening ceremonies for the highway were held in October 1996, some people still get together for the wagon train event, usually around the first weekend in July. See "Virtual North Carolina" at the back of this book for website information.

DID YOU KNOW?

The Cherohala Skyway was named by Charles Hall, who combined the names of two forests the highway spans: Cherokee National Forest on the Tennessee Side and the Nantahala National Forest in North Carolina. At the Unicoi Crest Overlook (elevation 4,470 feet), you can see three states: Tennessee from the west, North Carolina in the east, and Georgia to the southwest. Look for equally breathtaking vistas around the Santeetlah area (elevation 5,390 feet).

The Road to Nowhere

Just north of Bryson City and near the quiet village of Townsend, Tennessee, deep in the woods bordering Fontana Lake, is a road that ends abruptly at a long tunnel that traverses underground for several hundred yards.

The road is formally known as Lakeview Drive, but locals know it as the Road to Nowhere. It was begun in the late 1950s as a

Road to Nowhere (Atlas Obscura)

combined project of the U.S. Department of the Interior, the Tennessee Valley Authority, and Swain County. Lakeview Drive was intended to bring more visitors to Fontana Lake, and provide a more straightforward route from Bryson City to Townsend. Because of a lack of foresight, however, problems got in the way.

Twenty-eight family cemeteries were in the road's path, and people weren't willing to move their beloveds' remains. That, plus concerns about the environmental impact the road would create for the pristine wilderness around it, halted the building of the road.

You can drive most of the road in the wilderness at the North Carolina–Tennessee border, and when it comes to an end, you can explore the tunnel on foot. Both the road and the tunnel remain as mute witness to our sometimes-shortsighted ambitions.

Get Here However You Can: The North Carolina Transportation Museum

Located in the town of Spencer, the NC Transportation Museum is one of the biggest I've ever seen—roughly the size of two football fields. Located in what used to be the Southern Railway Company's 1896-era locomotive servicing facility, the museum staff continues to work on train engines, cabooses and train cars in need of work (these come from all over). Visitors can watch the staff work on these in the massive Back Shop. They can see the largest roundhouse in North America and see the turntable in operation.

Kids of all ages love to take the roughly half-hour train ride around the museum grounds, with ticket-takers dressed in turn-of-the-century costume. The museum has all kinds of interactive exhibits of antique cars, steam locomotives, classic trucks and more. The museum also features a full-size replica of the Wright Flyer. Kids love to celebrate their birthdays with a party in a train caboose, and the museum has special events such as rides with "Thomas the Tank Engine."

North Carolina Transportation Museum (Wikiwand)

TRANSPORTATION TRIVIA

Q. In what North Carolina county was the hot-air balloon made that was used by Tracy Barnes, the first person to travel across the United States in a hot-air balloon?

A. Iredell County (The Balloon Works).

Q. How did High Point, North Carolina, come by its name?

A. The town was founded on the highest point of land on the railroad that ran between Goldsboro and Charlotte.

Q. How many miles of highway does the state maintain?

A. At last count, approximately 80,000 miles—making it the largest state highway system in the United States.

Q. What is the name of the oldest known working tugboat? (Hint: when not on duty, it's located at Manteo's Salty Dog Marina.)

A. *The Lookout.*

Q. What is the name of the stretch of two-lane road that, from the state line at Deals Gap going north toward Maryville, Tennessee, contains 318 curves in only eleven miles of highway?

A. The aptly named and nationally famous "Tail of the Dragon," U.S. Highway 129. (Drive it in a sports convertible for a thrill!)

Q. What do locals call the stretch of U.S. 158 between Elizabeth City and Fort Raleigh?

A. The Virginia Dare Trail.

Q. What North Carolina city is the site of the largest display in the southeast of old work boats?

A. Wilmington.

Q. What year did work on the Blue Ridge Parkway begin?

A. 1935.

Q. What deep crevasse in North Carolina is known as the "Grand Canyon of the East"?

A. Linville Gorge, in Pisgah National Forest.

CHAPTER 4

BEFORE 'THE' WAR & PREHISTORIC NORTH CAROLINA

The Paul Revere of the South

In the early days of America's independence, twenty-seven delegates met at the Charlotte Courthouse and voted "Aye" on making Mecklenburg County independent from England. That day, May 20, 1775, Captain James Jack took the job of carrying copies of the resolution to the president of the Continental Congress and to the three North Carolina representatives.

In Salisbury, when Jack stopped to read the proclamation to the court in session, most of the people in earshot reacted with wild cheering—except for two lawyers who wanted to hold Jack and charge him with treason. The lawyers' objections were overruled, however, and Jack continued on his mission.

In all, Jack rode more than five hundred miles announcing the resolution and was met with either enthusiastic approval or threats of violence. As legend has it, he arrived on June 23, 1775, in Philadelphia to present the resolution. Upon his arrival he was dismayed to learn of Congress's plans to make an official statement to the King of England, denying Mecklenburg's request for independence.

Captain James Jack (UNC University Library)

Incensed, he is quoted as saying to those gathered there, "Gentlemen, you may debate here about 'reconciliation' and memorialize your king, but bear in mind, Mecklenburg owes no allegiance to, and is separated from, the crown of Great Britain forever."

Of course you know that separation of the colonies from Britain was imminent. Although he was perhaps a bit ahead of his time, Captain James Jack is still regarded as the Paul Revere of the South. You can learn more about this fearless patriot by visiting the Charlotte Museum of History. See "Virtual North Carolina" for website information.

THE FIRST "TEA PARTY" WASN'T IN BOSTON

The coastal village of Edenton saw the first political action by women in the American colonies. On October 26, 1774, the ladies of Edenton and five nearby counties gathered at the home of Elizabeth King (although some accounts claim it was at the home of Penelope Barker). They shared tea and wrote a declaration against the high taxes levied against American colonists by the English throne.

The document they signed eventually made its way to the British newspaper, the *Morning Chronicle & London Advertiser*, which voiced editorial disapproval of women's involvement in politics. After hearing of the ladies' patriotic stance, citizens in both the Carolinas and Georgia were inspired to swear off tea in opposition to the tax levied by the British. As a result, casks of tea sat unconsumed in warehouses in Charleston.

Ironically, when the Revolution broke out and patriots gained control of Charleston, they sold the casks of tea to help finance the war effort! Incidentally, the former home site of Elizabeth King on Court Street has a bronze tea pot sitting atop a cannon's mouth, commemorating the women's protest, for those who wish to go by and see it. Also, the home of Penelope Barker is now open for tours and is Edenton's Welcome Center. See "Virtual North Carolina" for website information.

The Days When Lawyers Were Revered

There are lots of jokes about lawyers these days, but in North Carolina, the American Revolution was led by barristers. North Carolina's own Declaration of Independence, known as the Halifax Resolves, was written by an attorney. Most of the members of the first Continental Congress (which included Tar Heels) were also attorneys, as were twenty-one of fifty-six signers of the Declaration of Independence.

Next time you want to tell a joke making fun of lawyers, consider going *out* of state to do it.

The Tale of the Overmountain Men

The Continental Army surrendered the city of Charleston, South Carolina, to the British on May 12, 1780. Before this, the army had been devastated by defeats at the battles of Cowpens and Waxhaws. The Continental Army was demoralized and things did not look good for the colonies. But no one realized how feisty the colonists in North Carolina could be.

North Carolina was the last bastion between the invading British general, Charles Cornwallis, and his final destination. Virginia was the largest colony in the Americas, and Cornwallis was determined to take it because this would bring the struggle for independence to a dismal and disheartening close. He, too, underestimated the fierce independent nature of the mountain men of the Tar Heel State.

The Continental Army was in disarray, and settlers in the mountain region of North Carolina heeded the call to arms to fight for America's independence. They were mostly farmers, hunters, and trappers by trade, most with no military experience whatsoever. So untrained were they that the British referred to them as "mongrels," and the invading Brits threatened that if the Americans did not submit to British rule, they would "lay waste the country with fire and sword." This, too, did nothing to dissuade the Tar Heel mountain men—it seemed to fuel their patriotic passions even more.

Seeing their numbers grow, other civilian soldiers from southern Virginia and Tennessee joined the ranks of the soldiers now known as the Overmountain Men. In a late fall campaign to stop the British from getting to Virginia, the patriots (including Daniel Boone) marched 313 miles, gathering forces as they went through four states, hot on the trail of their foe. More soldiers from Georgia joined the Overmountain Men in Polk County; then they met and defeated the British in the decisive Battle of Kings Mountain. In just one day—October 7, 1780—the farmer-soldiers won a pivotal battle for their beloved America. When he received news of the outcome of the battle, Thomas Jefferson declared it was "the turn of the tide that terminated the Revolutionary War."

Today, there are many ways you can learn more about this decisive battle and the men who fought for our country. Museums such as the Rocky Mount Museum (in Rocky Mount) and the North Carolina Museum in Raleigh both have exhibits about the Overmountain Men and the battle that decided the victory for America. In 1980, Congress established the National Historic Trail to commemorate the path the farmer-soldiers took to fight for our freedom; this greenway is open to the public. And, if you really want to get into the spirit of things, you can join the Overmountain Victory Trail

Association, which is a troupe of reenactors. See "Virtual North Carolina" for website information.

DID YOU KNOW?

The nation's oldest Revolutionary War drama, entitled *Horn in the West*, depicts Daniel Boone and the Battle of Kings Mountain and is held in Boone every summer. Also, the pivotal victory of patriot militia over the Loyalist forces is commemorated at Kings Mountain National Military Park in Cleveland County, South Carolina (just over the border from North Carolina). This beautiful military park features a lovely Visitor Center with interactive exhibits and a great film about the decisive battle. See "Virtual North Carolina" for website information.

Losing the Battle, Winning the War

The Battle of Guilford Courthouse on March 15, 1781, may be officially recorded as a loss for the colonies, but in the long run, it wasn't. Here's why.

General Charles Cornwallis had mounted his second attack on North Carolina in January 1781. General Nathanael Greene had always stayed a step ahead of the invading British, trying to keep himself and his soldiers strategically situated between Cornwallis and his supplies in South Carolina. As Cornwallis advanced, Greene retreated; this forced Cornwallis to begin abandoning supplies to make pursuit easier on his troops.

When Greene got Cornwallis as far as 230 miles from his South Carolina supplies, he took a stand at the Guilford County Courthouse. Cornwallis's side suffered badly. At the end of the fighting, the colonists had 78 dead and 183 wounded, compared to 93 British dead and 439 wounded.

Greene retreated to save his remaining men, and although Cornwallis continued his attempt to defeat the patriots, he and his men had been badly weakened and were ill supplied, thanks to Greene's ingenious maneuvers. The British were ultimately defeated by General George Washington and General Jean Baptiste de Vimeur, Comte de Rochambeau in Yorktown, Virginia, in October 1781. Today, when you visit the Guilford County Courthouse in Greensboro, you will know that a quick-witted patriot made sure that, although Cornwallis technically won that battle, he effectively lost the war.

At the time of the battle, the town was named Martinsborough. It was renamed Greensboro in honor of Greene, and Guilford Courthouse National Military Park became the nation's first Revolutionary War military park.

The Capital of North Carolina was Determined by a Drink Called "Cherry Bounce"

The Joel Lane House in Raleigh, which dates back to 1760, is not only the oldest existing building in Wake County, but is also part of an amusing story relating to the establishment of Raleigh as the permanent state capital.

Before Raleigh received this designation in 1792, the state capital had been moved many times. Edenton was first (1708 into the 1740s); followed by Bath (in the 1740s); Wilmington (later in the 1740s); New Bern (off and on between the 1740s and 1790s); Hillsborough, Halifax, and Tarboro (between 1770 and the 1780s); and then Fayetteville (1780s). The people of

North Carolina probably breathed one huge sigh of relief when everyone voted on making Raleigh the permanent state capital.

These facts you can find in virtually any North Carolina history book. While you can still visit the Joel Lane House, here's "the rest of the story" that you *won't* find in any history book, that I learned back in 2007 from docent LeRae Umfleet.

Raleigh didn't exist until it was founded as the state capital. As a matter of fact, there wasn't a single town in Wake County until Raleigh's founding. The state of North Carolina wanted to choose a new capital in the middle of the state, making it easier for everyone to travel to the capital for business. The previous state capitals had all been on the coast and were inaccessible for people in the mountains and the Piedmont areas. Wake County was close to the geographical center of the state, so the real decision was where in Wake County to put the capital.

The committee agreed on a general location within ten miles of Isaac Hunter's tavern, a popular stopping place. Several men, including Joel Lane, offered to sell the state's representatives land in the ten-mile stretch from Hunter's tavern. The committee reviewed the land offerings and decided to settle it with a vote. During the deliberations, Lane entertained the representatives at his home.

The first two votes on a Thursday in March were inconclusive, with no clear majority. They decided to adjourn and vote again the next day. This is when Lane worked his magic.

Oral tradition holds that he entertained his guests with a bountiful table and free-flowing spirits such as Cherry Bounce, a sort of cherry cordial and whiskey concoction.

There is no agreed-upon historic recipe for the drink but with each iteration of the tale, the brew has become ever more potent. The guests reportedly enjoyed a serving (or more) of Cherry Bounce.

Next morning, when the guests' collective fog lifted, they offered to buy a thousand acres from Lane for the site of the new state capital. It was named Raleigh in honor of Sir Walter Raleigh, the English explorer whose exploits led to the colonization of North Carolina in the seventeenth century.

North Carolina State Capital Building

Joel Lane's reputation has descended through history as a man who was an outgoing, well-mannered individual who used his influence and wealth to secure the location of the city of Raleigh in what was, literally, his front yard. His home is preserved and furnished as it was when he lived there and is open for tours led by costumed docents.

It's worth a visit—with or without being served the famous (or infamous) drink. If you do want to work your own Cherry Bounce magic, try this recipe suggested by LaRae

Umfleet, who says the drink improves with age and is "much better when it's two to three years old."

Cherry Bounce

4 quarts cherries, drained

2 quarts sugar

1 quart best whiskey or brandy

Stir together cherries and sugar and let stand overnight. In the morning, stir again and add whiskey or brandy. Store in a stone jar, put on a lid, and seal the edges with a cloth dipped in paraffin. Let stand for 6 weeks, squeeze out juices, and strain and filter it.

The famous 'Cherry Bounce' drink worked its magic at the Joel Lane house, and Raleigh was unanimously voted the Capital of North Carolina. (Photo by the Author)

Some Early Settlers

In the early 1700s a group of Siouan-speaking Indians settled in what is now Robeson, Hoke, Cumberland and Scotland counties. Growing and thriving, they were first referred to as Cheraws, then were thought to be Croatan, then in 1911 the North Carolina General Assembly changed their name to simply the "Indians of Robeson County." At one time they were also thought to be a part of the Cherokee nation, but their origin in still unclear. Finally, in 1956 the U.S. Congress recognized them as the Lumbees.

The Lumbee people have made many contributions. They helped defend this country, starting with the Revolutionary War. In 1887 the Lumbee people built Croatan Indian Normal School, today the University of North Carolina at Pembroke. They opened the first Indian-owned bank in the United States, the Lumbee Bank in Pembroke. It is the only tribe in this country to hold on to its native lands, without being forced onto a reservation.

Although the Lumbee tribe has grown to include more than 40,000 members on its rolls and the U.S. Government has recognized them as Indian, they have yet to receive full government recognition with its attendant benefits. The fight for full recognition continues today; you can track their progress on the tribal website (see Virtual North Carolina).

When a Tar Heel "Saved" George Washington

In 1814 when the British were attacking the city of Washington, D.C., they were bent on burning down President James Madison's home. Hearing of their intentions and knowing that everything in the home would be destroyed, the president's wife, Dolley, gathered what possessions she could as she prepared to flee the city.

Born Dorothea Payne from Guilford County, Dolley quickly saw that one thing in the home could never be replaced: a large portrait of George Washington in a splendid frame. Realizing that there was no time to unscrew the painting from the wall, she ordered that the frame be broken and the canvas removed.

The Redcoats arrived within minutes of her evacuation, looting and burning the house, and leaving only the charred shell of the executive mansion in their destructive wake.

Dolly Madison is the only first lady from North Carolina. When the British burned the executive mansion in 1814, she had the presence of mind to rescue the portrait of George Washington (Library of Congress)

Because of a Tar Heel with steel in her spine, the only original piece to survive from the executive mansion (later to be known as the White House) is that portrait of George Washington she saved August 24, 1814. A replica of this painting by Gilbert Stuart hangs in the East Room of the White House today. The original that Dolley saved is on display in the Smithsonian's National Portrait Gallery.

Dolley Madison is the only First Lady born in North Carolina. Her accomplishments are honored in exhibits at the Greensboro Historical Museum.

Unusual Town Names

Some towns in North Carolina have strange names, with sometimes offbeat reasons for their naming.

Kill Devil Hills: Early white settlers regularly imbibed a rum drink said to be strong enough to kill the devil himself.

Lizard Lick: One early resident regularly took his stroll alongside a local fence, knocking (or "licking") the lizards off the fence railing with his cane as he passed.

Cats Square: Unwanted cats were abandoned there.

Old Trap: This town in Camden County was originally given the derisive name of The Trap by "decent" women up in arms over the number of taverns and loose women in the area.

Pigeonroost: Passenger pigeons, now extinct, once roosted there.

Boogertown: People who made moonshine kept the curious away by letting it be thought that evil spirits, or "boogers," hid in the woods.

Rabbit Shuffle: Early settlers of this town in Caswell County thought the soil quality was so poor that even a rabbit had to shuffle to get sustenance.

Machelhe Island: This island on the Pasquotank River was named from the first two letters of each of the owner's four children (Mary, Charles, Eloise, and Helen).

An Accident Leads to an Invention

George Gist, the son of a woman from a prominent Cherokee family and a fur trader from Virginia, was hunting in the area of North Carolina that is now the Cherokee Nation. He had a hunting accident that forced him into a period of inactivity, and during this time, became fascinated with the marks white people made on paper. He called the papers "talking leaves," because he saw how people could communicate using a written language. Gist then decided he would create a written language and started working on one for the Cherokee language.

George Gist, better known as Sequoyah, invented the Cherokee syllabary. (Wikipedia)

He labored for more than ten years to create the eighty-five-character syllabary, using characters to represent syllables rather than individual letters. This was adopted by the Cherokee Nation in 1821 and became the basis for the written Cherokee language. Using this syllabary, the Cherokee people established their first newspaper, the *Cherokee Phoenix*. That paper no longer exists, but the *Cherokee One Feather*, an English language newspaper, is published weekly out of Cherokee, North Carolina. Also, two other newspapers--*The Cherokee Observer*, published monthly out of Blackwell, Oklahoma, and *The Cherokee Advocate*, published out of Talequah, Oklahoma—are published in Cherokee and English. In Cherokee itself, the newspaper *Cherokee One Feather* covered a new program on the reservation, in which Native children in daycares there are taught their tribal tongue. Editor Joe Martin wrote, "Children are fluent in Cherokee by the time they reach kindergarten."

Because of an accident and resultant forced inactivity, Gist, known better as Sequoyah, helped preserve an entire culture through the first written language of native North America. Now a bust of his likeness stands at the entrance to the Museum of the Cherokee Indian in Cherokee.

DID YOU KNOW?

TYRANNASAURUS ONCE ROAMED THE TAR HEEL STATE!

While fossils of prehistoric creatures aren't as numerous in North Carolina as, say, Montana or Utah, the cousin of the Tyrannasaurus, Appalachiosaurus, is thought to have roamed what became the Tar Heel State. If you'd like to "dig into" more about prehistory in North Carolina, you're sure to find many answers to your curiosity about all things prehistoric in Asheville's Museum of Science. See "Virtual North Carolina" in the back of this book for website information.

World's only complete T. Rex Skeleton Housed in North Carolina Museum

Whales, Birds, and Sharks, Oh My!

Five miles outside the coastal town of Aurora is a large phosphate mine. The area is rich in phosphate—a key ingredient in fertilizer—caused by the biodegradation of prehistoric marine life. Sometimes phosphate miners would come across intact fossils five million to fifteen million years old.

The town of Aurora has capitalized on these finds, displaying them in its Fossil Museum. Here you will find evidence that this part of North Carolina was once deep under the sea: on display are huge whale backbones, prehistoric bird bones, and gigantic shark teeth. Across the street from the museum, people of all ages enjoy digging in the two spoils pits where they can find their own fossils. Every Memorial Day weekend they celebrate their "prehistory" with a Fossil Festival.

You'll "Dig" Seeing THIS State Park!

In the town of Creswell, archeologists have discovered thousands of relics, including approximately thirty dugout canoes, that were all found on the floor of Lake Phelps. Scientists have dated the canoes and determined some of them to be as old as the pyramids of Egypt. They say that this is proof of Native Americans being in this area as early as 8,000 BC. Some of the canoes are on display at the Information Center at Pettigrew State Park.

Q & A

BEFORE THE WAR & PREHISTORIC

Q. What is the official fossil of North Carolina?

A. The Megalodon. There's a full-sized fossil of a complete set of Megalodon teeth in the Fossil Museum of Aurora.

Q. Which county is home to shallow, oval-shaped craters, called "Carolina Bays," said to have been created by a Pleistocene-era meteor shower?

A. Bladen County.

Q. Where can you find the World's only Acrocanthosaurus fossil?

A. In the North Carolina Museum of Natural Sciences, Raleigh. (This you've got to see!)

Q. During the Tuscarora War, where did approximately 950 Indians lose their lives?

A. Nooherooka.

Q. What was North Carolina's first military school, established in Williamsboro in 1826?

A. Bingham School.

Q. What four states border North Carolina?

A. Tennessee, Virginia, Georgia, and South Carolina.

Q. What town hosts the Annual Soldiers' Reunion Celebration, the oldest patriotic event of its kind?

A. Newton.

The gardens outside Tyron Palace, New Bern, which was the administrative headquarters of British governors from 1770 to 1775 (Wikimedia Commons)

Q. What is the motto of North Carolina?

A. The Latin phrase, *Esse quam videri,* which means, "To be, rather than to seem."

Q. From what author was this quote derived?

A. Cicero, in his essay on friendship, *De Amicitia.*

Q. What Revolutionary War hero was such a colorful character that Wayne County was named in his honor?

A. "Mad Anthony" Wayne.

Q. What bordering colony so hotly contested the boundary with North Carolina that an official survey in 1728 was required to settle the dispute?

A. Virginia.

Q. When did North Carolina enter the Union?

A. November 21, 1789.

Q. When Sir Robert Heath was granted land from Albemarle Sound southward to Florida in 1629 and named it "Carolina," who was he naming it after?

A. King Charles I (Carolina is the Latin form of Charles).

Q. When were the Carolinas split into North and South, and why?

A. In 1663 King Charles II realized the area was too large to be managed efficiently and put eight "Lords Proprietors" in charge of what became North Carolina and South Carolina.

Q. What courthouse is the oldest still in use?

A. The Chowan County Courthouse, circa 1767.

Q. What three North Carolinians signed the Declaration of Independence, adopted by Congress on July 4, 1776?

A. William Hooper, Joseph Hewes, and John Penn.

Q. When did the North Carolina Legislature charter the University of North Carolina?

A. In 1789, making it the first state university in the United States.

Q. What Spanish explorer in 1540 came looking for gold in what are now Jackson, Cherokee, and Clay counties?

A. Hernando de Soto.

Q. In what year was the oldest recorded land deal in North Carolina?

A. In 1661, between Yeopin Indians and George Durant, in Hertford.

Q. What is the only National Historic Landmark in North Carolina to commemorate American Indian culture?

A. Town Creek Indian Mound in Mount Gilead (Montgomery County). Some of the settlement has been reconstructed and is open for tours.

CHAPTER 5

FAMOUS NORTH CAROLINIANS

A Kiss and an Obsession Led to a Museum!

The Barefoot Contessa was one of the movies that starred Ava Gardner and contributed to her enduring fame. Born December 25, 1922, in a rural area outside Smithfield, Ava Lavinia Gardner was one of eight children in the family of Jonas and Mary Gardner. To help make ends meet, little Ava's parents ran a boardinghouse for teachers of the rural Brodgen School, and the children often lent a hand.

After graduating from Rock Ridge High School in 1939, Ava went on to take secretarial courses at Atlantic Christian College in Wilson. She had completed her first year of study there when she visited her sister, Beatrice, and Beatrice's husband, Larry Tarr, a professional photographer in New York City. During that visit he took photos of Ava and

Ava Gardner was born in a rural area just outside of Smithfield. (Courtesy Johnston County Visitors Bureau)

displayed one on the wall of his studio. Someone saw her photo on the wall, and Ava was "discovered"—she was invited to do a screen test with Metro-Goldwyn-Mayer Studios and signed her first movie contract in 1941.

She later married actor Mickey Rooney, then swing-band leader Artie Shaw, and finally singer Frank Sinatra, but all of her marriages ended in divorce. She remained friends with each ex-husband throughout her life, and though she had no children, enjoyed close relationships with her nieces and nephews.

When she was thirty-three, Ava moved to Spain, where she lived for eight years; she then lived in London for twenty-six years until her death in 1990. She is remembered for many wonderful films, including *One Touch of Venus*.

But that's not the whole story about Ava Gardner. In 1939 an attractive secretarial student in Wilson had happened to kiss a twelve-year-old boy on the cheek. Two years later, the boy (Tom Banks) opened a newspaper and saw a photo of the face he couldn't forget, in an article about Ava's marriage to

Mickey Rooney. Only then did Banks learn the name of the beautiful girl who had kissed him.

The young man later became a doctor and married. He and his wife, Lorraine, spent much of their time collecting memorabilia relating to the beautiful actress. In the early 1980s, Banks bought the house where a young Ava and her family had lived in Smithfield, and for nine years he operated the Ava Gardner Museum in her former home.

Banks died of a stroke in August 1989 at the museum and, coincidentally, Gardner died in London of a stroke the following January. Lorraine Banks donated the collection to the city of Smithfield, and now the Ava Gardner Museum, relocated to Market Street in the heart of downtown Smithfield, can tell you everything else you'd like to know about the beloved and much-admired actress. See "Virtual North Carolina" for website information.

This Inmate Made Good Use of His Time!

The man everyone described as dapper and reserved with a slight Southern drawl had been convicted of embezzlement and sentenced to three years in an Ohio prison. He was the son of a North Carolina physician, lost his mother to tuberculosis, worked as a pharmacist, then worked on a ranch in Texas before becoming a bank teller. Convict Number 30664 seemed to carry with him an air of gentility that decried his tragic life and the crime of which he was convicted. Inmates and prison guards alike agreed: this well-spoken gentleman didn't belong behind prison walls and iron bars.

But the man served his time well and responsibly, and for the first time had a huge block of time in which to write. He took advantage of the three years, writing stories for magazines far from the Ohio prison walls. Most of his best friends and editorial associates in both North Carolina and New York were unaware of his incarceration or the conditions under which he was writing. It wasn't until his death that the truth finally came out: William Sydney Porter, who used the pen name O. Henry, had been imprisoned for three years for embezzling money from the First National Bank in Austin, Texas, where he had been a bank teller.

At the time of this charge, the young bank teller had jumped bond, supposedly heading to Honduras, which had no extradition treaty, but hastened back to Austin when he learned that his frail, sickly wife, Athol, was extremely ill. There he was tried for embezzlement and sent to the federal penitentiary in Columbus, Ohio.

William Sydney Porter, who used the pen name O. Henry

Scholars and biographers still disagree as to whether or not he committed the crime, but in 1898 he began serving the sentence he referred to once as when he "fell heir to enough spare time to take up fiction writing seriously."

Some people shine under difficult circumstances. During his incarceration the author refined his writing and became known as the literary genius from whose pen flowed more than two hundred stories, including such classics as *The Gift of the Magi* and *The Ransom of Red Chief*.

Incidentally, the city of Austin bears O. Henry no grudge. On the contrary, they celebrate him in annual "O. Henry Days" every summer, and the home where he lived is open for tours. In North Carolina, you can see some artifacts relating to the life of William Sydney Porter at the Greensboro Historical Museum, and can visit his burial place at Riverside Cemetery in Asheville.

The Man Who Couldn't Go Home

He was a big man, well over six feet tall and with large feet. The man the world would come to know and celebrate as North Carolina's and perhaps America's most famous literary figure was born in Asheville. Thomas Wolfe was more at home in cities such as New York and Paris, far removed from the Blue Ridge Mountains that he said "imprisoned" his imagination. The words he wrote, "You can't go home again," apparently were true for him.

Some of his peers were put off by what they perceived as Wolfe's intellectual snobbery and egomania. At age sixteen, he once addressed the Dialectic Society of Chapel Hill assembled at the University of North Carolina and announced that one day his own portrait would hang right next to those of Confederate generals and ex-presidents (he was right).

He is best known for his novels *Look Homeward, Angel* and *Of Time and the River*. The former book—said to be the most autobiographical work of fiction by an American writer—so inflamed and insulted the people of Asheville that when Wolfe returned to the city of his birth, they threatened to tar and feather him (as a matter of fact, *Angel* was banned from the city library and Wolfe did not revisit Asheville for eight years).

He died in 1938 of tubercular meningitis, just shy of his thirty-eighth birthday. Wolfe is buried with other family members in Riverside Cemetery in Asheville. The boardinghouse called Old Kentucky Home, which his mother Julia owned and where he grew up, still stands (in *Angel*, Wolfe called the boardinghouse "Dixieland").

The house was damaged by fire in July 1998, and for several years was closed for extensive renovations. In May 2004 it was once again restored and open to the public. Thanks to meticulous work by preservationists, the 6,000-square-foot home is more historically accurate than it was

Thomas Wolfe

before the fire, even down to the exact shade of yellow paint on its exterior. Today, you can see the house as it was in 1916, tour the grounds and learn more of Wolfe's history from the docents.

It strikes many visitors as ironic that the home of the man who couldn't go home again is a popular tourist stop.

Now known as the Thomas Wolfe Memorial, the home, now operated as a North Carolina State Historic Site, is frequented by fans and historians. Across the street and on a plaque by the curb of the Renaissance Hotel, you will find a pair of enormous shoes, a replica of the size thirteens worn by Wolfe. Bronzed by a local garden club, perhaps these wait for Wolfe to return, or for someone of his high literary caliber to come along and fill them one day.

Strange but True!

The Story of Thomas Wolfe's Real Angel

When Thomas Wolfe was a young boy, his father, William Oliver Wolfe, had a tombstone shop in Asheville. He once purchased an angel statue from Carrara, Italy—a marble piece with delicate details in which one hand held a lily, the other was raised in silent benediction, and one foot stood nearly on tiptoe. The angel sat on the front porch of the shop for years, and later was the inspiration behind Wolfe's first story, "Angel on the Porch." Most people believe the statue also inspired the title, *Look Homeward, Angel*, although those words were taken from Milton's classic poem, "Lycidas."

The angel statue now stands sentinel in Oakdale Cemetery in Hendersonville, about twenty miles south of Asheville.

"Good Night, and Good Luck"

Born Egbert Roscoe Murrow in 1908 in Greensboro, he changed his first name to Edward. Hardworking and ambitious, Murrow put himself through college at Washington State while working in logging camps, then became assistant director of the Institute of International Education. This was a far cry from the profession he finally chose, and for which he is best remembered.

Murrow went to work for CBS in 1935, then became the director of the European Bureau in 1937. His descriptions of the Nazi takeover of Vienna enthralled his radio listeners, and in London when he sat on a rooftop to make his moment-by-moment description of German bombing raids he became as famous as any newscaster today. His signature saying as he was going off the air was, "Good night, and good luck."

Returning to New York, he co-produced a weekly radio program, but it was his television series, *See It Now*, that turned the tide of public sentiment against Senator Joseph McCarthy, known for his vehement and career-destroying accusations of Communist activity (a movie entitled "Good Night and Good Luck," directed by George Clooney, was released in 2005 about Murrow and his role in bringing down McCarthy).

Cancer claimed the life of chain-smoking Murrow in 1965, but in his lifetime he helped set the gold standard for the journalistic profession. His hometown of Greensboro honors his memory with a street named after him (Murrow Boulevard) and a bust made by sculptor Ogden Deal, which stands on the grounds of the Greensboro Historical Museum. A permanent exhibit about Murrow, "Voices of the City," can be found inside the museum itself.

For you, Mr. Murrow, "Good night, and good luck."

A World War II Vet Still in Great Shape!

Lying at anchor on the Cape Fear River in the City of Wilmington, the Battleship *North Carolina* still looks great and is an impressive sight up close. She's more than 728 feet long, with a beam of a little more than 108 feet and has a displacement of 44,800 tons when fully loaded.

Commissioned in 1941, she was the first of ten battleships especially built for speed and power, a major naval force to be dealt with in World War II. The Battleship, well made for intensive confrontations, was a key player in every significant

The Battleship North Carolina lies at anchor in Wilmington. (Courtesy of N.C. Division of Tourism, Film and Sports Development)

naval offensive in the Pacific Ocean, including Guadalcanal and Okinawa. She was outfitted with three turrets, each containing three 16-inch guns that could fire 2,700-pound shells up to 23 miles away. She had enough additional firepower to bring 128 gun barrels to bear against any air target. With all this firepower in action, it often appeared from a distance that the ship was on fire.

In the Battleship's heyday, she was, for months on end, home to a crew of 2,339 men. The Battleship was its own self-contained city, with a bakery, hospital, movie theater, butcher shop, and general store. The crew slept stacked in bunk beds five-high and feeding such a massive number of people was a challenge.

As an example, here's a list of ingredients for a pumpkin pie recipe served onboard (don't try this at home):

6 cases pumpkin

100 pounds sugar

30 gallons water

30 dozen eggs

22 pounds cornstarch

The Battleship earned fifteen battle stars for her distinguished service, which took her the equivalent of three times around the world. Those and her other war decorations are on her side, just like on a soldier's chest. After her glory days at war, however, it seemed the government had other ideas for her: The *North Carolina* was decommissioned in 1947 and plans were announced she was going to be scrapped.

This spurred two Wilmington citizens, James S. Craig and Hugh Morton, into action. They, along with Governor Luther Hodges, launched a campaign to bring the ship to the port in Wilmington. More than 700,000 schoolchildren got involved, donating pennies, dimes and nickels to bring the ship home. Finally, the *North Carolina* was brought home to Wilmington. She was made into a memorial in 1961, dedicated to the World War II veterans who hailed from the Tar Heel State.

Now you can tour the Battleship, walk the bridge, and see the kitchen, the gun turrets, the engine room, the pilot house, and more. Besides being impressed and stirred by the size of the ship and her history as you walk around the ship and grounds, you might see or hear more: some workers say the ship is haunted by the ghosts of five crewmen who were killed by an enemy torpedo during the war. The ghosts have even frequented places outside the ship, such as the gift shop.

One gift shop employee told me, "My coworker and I were getting ready to close up for the night. We were in the stockroom putting up merchandise when there was an extremely loud crash that sounded like glass breaking in the gift shop. We knew it had to be the glass cases shattering." Thinking it might be someone robbing the shop, the employees fled. Returning later with help, they found nothing out of place and everything intact. "All the cases were just the way we left them," the employee said. "But no one could tell us we hadn't heard what we heard. The sound of all those cases breaking was deafening."

The ship has received much attention from paranormal investigators in the past few years, and it has been featured on the SciFi Channel's series, *Ghost Hunters*. Also, a book has been written by someone who has been working on the ship for more than 25 years: *Ghosts of the Battleship North Carolina*, written by Danny Bradshaw, will keep you awake long after the lights are off (I suggest reading it *after* you tour the ship).

When you visit, keep your eyes—and ears—open. Even in the gift shop.

It Started with a Mark on a Page

Governor Charles B. Aycock is known as North Carolina's "education governor." What is not so widely known is how and why he was so intent upon every person in the state being educated.

Born in Fremont in 1859 and the youngest of ten children, Charles was still a youngster when he witnessed something that altered his life. One day the county squire came by and needed Charles's mother's signature on a land deed. Instead of signing her name, his mother marked an X on the line where her signature would normally go. She admitted to a surprised Charles that she could neither read nor write. Even at his young age, Charles vowed to himself then and there that he would somehow see to it that every man and woman in North Carolina would have the chance to learn how to read and write.

Because of the Civil War, Aycock was unable to begin school until he was eight years old. This delay did little to

Governor Charles B Aycock took steps to assure that every person in North Carolina could learn to read and write. (Courtesy N.C. Dept. of Cultural Resources)

dissuade him. By the age of sixteen, Aycock was a teacher in a one-room schoolhouse. In 1877 he attended the University of North Carolina and graduated in three years. In 1881 he was elected superintendent of public instruction for Wayne County, the only office he held other than governor.

Aycock developed oratory skills that lifted him in prominence with both parties. He galvanized both Democrats and Republicans into action, taking steps to ensure every person in North Carolina could learn to read and write. During his term from 1901 to 1905, a schoolhouse was built every day Aycock was governor—including Sundays.

After his term, he became a nationally recognized spokesperson for education, traveling from Maine to Oklahoma to share his vision of universal education. On April 4, 1912, during a speech in Birmingham, Alabama, he suffered a heart attack and died, with the word "education" the last word from his lips.

In 1932 in Statutory Hall in the U.S. Capitol, Aycock was honored by one of the two statues representing the best of North Carolina. On the hundredth anniversary of his birth, his birthplace in Fremont was made into a State Historic Site, one of the first in the state. The site has been restored to the way it appeared when it was a farmstead in the late 1860s and early 1870s, and includes a one-room schoolhouse, similar to the one in which Aycock taught. It is open every day except public holidays. See "Virtual North Carolina" for website information.

Often it's not the moments shared by thousands that affect millions—a small moment witnessed only by one or two people may change history. Such was the case of Charles Aycock and a mark on a page that changed the history of North Carolina and made him known forever as the "education governor."

A Mother Immortalized

Anna McNeill was born in Clarkton on a plantation called Oak Forest. At age twenty-seven she married a West Point graduate, and had five sons, one of whom moved to live in Paris. Anna then lost her husband and three sons to illness. When the Civil War broke out, Anna felt unsafe in the South because she had been married to a West Point man, so she joined her son in France.

There Anna became immortalized and her son, famous. He was an artist and he had her sit for a portrait, entitling it *Arrangement in Grey and Black: The Artist's Mother.*

Had it not been for the Civil War and Anna McNeill Whistler's uneasiness at remaining in North Carolina, we might never have come to know her as *Whistler's Mother* and to know her son, James Whistler, and his resulting body of work.

Incidentally, the painting, owned by the government of France, is on exhibit at the Musée d'Orsay in Paris, and is a stunning work.

Guess Who?

This Winston-Salem native carved a niche for himself in sports journalism beginning in the 1950s. He often announced the matches of young boxer Cassius Clay (aka Muhammad Ali) and was a commentator for ABC's *Monday Night Football* in the 1970s. His name rapidly became well-known because of his unapologetically acerbic interview style and critical diatribes.

This announcer was none other than the inimitable Howard Cosell, who was born Howard Cohen and changed his last name while in college.

Welcome to Mayberry

The streets of Mount Airy bring to mind the fictitious village of Mayberry from the long-running television series, *The Andy Griffith Show.* Located just about seven miles south of the Virginia state line, the town is as colorful, warm, and quaint as your grandmother's handmade quilt.

It was here that Andy Griffith was born in 1935 to Carl and Geneva Griffith. A Depression-era baby, he learned the value of hard work and how to be resourceful with his talents. He had a quick wit, and many of his high school classmates at Rockford Street School referred to him as someone born to act.

Young Griffith also had musical talents; he learned to play the trombone from his minister, Reverend Ed Mickey, who presided over the Grace Moravian Church. The young man also took voice lessons and sang many solos at school and church events.

Griffith was possessed of a deep faith and pursued a degree in religion at the University of North Carolina at Chapel Hill. His acting talents would not be denied, however; he wound up as a member of the university theater group, The Playmakers, and changed his major to acting.

The rest is history: Andy Griffith got his first big break in Manteo, playing Sir Walter Raleigh in the play, *The Lost Colony*, about the missing colonists of Roanoke. From there he went to Broadway, starring in *No Time for Sergeants* and *Destry*. He made comedy records such as *What It Was, Was Football* and his own version of *Romeo and Juliet*. Most likely you know about his other blockbuster television series, *Matlock*.

What you may not know is that through *The Andy Griffith Show*, one of television's most successful programs, the young man who veered away from a possible degree in divinity is today indirectly inspiring people to explore their faith and values.

In 1998, preacher Joey Fann, who at that time presided over the Twickenham Church of Christ in Huntsville, Alabama, started a Bible study group that focused on Mayberry episodes to teach examples of Christian struggles, hopes, and life lessons.

Dubbed "The Search for Mayberry," the lessons caught on with hundreds of church groups around the country. Complete with lesson plans and other guides, the themed Bible study has been taught and used in about twenty churches in North Carolina, including the First Baptist Church in Albemarle, and Wrightsville United Methodist Church in Wrightsville Beach. In 2010, Joey Fann (who played "Goober") came out with his own book, *The Way Back to Mayberry: Lessons from Simpler Times*. The wave has continued to grow, with three volumes of a *Mayberry Study Guide* offered through Christian book retailers and on-line sources.

Although Andy Griffith passed away in 2012, he is honored with The Andy Griffith Museum located in Mount Airy. See "Virtual North Carolina" for website information.

Visiting Mayberry in Mount Airy

The Andy Griffith Show and the fictitious village of Mayberry continue to fascinate millions of Americans. In Mount Airy, Andy Griffith's boyhood home at 711 Haymore Street has been turned into a bed and breakfast, where die-hard fans can spend the night in the rooms young Andy lived in. "We stay pretty much booked up," said Trudy Willard, the guest services manager. "It's been amazing how many people have come through town to stay here at Andy Griffith's boyhood home. When folks stay with us, we play music from the show and also let our guests view films from the series while they're here."

In addition, the city itself in some ways replicates the *Mayberry* set, complete with Floyd's Barber Shop and a diner called Snappy Lunch. Mount Airy has capitalized on America's fascination with all things related to the series, and holds an annual *Andy Griffith Show*–themed festival called "Mayberry Days." During the celebration, many of the show's characters make special appearances in town.

If you've been looking for Mayberry, now you know where to find it.

GUESS WHO?

This remarkable woman is often hailed as a sort of "Renaissance" woman—she's known for being an educator, speaker, writer, activist—there's nothing, it seems, she hasn't done. She helped heal thousands of women who had also been victims of rape when she wrote about her own experience in a book she wrote called *I Know Why the Caged Bird Sings*.

Who is this remarkable woman? Maya Angelou, who died in Winston-Salem in 2014.

Helping Cure the Ills of Society

Near the middle of the nineteenth century a young girl named Elizabeth Blackwell decided she wanted to pursue a profession to which few women had aspired. She told her friend and minister-physician in Asheville, John Dickinson, that she would pay "whatever price demanded" to reach her goal of becoming a physician.

Blackwell was born in England and came to America with her parents when she was about ten years old. After her father's death, she and her two sisters started a private school in Cincinnati, Ohio. From there she taught in Kentucky, then found her way to North Carolina, where she took a teaching job in Asheville.

Blackwell, then twenty-five, realized that she had a penchant for curing the sick, and read everything she could about medicine. At this time she and Dickinson became friends, and he and his brother, a doctor in Charleston, South Carolina, loaned her medical reading materials.

Elizabeth Blackwell was the first woman in the United States to receive a medical degree. (Courtesy N.C. Dept. of Cultural Resources)

When Blackwell announced her intention to obtain a medical license, Dickinson sent her to his brother, an instructor at Charleston Medical College. There, Samuel Dickinson tutored her in the healing arts, for free.

Blackwell applied for admission to Harvard Medical School, then Yale, then Bowdoin. All three rejected her. Other medical schools in New York City and Philadelphia were equally discouraging. Finally, she was accepted to Geneva

Medical School in New York, now a part of Syracuse University. She had applied at thirty institutions before being accepted.

Her college experience at Geneva was difficult. As the only female, many of her fellow students refused to acknowledge her presence, and some professors turned her away from anatomy lessons. Despite this, Blackwell graduated in January 1849, with the highest honors of her class—becoming the first woman in the United States to receive a medical degree.

Blackwell's professional obstacles did not stop there. Turned away from clinics and hospitals, she went on to study obstetrics at a maternity hospital in Paris, then undertook further medical studies in London.

After returning to New York City, despite opposition and a lack of funds, Blackwell helped establish the New York Infirmary for Women and Children in 1857 and the first Women's Medical College in 1868. Because of the opposition she had faced, Blackwell became even more rigid in her resolve to further rights for women and became known as "a militant suffragette."

Throughout the rest of her life, Elizabeth Blackwell was active in the struggle for women's rights. By means of her stubbornness, vision, and perseverance, she opened the way for women to enter the world of medicine. You can learn more about this remarkable woman by visiting the North Carolina Museum of History in Raleigh. In Asheville, you can take their walking tour, where you will find a bronze sculpture on the side of a bank building near Patton Avenue and Church Street. The sculpture, an arbor created by artists James Barnhill and Joe Miller, features the leaves of many healing plants, all of which are indigenous to North Carolina, above the image of Dr. Blackwell. See "Virtual North Carolina" for website information.

GUESS WHO?

This broadcast journalist was born in Wilmington in 1920 and was later teamed with co-anchor Chet Huntley on a news-and-commentary show. Through his years as an objective news commentator, he won the Peabody, Sylvania, and Emmy Awards for his work. He published his memoirs, *Everybody is Entitled to My Opinion*, in 1996, and passed away in 2003. Who is this news icon?

David McClure Brinkley.

Famous North Carolinians Trivia

Q. What "poet of small-town America" who was also a newsman for CBS was born in Wilmington in 1934? (Hint: he is memorialized in a nature trail in Windsor, part of the Roanoke River National Wildlife Refuge.)

> A. Charles Kurault, who looked for stories down the side roads and in small towns. His show was *On the Road with Charles Kurault.*

Q. What TV personality and comedian, whose real name is Milton Hines, was born in Franklinton?

> A. Soupy Sales.

Q. What Emmy award–winning actress made her home in Siler City and played Aunt Bee on *The Andy Griffith Show*?

> A. Frances Bavier. Her home still stands at 503 West Elk Street.

Q. In what North Carolina town did Marjorie Kinnan Rawlings write her novel *The Yearling*?

> A. Banner Elk.

Q. What artist was fired from an Asheville construction company in 1924 for doodling on subdivision plats? (Hint: his first character was named Mickey.)

> A. Walt Disney, who moved to California after he was fired. The plats are still on file in the Buncombe County Courthouse.

Q. What famous writer of the Jazz Age lived in the Grove Park Inn in Asheville in 1936?

> A. F. Scott Fitzgerald.

Q. Who in 1953 was named North Carolina's first poet laureate?

A. James Larkin Pearson.

Q. What Chatham County slave wrote *The Hope of Liberty*, which was the first book by a black author in the South?

A. Known as "The Black Bard of North Carolina," his name was George Moses Horton. He was posthumously inducted into the North Carolina Literary Hall of Fame, located in the James Boyd House in the town of Southern Pines.

CHAPTER 6

FROM THE HILLS OF NORTH CAROLINA

Oh, to What Heights They Will Go!

The Smoky Mountains' highest mountain is named in honor of the late professor Elisha Mitchell, with an unusual story behind the naming of Mount Mitchell.

It started with a dispute between mountain explorer and Tennessee senator Thomas Lanier Clingman and Mitchell, a professor at the University of North Carolina, about what peak in the Appalachian Mountains was the highest. Mitchell claimed Black Dome in North Carolina; Clingman said Tennessee's Smoky Dome had that honor.

While doing altitude checks of Black Dome, Mitchell fell and drowned in a stream. After this, Clingman hired Arnold

Guyot, a Swiss-born geographer, to make a study of the mountains. At 6,643 feet, Smoky Dome (now Clingman's Dome) is the highest point in Tennessee—but Black Dome (now Mount Mitchell) won the contest, at 6,684 feet.

Today you can visit the Mount Mitchell State Park and Museum, which offers many ways to learn more about the mountain that caused such a stir.

This Should "Peak" Your Interest

The only county in the entire United States with a mountain range lying completely within its borders is the Piedmont's Stokes County. The mountain range is Sauratown Range, an ancient range named for the Saura Indians. This mountain is for experienced climbers only and is not accessible year 'round. A mountain climbing club, Carolina Climbers Coalition, has a 20-year lease (with nearby YMCA Camp Hanes) giving them permission to explore the mountain range; it is only with their approval that climbers are allowed to explore this challenging mountain range. See "Virtual North Carolina" for website information.

The Vanderbilt Legacy in North Carolina

At the time of his father's death in 1885, George Washington Vanderbilt was considered the world's most eligible and wealthy bachelor. The twenty-three-year-old heir to part of his father's $200 million estate, this youngest son had been raised in New York City and was both well educated (with a reading knowledge of eight languages besides English) and well traveled. But in 1888 he was bitten by the love bug.

This young heir was smitten not with a woman, but with a place. When he visited the mountainous and breathtaking area of Asheville, Vanderbilt knew he had to make his home in the area.

He initially thought to build a "modest winter retreat" to escape the inclement and cold weather in New York. To carry out his vision, Vanderbilt appointed experienced craftsmen especially trained in the ways of the Old World. For home design, he chose architect Richard Morris Hunt, and for the landscaping and grounds design, Frederick Law Olmsted, who designed New York City's Central Park. For this winter

The Biltmore house in Asheville is the largest privately owned home in the world. (Photo by James Valentine, © Biltmore Company, used with permission)

home he chose a lovely wooded area outside Asheville.

As time passed, architect Hunt's plans evolved and grew to resemble a European castle more than an Appalachian mountain retreat. Vanderbilt's acreage also increased as he continued to expand his landholdings, eventually reaching 125,000 acres, including Mount Pisgah.

As any homebuilder can tell you, construction always costs more and takes longer than you anticipate. Vanderbilt's house project took six years to complete, but what we know today as Biltmore House is unlike anything else in America.

From banquet hall to library (with walls of leather-bound volumes) to a swimming pool to its thirty-four bedrooms, Biltmore House impresses all who see it. It is now open to the public, preserved by Vanderbilt descendants. Biltmore Estate itself includes the house, a winery, vineyards, an equestrian center, lovely gardens, and an inn with more than two hundred rooms.

Biltmore House is listed in the *Guinness Book of World Records* as the largest privately owned home in the world. While much of the other Vanderbilts' fortunes have been spent on things long forgotten, George Vanderbilt created an enduring masterpiece with Old World elegance that continues to delight and inspire people. See "Virtual North Carolina" at the back of this book for website information.

Did You Know?

The first part of the name Biltmore was taken from the word "Bildt," which is the name of the Dutch town of George Vanderbilt's ancestors. The "more" part is an old English word meaning "open, rolling land."

A Tragic Page in History

On April 7, 1838, General Winfield Scott sent his superiors this message: "I shall probably call for the following detachments of militia to rendezvous at the places mentioned, two regiments of 1,840 Georgians to rendezvous at New Echota, one regiment of 750 Alabamians to rendezvous at Belfont, one regiment of 740 North Carolinians to rendezvous at Franklin, NC, one regiment of 740 Tennesseans to rendezvous at Ross Landing. 3,700 troops plus 2,200 regulars. Subsistence for the foregoing troops at the places mentioned will be required for 90 days, commencing about the middle of May."

Scott wasn't gathering the regiments for battle, but to round up Native American people living in and near there, for the long, bitter march we now know as the Trail of Tears. More than four thousand Native American men, women and children perished in 1838 as a result.

The infamous "Trail of Tears" forced march has been commemorated in a number of ways. The Cherokee Nation offers visitors ways to learn more about their ancient heritage through a visit to the Oconaluftee Indian Village; it is here they offer their iconic dramatic rendition of a play they call "Unto These Hills." The Indian Village gives visitors a glimpse of what life was like for the Cherokee in the 18th century. You can also learn more about the Cherokee People at the North Carolina Museum of History in Raleigh. See "Virtual North Carolina" for website information.

The Rebirth of a Nation

The Eastern Band of the Cherokee Nation has a long and proud history of not only surviving but thriving despite circumstances that would have wiped out lesser people. Known as one of the "Five Civilized Tribes," before encroachment of white settlers, the Cherokee had a constitution; a capitol in New Echota, Georgia; their own written language; and their own newspaper, the *Cherokee Phoenix*.

You might think that these attributes would have encouraged white settlers to live peacefully with the Cherokee, but this was not the case. Whites seemed even more determined to take over the Cherokee tribal lands.

In 1835 tribal leaders saw resistance was futile, so they signed the Treaty of New Echota, which stated they would move to seven million acres "in the Arkansas River region" as their new homeland. In turn, the U.S. government under President Andrew Jackson agreed to set aside two thousand dollars annually to educate Cherokee children and provide the departing families with various equipment and supplies. It also agreed to replace the printing press and type that white people had recently destroyed.

Scouts began rounding up Cherokee people. Approximately a thousand hid out in the mountains under the leadership of Utsali, also known as Lichen. One Cherokee man, Tsali, was in his cabin with his wife and children when scouts arrived and ordered them to pack what they could carry and walk to the stockade in Bushnell (now under the waters of Fontana Lake). They were joined by Tsali's brother-in-law and proceeded to the stockade under guard.

The march west, known today as the Trail of Tears, began in 1838 from Bushnell, led by General Winfield Scott. Along the trail, many of the Cherokee began dying. The old people and the very young were the most vulnerable to illness and death, as the uniformed soldiers prodded them along—sometimes with bayonets.

When Tsali's wife, Wilani, stumbled and fell, she was prodded with a soldier's bayonet. Tsali held his anger in check and decided on a course of action. Speaking in Cherokee, Tsali told his relatives that at the next

The Trail of Tears and Tsali's sacrifice are remembered in the drama Unto These Hills performed at Qualla Boundary. (Courtesy Cherokee Historical Association)

bend in the trail, he would trip and fall, saying he had injured his ankle. By creating a distraction, Tsali and his family escaped the soldiers, but during the struggle one soldier was killed. Suddenly Tsali and his family were not only fugitives, but wanted for murder. The family took refuge in a cave under Clingman's Dome. Meanwhile, Utsali's band of Cherokee continued to elude capture in the mountains.

Through a trader, Scott offered to let Utsali's band stay in the mountains if Tsali, his brother-in-law, and sons surrendered. Tsali agreed.

Although his youngest son (Wasituna, called Washington by white people) and Wilani were spared, Tsali (his brother-in-law) and two of his sons were taken to be executed. Tsali's last request was that he be shot, not by white soldiers, but by his own people. Three Cherokee men were chosen to be the executioners.

Because of Tsali's sacrifice, the Cherokee who remained in the mountains began to thrive. The descendants of those who escaped the Trail of Tears now live on the Cherokee Reservation known as the Qualla Boundary, near western North Carolina.

Today, the reservation is a thriving community and popular tourist stop, with various attractions. The play, *Unto These Hills,* depicts the history of the Cherokee and Tsali's sacrifice, and more than one hundred thousand people saw it during its opening season in 1950 (as of 2022, more than 6 *million* people have been in the audience since then). There is also a new production of the play entitled *Unto These Hills...A Retelling,* which is growing in popularity as well. The "Eternal Flame" at Cherokee's Mountainside Theater will soon have a monument in the form of seven slabs of granite in a sacred spiral, with the names of loved ones, departed or still living, engraved on the stones.

Also within the reservation is the aforementioned Oconaluftee Indian Village, a unique recreation of a Cherokee community in the eighteenth century. This was created in 1952 by a cooperative effort of anthropological experts from the University of Georgia, University of Tennessee, and University of North Carolina, under the supervision of the reservation-based Tsali Institute for Cherokee Indian Research.

The Museum of the Cherokee Indian, one of the oldest Indian museums in the United States, is itself a must-see, with state-of-the-art exhibits and interactive displays. The museum also publishes the *Journal of Cherokee Studies,* the oldest journal devoted specifically to one tribal group.

Today the reservation of fifty-six thousand acres is visited by more than a million people a year. Located at the North Carolina entrance to the Great Smoky Mountains National Park and at the terminus of the Blue Ridge Parkway, the Qualla Boundary offers easy access to visitors from those destinations. You can visit and learn more about a people who might have been lost were it not for the sacrifice of Tsali and his family.

A Moonshine Story

The Appalachian Mountains of western North Carolina have historically been home to people who made illegal whiskey, called moonshine. It might be illegal, but to those in the mountains, it was tradition and a right uniquely handed down by each generation.

The making of moonshine has long been a cherished family tradition among the people of this area, dating to the post–Revolutionary War years. In appreciation for their contribution, veterans of this war were given certificates from the new government, exempting these veterans from the law that made it illegal to make and sell whiskey. They took advantage of this and industriously created their own versions of various homemade spirits. The next generation followed suit, as did the next. The practice became a family tradition, with descendants of the original moonshiners believing that the exemptions their fathers had enjoyed were "passed down" to them. Being upstanding, God-fearing citizens didn't interfere with making moonshine, which they considered their right. Although the numbers of moonshiners have dwindled, they still exist.

In January 1951 a magazine called the *State* reported that in one county alone, 264 stills were seized and fourteen operators arrested the previous year. If you want to see a still up close, one captured by agents in the 1960s is on display in the Appalachian Cultural Museum, which is part of Appalachian State University in Boone. See "Virtual North Carolina" for website information.

DID YOU KNOW?

The term "moonshiner" came about because the illegal whiskey-making business was more safely carried on by dark of night. Those who sold this contraband were known as "bootleggers" because they often hid bottles of whiskey in the tops of their loose-fitting boots. What started as moonshine running (or whiskey tripping) in automobiles, racing to escape "revenuers," became the billion-dollar industry known today as stock car racing.

An Odd Population

In Flat Rock you'll find the former home of famous author Carl Sandburg—poet, "champion of the common man," and biographer of Abraham Lincoln. His home, now maintained as a National Historic Site by the U.S. Park Service, was named Connemara by the original owner, who was Irish. Although during the pandemic the home was closed for tours, as of press time, the home was in a re-opening phase. Today you can learn more about the man who was known as the "Poet of the People;" Connemara is under the auspices of the National Park Service.

DID YOU KNOW?

The oldest frame house west of the Blue Ridge Mountains is the Allison-Deaver Home in Brevard, dating back to 1815. Open for tours, events and school field trips, the house is unique because nothing has been changed in any way. The wall paneling, paint, structure, and the interior furnishings remain as they were in the early 1800s. The only work done on the house has been for necessary repairs and restoration work.

FROM THE HILLS OF NORTH CAROLINA TRIVIA

Q. What county is known as the Heart of the Blue Ridge?

A. Yancey.

Q. What county calls itself the Jewel of the Blue Ridge?

A. Madison County, because it offers diverse outdoor activities, scenic beauty—and the only hot mineral spring in the state.

Q. What county calls itself the Land of Waterfalls?

A. Transylvania, with more than 250 waterfalls within its borders.

Q. Approximately how many visitors come to see the Biltmore House annually?

A. 1.7 million annually, according to their latest records at press time (2022).

Q. What is the name of the largest recreation area on the Blue Ridge Parkway?

A. Doughton Park.

Q. What town is known as Sourwood City because of its many sourwood trees (which produce a delicious honey as well), and is home to the annual Sourwood Festival?

A. Black Mountain, North Carolina.

Q. Where can you find the annual Gee-Haw Whimmy Diddle (a toy unique to Appalachia) Competition?

A. Southern Highland Handicraft Guild Folk Art Center, just outside Asheville.

Q. Where was the site of the first execution (and only hanging) of a woman in North Carolina?

A. Morganton, which was where convicted murderess Frankie Silver was hanged in 1832.

Q. What was the first ski resort in the South?

A. Cataloochee Ski Area, in Maggie Valley.

CHAPTER 7

RELIGION AND UTOPIAN COMMUNITIES

Cursed by a Man of the Cloth

In 1705 Bath was the first settlement the North Carolina Assembly incorporated as a town. By the early eighteenth century, Bath was a thriving seaport (and home to a few pirates—but that's in another chapter) on the shoreline of North Carolina and at the mouth of the Pamlico River. However, one evangelist is said to have changed the luck of the town.

Evangelist George Whitefield came to Bath around 1747. He began exhorting the people against what he called deadly sins—cursing, drinking, and dancing. He was most adamantly against the latter.

This traveling preacher apparently was always prepared for his own trip to Heaven, because oddly enough, he carried his coffin in his wagon wherever he went. "When I pass on," he reportedly said, "I want my coffin right here." Even more bizarre was his habit of sleeping in his coffin at night, supposedly to avoid the inn and its attendant shady goings-on.

Whitefield finally gave up on converting Bath and the people who looked at him with more than a little suspicion. Just like the disciples of old, he drove his wagon to the outskirts of town, removed his shoes, shook the dirt from them, and put a curse on the town. He told onlookers that the Bible said people who couldn't get sinners to reform were to do just what he had done, and by shaking the dust of Bath from his shoes, the town would be cursed for its hardness of heart against the Word of God.

He is quoted as having said, "I say to the village of Bath, village you shall remain, now and forever, forgotten by men and nations until such time as it pleases God to turn the light of His countenance again upon you."

Since Whitefield's curse, downtown Bath has been struck three times by fire, and it remains a sleepy (but charming) little village on the coast, with its permanent population being only (as of press time) 220 souls.

Since this book first came out, Rev. Mark Creech, Executive Director of the Christian Action League of North Carolina, used my story about Bath to write a column, using the village as an example. His title was "Forgotten by Men and Nations," and in the column, he exhorted Americans to relate the story of Bath to our own hard-heartedness, and to turn away from sin.

Cursed or not, the town of Bath recently celebrated its tricentennial in 2005 and is a lovely town to tour. See "Virtual North Carolina" for website information.

Stories of Snake Handlers

Differences in interpreting the Holy Scriptures have often led to new and sometimes unusual religions and cults. One of these religions involves serpent handling, founded on the Gospel of Saint Mark (16:18): "And they shall take up serpents...." The Gospel of Mark also referred to spirit-filled people having the ability to speak in tongues and drink "any

Preacher Charles Prince was arrested for handling deadly snakes during an outdoor worship service held behind his bait shop in Canton. (One of the arresting officers was bitten by a yellow timber rattlesnake and required hospitalization) (Photo © Mike Dubose)

deadly thing" without injury.

Many people who participate in speaking in tongues and drinking deadly substances (including strychnine and lye) consider themselves to be simply following the word of God, and not doing anything unusual. If they get bitten or die, then it is God's will that it is "their time" and has nothing to do with their lack of faith or God's protection.

George Went Hensley is generally given credit for introducing handling of serpents as a religious rite. It began in Ooltewah, Tennessee, at Rainbow Rock on White Oak Mountain around 1905 (although some accounts place the first handling around 1908). Hensley had led a tumultuous life but was converted and began to follow all the teachings of God, including what he believed the Gospel of Mark dictated: that the truly faithful should handle serpents and drink toxic substances as part of their religious practices.

Many churches took up the practice back then, and it was most popular in Tennessee, West Virginia, Kentucky, and North Carolina. While believers saw snake handling as following the word of God, the rest of society considered it bizarre and abnormal. Finally, in the 1940s state legislatures began to make snake handling illegal, and North Carolina outlawed it in 1949. Despite this legislation, many refused to cease handling snakes, saying they were following God's law (and were therefore above man's law). Many died from being bitten—including Hensley in 1955, after handling his last rattlesnake.

The House of Prayer in the Name of Jesus Christ in Marshall still practices snake handling and as of press time, remained the only place of worship in the Tar Heel State that still clings to this literal interpretation of the writings of the

Gospel of Mark. The preacher at the House of Prayer declined interviews, and if you go to a service there, no one can guarantee you'll see snake handling. Believers say that particular activity is a spontaneous, spirit-led phenomenon—and not something one can schedule into a service.

The Religion of the Lost Cause

Before the Civil War, preachers shouted sermons from pulpits in support of the South. When war broke out, those preachers fervently rallied their flocks to stay true to the South's cause. They claimed that every Confederate victory was a sign of God's love for the new nation, every defeat an indication of God's wrath.

After the Civil War, those religious leaders strove to help people make sense out of their defeat and created a religion: The Religion of the Lost Cause. After all, Southerners observed, we can only become perfect through suffering.

Every faith has its martyrs and the Confederate States of America had many, from its generals to its president to its fallen sons and daughters. Robert E. Lee, Stonewall Jackson, and Jefferson Davis became mythic figures—to some, almost saint-like.

Terry Matthews, Ph.D., of Wake Forest University has lectured on this religious phenomenon in his course, Religion in the South. He describes this post-war religion as a "mixture of Southern nationalism and evangelicalism" aimed at recreating a perceived "golden age." Many Southerners saw some instances in Lee's life, he says, as parallel to the life of Jesus Christ. For example, Lee's decision to reject command of the Union Army was seen by followers as "the equal of

Christ's temptation in the wilderness" and fighting the Union Army was an example of Good fighting Evil. In the new religion, the North was an evil "marauding monster," and the South everything that was pure and godly.

In his lecture, "Baptized in Blood: The Religion of the Lost Cause," Matthews says this new religion helped further the dream of "a cohesive South with a separate cultural identity," which became even more important after the war. This fervor with which followers embraced the notion of keeping the South "pure" later contributed to rampant and widespread incidents of lynching.

In keeping with this new faith, Southerners boycotted national holidays such as Thanksgiving and the Fourth of July, but Lee's birthday of January 19 became a holiday throughout

General Robert E. Lee became the Christ figure of the Religion of the Lost Cause. (National Archives)

the South. Among the many Civil War memorials and statues the South erected between 1890 to 1910, there was one at Duke Chapel in Durham: a statue of Lee, standing right there with the saints. Following protests, the statue was removed in 2017 and placed in an undisclosed location where, according to *National Public Radio* news, "it would be preserved and protected."

The Enduring Mystery and Legacy of Roanoke

In the 1580s, England decided to send a fleet of ships and colonists to the New World, where Spain and France had failed at colonization. What piqued the interest of Queen Elizabeth I (daughter of Henry VIII) were rumors of Spanish galleons returning to their home ports laden with treasures of precious metals and lumber from the New World. While Spain retained claim to the newly discovered continent, England decided that a colony far enough away from Spanish efforts might just work, and Elizabeth sent Sir Humphrey Gilbert, who returned home after a brief stay in Newfoundland.

The next person chosen to carry out the charter was Gilbert's cousin, Sir Walter Raleigh, who had a burning desire to show England the feasibility of a colony in the New World. Raleigh worked quickly to gather a crew to send on the venture.

On July 4, 1584, the crew sighted land—the shoreline of what is now North Carolina—and gathered specimens of plant and animal life and drew maps of the area. They took these back home, along with two Native Americans, Manteo and Wanchese, as specimens of humanity that existed there. Raleigh's marketing tactics were on target: the English people were enthralled by the sight of the two aboriginal men and the amazing stories of the New World. Raleigh received more money to supply and fund the next voyage and additional ships.

After one bungled attempt at a settlement (they arrived too late to plant crops to tide them over the winter) in May 1585, Governor John White arrived in Roanoke with 113 men, women, and children. They repaired the cottages left by the first settlers and built new ones. On August 18 the first English child born in the New World was delivered. Her name was Virginia Dare.

Like the previous settlers' attempt, these people had also arrived too late for crops to sustain them through the winter. Governor White returned to England to expedite shipments in order for his colony to survive that brutal season.

When White arrived in England, however, no ships could be spared; England was about to defend herself in a war against Spain. White would not return to Roanoke Island until three years later, in 1590. When he did, he found the colony deserted, with deer and other wildlife roaming the houses and weeds growing in abundance. The only clues about what had happened to the New World's first colonists were carvings on a tree and a post: CROATOAN and CRO. The colonists were never seen again, and White eventually returned to England.

What happened to the people of what is now called the Lost Colony? No one will ever know for certain, although quite a few have ventured hypotheses. Many historians believe that the carvings indicated the colonists had moved to Croatoan Island, fifty miles away, now the southern part of Hatteras Island. This theory is borne out by a report that in 1701, surveyor John Lawson traveled to Croatoan Island and met gray-eyed Hatteras Indians who were familiar with books and indicated that their ancestors were white people. If this theory is correct, then the settlers of the "Lost Colony" were never lost, just absorbed by their environment and their new friends. Findings from archaeological digs, including copper farthings, lead shot, and gun flints, seem to support this conclusion.

Today, two groups are working to try and solve at least some of the mysteries surrounding the Lost Colony. Phil Evans, who formed the First Colony Foundation (FCF), is an attorney in Durham, North Carolina; since in 1982 he first stumbled upon the remains of an old well in what is now thought to be the colony site, he has been so fascinated with the mystery that he formed the foundation to raise funds for exploration and excavation of the area. Another group, the Institute for International Maritime Research (based in Washington, NC) has been working with the FCF to locate and identify remains of the settlement.

Historians believe that the Roanoke colony was a success. The information from the initial explorers on Roanoke's first sailing proved invaluable toward establishing a successful colony further north.

That colony was Jamestown, Virginia, settled in 1607. While Raleigh's dream of establishing the first permanent colony in America was not realized, he did manage to fuel the imaginations of English people everywhere. As for some of the new explorers of the area such as Evans, although they're digging for answers many of them would just as soon remain fascinated with the enduring mystery of Roanoke.

For more about the FCF, see "Virtual North Carolina" at the back of this book.

133

DID YOU KNOW?

One of the indigenous people Sir Walter Raleigh brought to London was named Manteo. North Carolina eventually named a coastal town after this man. It is here, in the city of Manteo, that every year the drama, "The Lost Colony," is performed on stage during the summer months.

The Roanoak Mystery is Dramatized by "The Lost Colony," performed in Manteo. (Courtesy of N. C. Division of Tourism, Film and Sports Development)

The Serendipitous Utopia

While most, if not all, utopian colonies and societies are planned, this one happened in a rather serendipitous fashion. Even odder is the fact that it came about because of World War I.

Once war was announced in April 1917, the enemy's commercial ships were seized in American ports. One of the ships seized on April 6, 1917, was the largest ship in the world, the *Vaterland*. The seized *Vaterland* and other German and Austrian vessels were overhauled and converted to U.S. troopships, and the U.S. government set about trying to find a place in which to house their sailors, referred to as "enemy aliens."

In looking for a temporary home for the detainees, the government search team discovered the small, quiet town of Hot Springs, North Carolina. The town had a beautifully appointed and large inn called the Mountain Park Hotel. On two hundred acres of rolling lands, it was a resort famous for the health-giving hot bubbling springs for which the town was named. Once the hotel owner agreed to the terms set by the government (a monthly payment, among other things), the hotel's guests were asked to leave; preparations began for the arrival of the more than two thousand Germans, mostly civilians. New structures such as a barracks, water tower, mess hall, and guardhouses were built, as well as everything else this strange "city" would need, including a hospital (which was transformed from Hampton College). An eight-foot board fence topped with barbed wire was installed around the 2,251-foot perimeter of the former resort. Seven acres of the hotel grounds were made into a garden for these new "guests" to grow crops.

It is difficult to imagine the reaction of the 650 inhabitants of that small village on June 8, 1917, when the first eighteen unwilling guests the locals called "Germanies" arrived. The population of the camp continued to swell until by 1918 it had reached 2,185 men—more than triple the town's inhabitants.

Nearly thirty of the sailors' wives and children also arrived and boarded with Hot Springs families so they could be near their husbands and fathers. After a time, the townspeople realized that there were talents and skills to be shared with and learned from their new, unexpected neighbors. German was spoken on the streets, the children attended school together, German housewives taught some of the local women fine needle working, and "alien" wives were regularly invited to tea with their American neighbors. The German internees showed their industriousness by using their skills in the garden, in raising animals, or in shoe cobbling or cooking. Guards and their captors formed friendships, and guards began taking these new friends home for dinner. With the internment of the thirty-five-member German Imperial Band, many a Sunday afternoon found the locals enjoying the band's performances, described by one news reporter as every bit as good as the Boston Symphony Orchestra. The teachers at nearby Dorland Institute arranged for some of the camp members to come give talks to their students, in a cultural exchange of sorts. The prison had become a type of paradise, it seems, for only one German ever tried to escape—he was, in fact, successful and never seen or heard from again.

The interned men created their own German village with cottages, fences, and even a chapel, all in the Old World style. Some of the buildings became artists' studios and woodworking shops. Newspapers from New York to San Francisco carried stories of the internment camp; the *New York Times* expressed the hope that American prisoners of war would be treated just as well.

But this utopia was not to endure. In July 1918 the Department of Labor and the secretary of state made a joint decision to concentrate all prisoners of war, both civilian and soldier, at the War Prison Barracks in Fort Oglethorpe, Georgia. The Hot Springs "aristocrats," as the *Asheville Citizen* called them, would have to live the life of other prisoners of war.

On the day the men were to leave, some speculate that, in an attempt to stay, they deliberately poisoned their drinking water. Whatever the cause, by the end of the day on August 1, 1918, more than 110 cases of typhoid fever had gripped the camp. Seventeen of the men died at Hot Springs, eighteen others died at a hospital in Asheville, and twenty-six stayed behind until they were fit for travel. On August 31 the remaining men were taken to Fort Oglethorpe, and by the end of September, the formerly bustling town of nearly 3,400 had shrunk to its original 650 residents.

Shortly after Armistice Day in November 1918, the charming, painstakingly erected buildings of the compound were blown up, one by one, by the townspeople. The Mountain Park Hotel and last remaining vestiges of the camp burned in 1920. The "accidental utopia" was no more; all that remains are the steps of the old inn.

In 1932 the American Legion of Asheville held a dedication ceremony on the camp site. It was attended by German dignitaries and nearly four thousand spectators and aired both in the United States and over German airwaves.

Although unplanned and unforeseen, the Hot Springs internment camp led to understanding between some of the two countries' people. Author Jacqueline Burin Painter wrote in *The German Invasion of Western North Carolina* (Asheville: Biltmore Press, 1992) that this camp was "an example for the world...truly one of western North Carolina's finest hours."

Today, you can see and learn more about this unexpected utopian experiment; the Hot Springs Welcome Center has quite a number of photographs of the buildings and the German people who, for a brief span of time, called Hot Springs home. See "Virtual North Carolina" for website information.

Bethabara: The Moravian Settlement

The Moravian Church is a Protestant denomination with roots in Hernhut, Saxony, in the early eighteenth century. In 1753 the site was chosen for what would become the first Moravian settlement in North Carolina. Named Bethabara, which translates to mean "house of passage," it was meant to be a temporary settlement until the town of Salem could be completed. Bethabara flourished and until 1772 served as the area's trade and religious center.

Costumed guides give tours of the 1788 Germeinhaus (German for 'Peoples Church') in historic Bethabara Park, the site of the first Morovian settlement in North Carolina. (Courtesy of N. C. Division of Tourism, Film and Sports Development)

Near Bethabara, some Moravian Germans settled in Salem. Salem later merged with Winston, becoming Winston-Salem. Now both Bethabara and Winston-Salem are popular with visitors who love history, shopping, and stepping back in time. The area remains one of the most authentic and documented colonial sites in the United States, and Bethabara itself is a National Historic Landmark.

Also called the *Unitas Fratrum*, or the American branch of the Renewed Church of the Unity of Brethren, the Moravian Church is separated into north and south provinces. The Northern Province has its U.S. headquarters in Bethlehem, Pennsylvania; the Southern Province, in Winston-Salem. Moravians emphasize fellowship and missionary work, and their church music (especially their singing) is known around the world. Bethabara Park is open for tours and has special events throughout the year. See "Virtual North Carolina" for website information.

DID YOU KNOW?

The tiny town of Bolivia has a Buddhist temple. Dedicated to the much-beloved and venerated king of Thailand, the Wat Carolina Buddhajakra Vanaram (wat is Thai for "temple") houses monks who represent an unbroken lineage of twenty-five hundred years.

The Dam That Built a Town

The year was 1941, just a few weeks after the disaster at Pearl Harbor. To fuel the United States' efforts in World War II, hydroelectric power was needed. Government officials from the Tennessee Valley Authority picked a spot to establish a dam that would provide such power, in an isolated area between Joyce Kilmer Memorial Forest and the Great

Smoky Mountains National Park. Within a few more weeks, more than six thousand workers, accompanied by their families, arrived to build the dam.

There is always time for family fun at Fontana Village. (Courtesy Fontana Village)

The workers and their families needed accommodations and in short order cottages, a school, a church, and a hospital were built. For years the incidental community was home, supplying the workers and their families with a social life, an education, and a sense of history. In 1945, with the dam completed, the workers were no longer needed and they scattered, abandoning the place known as Fontana Village.

Today, Fontana Dam is open for tours, with a tram to take visitors to the bottom. The top of the dam is accessible by foot and is where the Appalachian Trail continues.

And what of the small community that was once home to the dam builders and their families? Fontana Village was turned into a vacation spot after the war, and the cottages originally built as part of the war effort are now available for families coming to visit the area. Now known as Fontana Village Resort and Marina, the village created for dam workers and their families is now available for experiences you can share with your family.

One interesting footnote is about the club called the "Dam Kids," made up of workers' children who lived at Fontana Village during the years the dam was constructed. Every October, the "Dam Kids" hold their reunion at Fontana Village, the place they all once called home.

See "Virtual North Carolina" for website information.

Ethics: Alive and Well in the Tar Heel State

Founded in 1987, the North Carolina Society for Ethical Culture meets every Sunday at the Community Arts Center in the town of Carrboro. Headquartered in Chapel Hill, this is one of twenty-two societies in the United States that make up the American Ethical Union. Ethical Culture was founded by social reformer Felix Adler in 1876 as a movement toward humanistic, educational, and religious concepts. Members are committed to ideals such as the worth of the human individual, improving relationships, and bringing out the best in oneself and others.

Like any other church gathering, this forty-five-plus member group also regularly gathers for potlucks. If you're in Carrboro around midday any Sunday, sit in on a meeting and become enlightened—and maybe fed, too.

Plaid to the Bone

Many colonists came to America in search of religious and political freedom, and many descendants of the Highland Scots live along the coast in the Tar Heel State. The Highlands of Scotland is a mountainous region that was once led by lords who ruled their own clans. After the Jacobite uprisings of 1715 and, later, 1745, many fled from Scotland to America, specifically North Carolina, to escape persecution (during these uprisings they attempted to place the heirs of James II on the throne of England).

The annual Highland Games held at Grandfather Mountain celebrates the area's Scottish Heritage. (Courtesy of N. C. Division of Tourism, Film and Sports Development)

Today, there is a huge community of the descendants of "Scotland's greatest export." They reside in the Cape Fear River region and have greatly influenced the progress of the area. In the town of Red Springs, they founded a women's college in 1896. Named after Flora Macdonald, a Scottish heroine and political activist who briefly made her home in the area (between 1774 and 1780), it was the only women's college in southeastern North Carolina until the middle of the twentieth century. Although Flora Macdonald College closed its doors in 1961, the campus of Flora Macdonald Academy (it has been renamed and is now a private school for pre-kindergarten through twelfth grade) is a National Historic Site. Ten acres adjacent to the academy have been turned into a lovely garden, also named after Macdonald. Both the academy and the gardens are open to the public.

Red Springs is also the home of the Flora Macdonald Highland Games, in which the people celebrate their Scottish heritage with music, dancing, kilt wearing, and various competitions. To complement this festival, the "Highland Games and Gathering O' Scottish Clans" is held in mid-July every year at Grandfather Mountain; also located on Grandfather Mountain is a newly-completed Scottish Heritage Center.

See "Virtual North Carolina" for website information.

The "Miracle" of Crossmore School

In the early 1900s, a couple of doctors who were medical missionaries, Doctors Mary Martin Sloop and her husband Eustace Sloop, arrived in the town of Crossnore (Avery County). While Dr. Eustace Sloop focused on providing for the health needs of the townspeople, Dr. Mary Sloop concerned herself with educating the youth, who were among the poorest in the Tar Heel state. She sought to break the vicious cycle of ignorance and poverty, especially among young girls, who married early and then bore large numbers of children who would also not have access to education.

Dr. Mary Martin Sloop founded the Crossnore School in 1913 as a one-room schoolhouse, then added a boarding house for children who lived too far away to travel every day to the school. Early in the history of The Crossnore School, the Daughters of the American Revolution (DAR) became a supporter of this work; their support continues today. In the late 20th century, Crossnore began working with the state Department of Social Services to care for children in foster care.

Crossmore School

Today, the Crossnore School is known as Crossnore Communities for Children and has three locations in western North Carolina: the original Avery County campus, a campus in downtown Winston-Salem and an office in Hendersonville. These locations offer a unique place, where students and faculty become a special sort of family. They offer a broad base of services for North Carolina youth who are part of the child welfare system, including young adults who have aged out of the system. This place, where children may, for the first time in their young lives, feel safe and nurtured, offers education, therapy services, medical care, and a variety of enrichment activities.

The Crossnore School has expanded since those early days, both physically and in outreach. The campus in Avery County has grown to include a weaving school, the Sloop Chapel (which includes a beautiful fresco by famed artist Benjamin F. Long), Blair Fraley Sales Store, Crossnore Fine-Arts Gallery and Miracle Grounds Coffee Shop & Café. The proceeds of each business support the Crossnore mission.

Crossnore is a non-profit, 501 (c)(3) organization and continues to receive support from the DAR, churches, organizations, foundations and individual donors.

They also offer their facilities and experiential learning to the public. Crossnore Weavers offers three separate weeklong classes for those who wish to learn the art of traditional Appalachian hand-weaving. "Miracle Heights Adventures" on the Winston-Salem campus offers participants a variety of activities, from rock-climbing to riding zip-lines.

Brett Loftis, JD, serves as CEO of Crossnore Communities for Children. As a lifelong child advocate and attorney, Brett Loftis came to Crossnore in 2013 and has since led Crossnore's expansion to serve the western half of North Carolina and the formation of Crossnore's training division, The Center for Trauma Resilient Communities. His passion for protecting, nurturing and educating children is contagious and apparent in the school's continued success. For more on Crossnore, go to "Virtual North Carolina" at the back of this book.

The "Pope of Protestant America"

I will never forget the night I went to hear someone my Momma told me would change my life for the better. It was a minister, preaching the Gospel in a stadium in Birmingham, Alabama, around 1968. When we arrived, the stadium was packed with people eager to hear this man's words. At the end of his soul-stirring sermon, he had what Southern Christians refer to as an "altar-call": this preacher had the choir sing verse after verse of "Just as I Am," a simple yet beautiful hymn of sin, salvation and forgiveness, written in 1836 by Charlotte Elliott. Thousands of the sinful, seeking Grace, thronged down to stand near this humble, simple man, who offered the peace of God. Even those who already had dedicated their lives to God wept in their seats, joyfully witnessing the many who gave or rededicated their lives to Jesus.

Born in 1918 to a farming family in Charlotte, NC, the young William Franklin Graham, Jr., came from humble beginnings. Although he was raised in the Presbyterian church, it wasn't until he was 16 that, in a series of revival meetings in Charlotte, he became converted and gave his life to Christ. After graduating high school, he enrolled in Bob Jones College. The namesake of the college, Bob Jones, Sr., saw a rare potential in the young Billy Graham, saying, "You have a voice that pulls. God can use that voice of yours. He can use it mightily."

After transferring to the Florida Bible Institute in Temple Terrace, Florida, Graham enjoyed an occasional game of golf. It was during a game played at the Temple Terrace Golf and Country Club that Graham is said to have received his calling. He began to take some time paddling to an island in the Hillsborough River and practicing his sermons to the

William Franklin Graham, Jr
(Wikipedia)

animal residents there—the egrets, herons and alligators.

Ordained in 1939, Graham graduated with a Bachelor of Theology degree the next year. This was followed by a degree in anthropology from Wheaton College (in Illinois); during his time there he accepted the Bible as the infallible

Word of God, and launched a series of sermons he dubbed "Crusades." With his wife Ruth by his side, Graham began the Crusades in 1947, and over the years, he held more than 400 such Crusades in 185 countries on six continents. In 1950, Graham founded the Billy Graham Evangelistic Association, with its permanent headquarters in Charlotte, North Carolina (and with offices in such far-flung places as Tokyo and Buenos Aires).

He was one of the first ministers to declare racism a sin, and invited Dr. Martin Luther King to share the pulpit with him in 1955 during the Montgomery bus boycotts. In 1973, Graham preached against apartheid in Durban, South Africa—the first mixed-race event in South Africa, which at the time was in the grip of such racial segregation.

Over the course of his lifetime, he would come to influence world leaders, especially a number of U.S. Presidents, including Dwight D. Eisenhower, Harry S. Truman, Ronald Reagan (who in 1983 awarded Graham the Presidential Medal of Freedom, the highest honor accorded to American citizens), Richard Nixon, Lyndon B. Johnson, John F. Kennedy and Barack Obama.

Between them, Ruth and Billy Graham had five children—Virginia ("Gigi"), Anne, Ruth Bell (Bunny), Franklin and Nelson (Ned). When Billy Graham passed on to his heavenly reward, he left behind 19 grandchildren and a number of great-grandchildren.

He is buried on the grounds of the Billy Graham Library in Charlotte, NC, next to his wife Ruth, who preceded him by death in 2007. Graham's son Franklin and his son, Will Graham, have continued Graham's legacy—both have given sermons around the world. Franklin is President and CEO of both the Billy Graham Evangelistic Association and the Christian organization, Samaritan's Purse, which professes that its workers are "the hands and feet of Jesus." Daughter Anne, herself a minister, leads a Christian organization known as AnGel Ministries. Grandson Will, oldest son of Franklin Graham, is associate evangelist and vice president of the Billy Graham Evangelistic Association in Charlotte, NC. He also serves as executive director of the Billy Graham Training Center at The Cove in Asheville, NC.

See "Virtual North Carolina" at the back of this book for websites.

Q & A

Q. What museum in Lake Junaluska features the largest U.S. collection of artifacts pertaining to John Wesley and other Methodist church founders?

A. The World Methodist Museum.

Q. What religious group, dating to the Middle Ages, settled the town of Valdese?

A. The Waldensians. There is now a dramatic production, held throughout the summer in Valdese, which tells the story of their colony.

Q. What city in North Carolina once was nicknamed the City of Temples?

A. Asheville.

Q. Where does the Southern Baptist Convention hold its conferences in North Carolina?

A. Ridgecrest.

Q. In the early eighteenth century, what religious group settled the town of Belvidere?

A. The Quakers.

Q. The Southeastern Baptist Theological Seminary makes its home in what town?

A. Wake Forest.

Q. What colony with an Alpine flavor did Heriot Clarkson establish in 1910?

A. Little Switzerland.

Q. What Amish-Mennonite community existed only from 1907 to 1935 in the northeast corner of the state?

A. Pudding Ridge.

Q. What was the name of the Methodist preacher who rode circuit around the 1780s and named the town of Sligo after his birthplace in Ireland?

A. Reverend Edward Drumgoogle.

CHAPTER 8

SPORTS STORIES

You Never Forget Your First Home Run

It was 1914 and the young man named George had arrived with his Baltimore Oriole teammates for three weeks of spring training in Fayetteville. It must have been a big year for the eighteen-year-old, staying for perhaps his first time at a hotel (Lafayette Hotel) with his teammates, away from St. Mary's boarding school where he had been raised.

Playing an intra-squad game at the former Cape Fear Fairgrounds near Gillespie Street, the rookie player came up to bat. As batboy Maurice Fleishman watched, bat connected with ball in the "c-r-a-c-k" sound every ball player and fan loves to hear, then the ball arched up, up, and away, for a total of 405 feet. Out of the park it went, over a nearby cornfield it flew, then it plopped into a lake, as young George enjoyed his first home run as a professional baseball player.

Then a smile lit up his cherubic face, which was so youthful that the other team members had nicknamed him "Babe." This was George Herman Ruth Jr.—the man the world remembers as Babe Ruth.

The Babe went on to enjoy an illustrious career, first with the Orioles, then the Boston Red Sox, and finally the New York Yankees (who won seven pennants and four World Championships from 1920 to 1933, when he was on the team), and hit 714 official home runs.

And thanks to the efforts of the batboy, Maurice Fleishman, a historic marker was erected by the state at the site in Fayetteville where the Babe hit that first home run.

Family Racecar Dynasties

The racing world seems to attract competitors who make their profession a family tradition, such as the Petty and Earnhardt families.

The Petty family is full of NASCAR professional racers. Patriarch Lee Petty, from Randolph County, won fifty-four NASCAR Grand Nationals and the title of NASCAR Grand National Driving Champion three times. His son, Richard, and grandson, Kyle, also are racers, as was Kyle's son, Adam Petty.

Lee Petty passed away April 5, 2000, at age eighty-six. On May 12, 2000, tragedy again struck the Petty family when nineteen-year-old great-grandson Adam died in a practice run.

A Kannapolis native, Dale Earnhardt learned the thrill of racing from his father Ralph, who amassed 350 victories in his own twenty-three-year racing career. Making his own debut at Charlotte Motor Speedway in 1975, Dale was named Rookie of the Year for his stellar performances on the track. In his second year of racing he won his first Winston Cup Series—and this was the first of seven such victories.

He was called "the Intimidator" for his fearless and aggressive racing style and continued to win victories and gain fame during his career. He died on the racetrack in an accident during the last lap of the Daytona 500 on February 18, 2001. Ironically, the race was won by his teammate Michael Waltrip, with his son Dale Earnhardt Jr. coming in second. Dale Earnhardt Jr. continues to race, and his racing team is based near Mooresville.

You can learn more about these and other racing stories at the NASCAR Hall of Fame in Charlotte.

For Fans of the Petty Dynasty, There's Even More to Know About Them

For die-hard fans of the Petty family of racing greats, you already know about the Petty Museum in Randleman, North Carolina. You probably had your heart beating a little faster when you got to see close-up displays in the museum, such as the 1992 Pontiac Grand Prix SE that was driven by Richard Petty.

But the Petty family has a collective heart as big as their racing legacy. Some years back, they founded Victory Junction, a camp for children with disabilities or diseases. At this 84-acre camp in Randleman (near Greensboro), children discover freedom from worry about their disease or disability while they re-discover the joys of just being a kid. At Victory Junction, they learn to zip-line, excel at swimming or archery

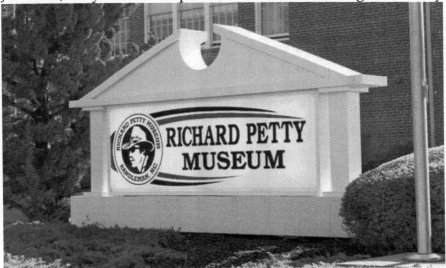

or fishing, and come away from the experience with a newly discovered confidence. The kids spend a week with other children with similar disabilities or diagnoses. Many say it was the week that changed their lives.

The inspiration behind the camp came from Adam Petty, great-grandson of NASCAR pioneer Lee Petty, grandson of racing legend Richard Petty and son of NASCAR driver Kyle Petty.

Before he lost his life in a racing accident at the age of 19, Adam Petty had always expressed an interest in helping children with devastating illnesses or disabilities. When not racing, he often visited children's hospitals, and told his family how much he wanted to start a camp in North Carolina similar to one he had discovered in Florida called Camp Boggy Creek, a SeriousFun camp.

Richard and Lynda Petty donated land to start the camp in 2002, and the NASCAR-themed camp opened its doors to the first campers in 2004. There is no charge to the campers or their families, but donations are gratefully accepted.

For Fans Who Like All Things Fast, Be Quick to Visit This Museum

For fans of all kinds of racing, from drag-racing to NASCAR, the place to go is the North Carolina Auto Racing Hall of Fame.

Located in Mooresville (also known as Race City USA), this combination museum, art gallery and gift shop just 20 miles north of Charlotte will satisfy the curiosity of any race fan. On display here is just about anything you would hope to see about racing, from film footage of races "back in the day," to exhibits pertaining to NASCAR legends.

...And Go See Speed at "The Rock"

In Rockingham, NC, you'll find entertainment that will thrill any racing fan. Rockingham Dragway, affectionately known as "The Rock," offers a variety of racing, including diesel truck racing, motorcycle racing, and auto racing.

Fans never know what they might witness at a race at The Rock. In a recent quarter-mile race, for example, one auto-racer broke the 8-second barrier, posting a best time of 7.85 seconds at a rate of more than 175 miles per hour.

He's About a Lot More Than "Air"

You probably know that Michael Jordan had a brilliant career with the Chicago Bulls and was named NBA Most Valuable Player of the Year five times. You may be familiar with his Nike commercials or his restaurants, such as Michael Jordan's 23 in Chapel Hill, featuring his retired number. You may know that he returned to play with the Washington Wizards and that he's a cigar aficionado. But Jordan is about more than business, competition, and basketball—he's got the heart of a philanthropist, which all started with his father and that father's love.

Michael Jordan
(Wikimedia Commons)

James R. Jordon was a family man. He often said that his family was his life, and showed this with the way he lived, caring for and spending time with his children, Deloris, Larry, Michael, and Roslyn, in Wilmington. A sign of greatness is in how those who have achieved success give back, and Michael Jordan has given back in several ways. In October 1996, after his father's death, Michael, his siblings, and his mother had a ribbon-cutting ceremony for the Jordan Institute for Families, part of the School of Social Work at the University of North Carolina in Chapel Hill. Michael Jordan's $1 million gift supplied seed money to support the work of the institute.

Jordan said at the dedication ceremonies that he felt "very blessed to have had a family structure" that nurtured him and his siblings, and he added that many youngsters today lack that home nurturing.

Michael Jordan's efforts have had a ripple effect: In November 1996 Jordan's teammates opened the James R. Jordan Boys and Girls Club and Family Life Center in Chicago to serve the children of the West Side community. The programs and services offered include education, employment skills training, a community health center, and more. And since Jordan started playing with the Wizards, he has pledged half of his earnings to the victims of the September 11, 2001 terrorist attacks on the United States.

The philanthropist with a basketball continued to "net" good things: playing for the Wizards, he has earned the title of Eastern Conference Player of the Week (2003), became the first NBA player to score more than 40 points (in a game in February 2003 over the Nets), and more.

Although he wrapped up his career in April 2003, Michael Jordan continues to be a role model to generations of children and adults because of the love he knew when he was brought up in North Carolina.

Not Tall Enough? Try This!

When Michael Jordan was a very young boy, he was dwarfed by some of the other players on the basketball court. Discouraged, he asked his mother what he could do to make himself taller. She suggested two things: prayer and a dash of salt in his sneakers, to be done nightly. Who's to say it didn't work?

SPORTS TRIVIA I

Q. Where was North Carolina's first jockey club?

A. Wilmington.

Q. What county is famous for its equestrian events, such as the Tryon Riding and Hunt Club Blockhouse Steeplechase (which has been occurring for nearly sixty years)?

A. Polk County.

Q. What Wilmington native won the 1976 Olympic gold medal in boxing and five world boxing titles, won twenty-five of thirty-six matches by knockouts, and was inducted into the International Boxing Hall of Fame in 1997?

A. Sugar Ray Leonard.

Q. What North Carolina museum exhibits hundreds of hand-carved decoy ducks?

A. The Core Sound Waterfowl Museum, on Harker's Island.

Q. What two teams played the first "scientific" game of football (according to intercollegiate rules) in North Carolina in 1888?

A. University of North Carolina played Trinity College (now Duke University) at the State Fairgrounds in Raleigh. Trinity won, 16-0.

Q. In what year was the first-ever intercollegiate football game between black colleges?

A. 1892, with Salisbury's Livingstone College hosting Biddle Institute (now Johnson C. Smith Institute). Livingstone won, 4-0.

Q. When was the first intercollegiate basketball game in the Tar Heel State?

A. February 6, 1906, between Wake Forest and Guilford. Guilford won, 26-19.

Q. What University of North Carolina coach developed a football team that became known as the "Team of a Million Backs"?

A. Chuck Collins, coach from 1926 to 1933.

Q. In 1935, what collegiate football team gave the University of North Carolina its only defeat that year, preventing it from reaching the Rose Bowl?

A. Duke University. The two teams have one of the fiercest rivalries in the South.

Q. What player in the negro leagues was from Rocky Nount and nicknamed "the black Lou Gehrig"?

A. Walter (Buck) Leonard, who played with the Baltimore Stars, the Brooklyn Royal Giants, and the Homestead (Pennsylvania) Grays, and was inducted into the National Baseball Hall of Fame.

Walter (Buck) Leonard
(Courtesy Baseball Hall of Fame, Cooperstown,
New York)

Challenging Color Codes and Exceeding the Odds

Today, thanks to African American golfers who in the 1950s challenged the PGA's rule prohibiting them from competing in the "Game of Kings," no one can be proclaimed ineligible because of race. One of the golfers who fought against racial discrimination, both on and off the links, was golfing great Charlie Sifford.

Sifford was a Charlotte native who fell in love with the game the moment he saw his first course. He became a caddy and learned the game from the greens up. Although he wanted to compete with players on equal turf, doing so was not easy.

He and his friends were barred from playing at country clubs, which didn't allow nonwhites. Caddies were allowed to play one

Charlie Sifford
(Wikimedia Commons)

day a week, however, and the young Charlie jumped at every such opportunity. Also, after hours he and his friends would sneak back onto the links, hitting balls until they were run off by the golf pros or security. That helped Charlie learn to play fast—although he never got to pay much attention to his putting, a part of the game he knew was his weakness. Putting takes time and concentration and playing under such circumstances wouldn't allow for either.

In the late 1940s, three African American golfers (Ted Rhodes, Bill Spiller, and Madison Gunter) brought suit against the PGA for barring nonwhites from PGA competition. The PGA responded by dropping the nonwhite rule—but declared the tournaments to be attended by invitation-only, effectively barring African Americans.

Sifford endured countless humiliations while he was trying to play the game he loved. In the early days, he wasn't allowed to dine in the country club restaurants and took more meals than he cared to in the locker room. Sometimes he wasn't allowed to use any of the facilities where he competed—including the locker rooms and the restrooms. He didn't let any of this stop him.

In August 1955 he and fellow golfer Ted Rhodes played the Canadian Open, which had no such race barrier. Sifford played well enough to feel more confident about becoming a professional golfer. The next year, he signed up to play the Rhode Island Open, and won his first "white" tournament. It wasn't PGA, but it was a foot in the door. Now Sifford was determined to enter and win a sure-enough PGA tournament. First, though, he had to become a member.

Sifford went through legal channels to force the PGA to change its membership rules, which as recently as 1961 only allowed whites. The rule was removed in 1962 but holding a member's card still wouldn't get Sifford through the country club gates. Sifford decided to go through the back door by competing in open tournaments (ones that were open to all, regardless of membership or rank).

In 1961, Sifford signed on to play as the first African American golfer in the PGA Greater Greensboro Open. This was during the time of lunch-counter sit-ins and the beginning of the civil rights movement, and Charlie Sifford was right in the middle of it. The night before he was to play for the first time on a PGA course, he got a phone call. It was a death threat, with racial slurs thrown in.

On the greens that day, he was hounded by hecklers. Sifford kept his cool and concentrated on the game. He finished, amazingly enough, at 72, only one over par—but realized he would be the one to open the door to other black golfers, and the difficulties he would face would mean sacrificing his full potential as a golfer. "That first year as a PGA rookie," he wrote in his autobiography, "was one unlike that of any other rookie." He went on to win the Hartford Open in 1967, becoming the first African American to win in PGA competition.

In 2004, another of Sifford's dreams was realized when he was inducted into the World Golf Hall of Fame—the only African American out of the hundred golfers to be in this exclusive "club." Once again, he had opened doors and broken barriers.

As he wrote in his memoirs, all he had wanted to do was to play. Thanks to Charlie Sifford, today's golf greats don't have to break down racial barriers, and the competition is wide open in the "Game of Kings."

The Queen of NC State Basketball

Born in Gibsonville, Kay Yow was one of four athletic children. She and her sisters, Debbie and Susan, all played basketball in high school (and all wore the Number 14 jersey, which has since been retired), and her brother, Ronnie, played football. Yow was dismayed, however, to find little opportunity to play basketball in college. Very few colleges offered varsity women's sports, let alone athletic scholarships.

Yow satisfied her athletic streak and natural ability by playing softball.

Yow majored in English, then earned a master's degree in physical education and landed a job teaching English at Allen Jay High School in High Point. In 1964 a position opened for the girl's basketball team coach and Yow jumped at the opportunity. She realized she could combine her teaching talents with her athletic ability, and coached the team to four straight league championships, the highest honor available to a girl's basketball team in North Carolina in the 1960s.

From there, she coached at her alma mater, Gibsonville, then took a coaching job at Elon College, where from 1971 to 1975 she had a 57-19 record and led her teams to two state championships. In 1975 she became head coach of "the Wolfpack Women" basketball team at North Carolina State University.

Coach Kay Yow led the "Wolfpack Women" to victory and helped make women's basketball the high-profile sport it is today. (Courtesy N.C. State University)

Yow has inspired her players to excellence, both on and off court. Her team won the silver medal in the 1981 World University Games. In 1986 her teams took gold medals in the World Championships and the Goodwill Games. In 1988 her team won the gold medal in the Olympic Games—probably especially satisfying for Yow as women's basketball wasn't even an Olympic sport until 1976.

Some of her achievements have included breaking the five hundred–win mark in 1996 and being named the Women's Basket-ball Coach of the Year by *College Sports News* when she directed the Wolfpack Women to the Final Four in 1998. She received the President and Mrs. George Bush Community Impact Award, and in 2000 was inducted into the Women's Basketball Hall of Fame in Knoxville, Tennessee. In March 2007, Governor Mike Easley presented Yow with the state's highest athletic award—the Laurel Wreath.

In 2009, Yow succumbed to stage 4 breast cancer, but has left a legacy of being one of the most admired and respected coaches in international and collegiate basketball. Perhaps she didn't realize that when she left the English classroom to coach, she would help make women's basketball a high-profile sport.

Sir Archie and the Culture of Horse Racing

In 1805 in Virginia, a foal destined for fame was born. His parents were of English racing stock, and his mother had won the English Derby in 1780. Eventually named Sir Archie, the horse went through several owners and eventually arrived on Marmaduke Johnson's plantation in Warren County, North Carolina, where he trained for the 1808 season. In that season, he beat all other competition on hooves.

His final race of the season was at the Scotland Neck racetrack in Halifax County, and because Sir Archie was racing an unbeaten horse named Blank, no one thought Sir Archie could win. When Sir Archie won, the race became the most famous in North Carolina. Sir Archie, of course, became famous as well.

When Sir Archie had beaten all the competition and no takers answered to a challenge, Johnson sold him. After several different owners, Sir Archie finally came to spend the rest of his life at William Amis's plantation, Mowfield, in Northhampton County. Here, from 1816 to 1831, Sir Archie may have spent his happiest days. During these years he was a stud horse, and with his racing and genetic history he was quite popular with the owners of mares.

So popular was he that during those years, Sir Archie sired more than four hundred sons and daughters, earning the name Foundation Sire of the American Thoroughbred. Sir Archie's progeny carried on his racing ability to such an extent that by 1827, Northern racing clubs began to exclude the "Roanoke Racers" from their events.

Sir Archie went to the great racetrack in the sky in 1833. He was inducted into the National Museum of Racing and Hall of Fame in 1955.

For Some "Reel" Adventures

North Carolina has some of the best fishing to be had, both on the coast and along its forty thousand-odd miles of rivers and streams. You can try to beat these freshwater records:

- ❖ **Bodie bass:** 17 pounds, 7 ounces, Lake Chatuge, 1996
- ❖ **Smallmouth buffalo:** 88 pounds, Lake Wylie, 1993
- ❖ **Blue catfish:** 89 pounds, Badin Lake, 2006
- ❖ **Brown trout:** 24 pounds, 10 ounces, Nantahala River, 1998

Those who love fishing ocean waters could try for the World All-Tackle Records (a world record regardless of what type of tackle used). Those include:

- ❖ **Bluefish:** 31 pounds, 12 ounces, Cape Hatteras, 1972
- ❖ **Red drum:** 94 pounds, 2 ounces, Hatteras Island, 1984
- ❖ **Spanish mackerel:** 13 pounds, Ocracoke Inlet, 1987
- ❖ **Amberjack**, 128 pounds, off Swansboro, 2008

So whether you fish with a fly rod, casting rod, or deep-sea rig, try your luck. Just wear your lucky fishing hat!

If You're A Sports Fan, This Is The Place For You!

Located originally in Charlotte, the North Carolina Sports Hall of Fame is in Raleigh, where it shares space with the North Carolina Museum of History. The first five inductees in 1963 were Jim Beatty (runner), Wes Ferrell (baseball pitcher), football players Ace Parker and Charlie Justice, and Estelle Lawson Page (golfer).

This Activity Helped Him Become "Some Bunny"

National Baseball Hall of Fame legend Enos "Country" Slaughter, a native of Roxboro, became a noted outfielder in the 1940s and 50s. He had a lifetime batting average of .300 and an unusually strong pitching arm. He gave credit for his prowess in pitching to a boyhood activity unrelated to baseball.

When he was young, he hunted rabbits, by throwing rocks at them!

SPORTS TRIVIA II

Q. Who was the first football All-American in North Carolina?

A. Fred Crawford, who played at Duke and was All-American in 1933.

Q. What Duke University football coach turned the Blue Devils into a winning machine and produced the team of 1938 known as the Iron Duke?

A. Wallace Wade, head football coach at Duke from 1931 to 1941.

Q. What football great played at Duke University during the mid-1930s, played both pro baseball and pro football between 1937 and 1946, and was named the NFL's Most Valuable Player in 1940?

A. Clarence (Ace) Parker, who was enshrined in the Pro Football Hall of Fame in 1972.

Q. Who are the only two siblings to be awarded the Cy Young Award?

A. Jim and Gaylord Perry, Williamston natives.

Q. Who finished second in the Heisman Trophy voting in 1948 and 1949 and has been called the most well-known football player in North Carolina history? (Hint: he played for Coach Carl Snavely at the University of North Carolina in Chapel Hill.)

A. All-American Charlie (Choo-Choo) Justice.

Q. What is nicknamed the "Mecca of Motor Sports"?

A. Lowe's Motor Speedway, near Charlotte.

Q. What town won the 1940 Little World Series, a game sponsored by the American Legion and played by Little League ballplayers?

A. Albemarle, which defeated San Diego, 9-8.

Q. What National Basketball Hall of Famer from Cleveland County, who played for North Carolina State and the Denver Nuggets, is called "the Michael Jordan of the 1970s"?

A. David Thompson.

Q. What North Carolinian invented hang gliding?

A. Francis Rogallo, who lives near Jockey's Ridge.

Q. What baseball player from Hertford made his Major League debut in 1965, pitched five victorious World Series games the the Oakland A's and the New York Yankees, won the 1974 Cy American League Young Award for best pitcher of the year and was later inducted into the Baseball Hall of Fame?

A. Jim "Catfish" Hunter.

Q. What golf legend became not only well-known for his love of Wake Forest University but designed golf courses and branded his own labels of tea and lemonade?

A. Arnold Palmer.

Q. What two brothers from Greensboro were both famous for being baseball greats and were both inducted into the Baseball Hall of Fame (Cooperstown, NY) in 1984?

A. Brothers George and Rick Ferrell.

Q. Where is the annual three day Hang Gliding Spectacular held?

A. Jockey Ridge in Nag's Head, the tallest sand dune in the United States (More than 100 feet)

(Courtesy of N. C. Division of Tourism, Film and Sports Development)

CHAPTER 9

THE CIVIL WAR IN NORTH CAROLINA

The Tar Heels: First, Farthest, and Last

A Civil War saying popular in North Carolina was "First at Bethel, farthest at Gettysburg, and last at Appomattox." Here's why.

The first Confederate soldier to die in a Civil War battle was a North Carolinian. Henry L. Wyatt of the First North Carolina died on June 10, 1861, in the Battle of Big Bethel, an early Confederate victory. Wyatt's commanding officer, Colonel John B. Magruder, called him "a brave soldier and devoted patriot," and Wyatt was buried in Richmond and his tombstone inscribed "First at Bethel." There's a memorial garden dedicated to Wyatt and his sacrifice on the grounds of the city of Tarboro.

Henry L. Wyatt's death at the battle of Big Bethel was the first Confederate loss of the civil war (Courtesy N.C. Dept. of Cultural Resources

"Farthest at Gettysburg" was added to the saying when the Twenty-sixth North Carolina, under Colonel Zebulon Vance, suffered the most Confederate casualties at that battle.

"Last at Appomattox" became part of the credo when the brigade of North Carolinians under General William Ruffin Cox and the Army of Northern Virginia fired the last shots of the war in the vicinity of the Appomattox Courthouse on April 9, 1865, the day General Robert E. Lee surrendered.

New Bern, Cover-Girl City of the War

Just after the Battle of New Bern on March 14, 1862, Federal troops occupied the city until the end of the war. That might have seemed to be a terrible fate for the loyal Confederate citizens of New Bern, but it ultimately saved their town from torching and pillaging. Because it was occupied so early in the conflict, New Bern was spared from destruction. It was so untouched by war's devastation that it was the most photographed Southern city during the war — and remains a picture-perfect town.

The Civil War Meets Modern Archaeology

As soon as North Carolina seceded from the Union, Tar Heels realized that they needed to protect the coast, and set to work constructing forts along the banks. On Beacon Island, soldiers and volunteers constructed a fort in May 1861 from barrels of sand and many layers of sod. Dubbed Fort Ocracoke, it was armed with two cannons called Columbiads, four eight-inch shell guns, and fourteen smooth-bore cannons. It was also shored up with ballast stones as a breakwater to prevent the tides from washing it out. Fort Ocracoke was planned to be a coastal bastion of the Confederacy, but history would have it otherwise.

In August 1861 Union armies assaulted and took over nearby Fort Hatteras and Fort Clark. Realizing the inevitable fate of their own fort, the Confederates manning Fort Ocracoke set fire to her gun platforms, then fled in a gunboat. Union soldiers vandalized and burned what was left of the earthen fort. Time did the rest, and early in the twentieth

An artist depicted Fort Ocracoke after it was partially destroyed by Confederate forces in August 1861 (Courtesy Ocracoke Preservation Society)

century, the remains of Fort Ocracoke and Beacon Island itself were submerged under the waters of Ocracoke Inlet.

In 1998, 137 years later, charter boat captain Donald Austin spotted what he thought was a shipwreck in the inlet, and tipped off divers working for Surface Interval Diving. This Beaufort-based nonprofit marine archaeological company was searching for the pirate Blackbeard's sunken ship, and thought Austin might have spotted the famed *Queen Anne's Revenge*.

What they found were the remains of Fort Ocracoke. Ballast stones, pieces of

Ocracoke Preservation Society.

pottery, and other debris were tested and determined to be Civil War artifacts from the doomed earthen fortress.

In April 2000 the marine archaeologists who discovered the remains held a ceremony to commemorate the history behind the fort and to honor the soldiers who had served from Ocracoke and Portsmouth Islands. Today you can see the artifacts on display in a museum operated by the Ocracoke Preservation Society. Offshore, captains conducting small private boat tours point out the historic submerged site to their passengers.

Cherokee in the Civil War

Thomas's Legion was a Civil War regiment credited with firing the last shots of the Civil War in North Carolina. The legion was raised by William Holland Thomas, who lived among the Cherokee in the mountains of North Carolina. When the enforced march now known as the Trail of Tears was imminent, Thomas persuaded President Andrew Jackson to allow some of the tribe to stay in the mountains. As Thomas was an attorney and state senator, his request carried weight.

Thomas's legion of Cherokee Indian Confederate veterans pose for a photograph at a post war reunion. (Courtesy N. C. Dept. of Cultural Resources)

When the Civil War broke out, Thomas recruited his tribal friends to join him. At the beginning, "Thomas's Legion" consisted of about 130 Cherokee soldiers, but this number quickly grew to include more Cherokee and also their white mountaineer neighbors.

Varying historical accounts claim that Thomas's Legion scalped some of its opponents. Whether these tales were true or not, Thomas's Legion's reputation for ferocity spread like wildfire, and the group retains the distinction of being one of the Confederacy's most distinguished fighting units.

Because it was composed mostly of Cherokee, Thomas's Legion is now honored in the Museum of the Cherokee Indian in Cherokee.

"Waterloo Teeth" and Civil War Dentistry

Before the advent of today's dentures, teeth were more often pulled than saved, and many different types of materials were used to make dentures. Bone, ivory, and wood were carved to make rudimentary replacements.

Sometimes, too, human teeth were used. Called Waterloo Teeth because they were often gathered from dead soldiers as they lay on the battlefield, the Civil War resulted in the manufacture of many "real" dentures. During the war, entire barrelsful of teeth were taken from dead soldiers and shipped to England.

The Brief Reign of the Smithville Home Guard

Like many towns during the Civil War, Smithville saw a need for a Home Guard. Home Guards were created to protect the town's inhabitants and their possessions while so many of the able-bodied men were off fighting.

In late May 1861, the concerned residents met at the courthouse and voted to create a Home Guard comprised of all those men who were not able to go to war. A Smithville citizen named John Bell was appointed captain, although a historian later said Bell must have been too "good natured and not likely to enforce any military discipline whatsoever."

When the newly elected Captain Bell suggested that the Guard meet the next morning for its first drill, some of the elderly "guardsmen" proposed that they bring stools so when they got tired, they could sit and rest. Following this suggestion, perhaps in an effort to prove who was in charge, Bell ordered the Guard to attention and had them march around town. But as each guardsman passed near his residence, he disappeared.

As the ranks were so alarmingly diminished, Bell did the only thing he probably could do, given the circumstances and his own personality. He made a motion to dissolve the Home Guard, which was unanimously carried—by all who were left to hear the motion, anyway.

This may well be the shortest-lived Home Guard unit in the entire Civil War.

...And More About Smithfield

Smithfield's Hastings House served as the Confederate headquarters in March 1865 while General Joseph E. Johnston met with General Braxton Bragg to form a battle plan that they hoped would block Union General Tecumseh Sherman's march from Savannah. The battle raged for two days just 15 miles outside Smithfield and resulted in a Confederate loss. General Sherman then used Smithfield's Courthouse Square for his soldiers to encamp there in April 1865. It was here that he received news that the Civil War was over, and he had his men move to Appomattox for the formal surrender of the Confederacy.

Smithfield celebrates their city's role in "America's cruelest war" with an annual celebration of its history. There are guided tours of Hastings House and candlelight tours of the city's Civil War sites, as well as living history demonstrations and Civil War re-enactors encamping near the Town Commons as well as living history demonstrations. See "Virtual North Carolina" for website information.

The CSS *Neuse*

This ironclad vessel was the hope of the Confederacy, one of twenty-two such vessels commissioned by the navy. Flat-bottomed, measuring 158 feet long and 34 feet wide, CSS *Neuse* resembled a barge more than a warship. Her mission was to recapture Union-held New Bern, and help the Confederacy stem the tide of war. But the *Neuse* was destined never to see action south of Kinston, where she was constructed. First she was beset by construction delays; then low tides and insufficient ground support prevented her from seeing much combat to the south.

Her fatal blow was in March 1865, when Union soldiers took over Kinston. As Confederate soldiers were obliged to do when the enemy was threatening to take over one of their own vessels, the sailors of the *Neuse* set her afire. The *Neuse* sank in the Neuse River, and there she lay until raised in 1964. The hull was transported to what is now the CSS *Neuse* Civil War Interpretative Museum in Kinston, where you can see her today.

The hull of the CSS Neuse, one of only three Confederate ironclads to be recovered and displayed can be seen in Kinston. (Courtesy CSS Neuse Historic Site)

The *Neuse* is one of only three Confederate ironclads ever recovered and displayed. At the historic site are the remains of the hull and other artifacts that relate to this tragic era in America's past.

The Tragic Story of the Harper House

The Battle of Bentonville in the final year of the Civil War was a long and bloody one, and the climax of the Carolinas Campaign. What happened to the people who lived near these battlegrounds, however, is not often considered.

John and Amy Harper lived with their six children in a two-story home near the site. Once the battle commenced, their home was turned from a peaceful haven into a makeshift field hospital. The house was filled with the screams and moans of wounded and dying soldiers. One historian estimated that five hundred soldiers were brought in during a twenty-four-hour period. One officer, Lieutenant Colonel William Douglas Hamilton of the Ninth Ohio Cavalry, said the hospital "resembled a slaughterhouse. A dozen surgeons and their attendants in their shirtsleeves stood at rude benches cutting off arms and legs and throwing them out of the windows, where they lay scattered on the grass."

Today, you can visit and tour the Bentonville Battleground State Historic Site and the Harper House, on the grounds of the site of the last full-scale Confederate offensive. There are also re-enactors who come to dramatize this part of Civil War history

Incidentally, there was recently another dedication of the battlefield: on March 14, 2005, the North Carolina Civil War Trails Program and Roadside Pull-off Exhibits were officially dedicated on this historic site. North Carolina has joined forces with two other states, Maryland and Virginia, in a three-state Civil War-trails tourism campaign, and the site of Bentonville is the jewel in the crown of North Carolina.

See "Virtual North Carolina" in the back of this book for website information.

School's Not So Tough After All!

The first students to go into battle during the Civil War were teenage cadets at a military school. Fifteen such cadets, enrolled in the North Carolina Military Institute in Charlotte, took part in the battle of Big Bethel, Virginia, on June 10, 1861. This was also the first significant military clash of the war and was a Confederate victory.

Lion-hearted Flusser

Southern-born Charles Williamson Flusser was handsome, with dark hair and steely eyes. He was also unmoving in his convictions, and when the Civil War broke out, his loyalties remained with the Union, although his family sympathized with the South. Despite family friction because of his Union steadfastness, the 1853 Annapolis graduate had a single burning goal during the war: to captain a steam-powered warship.

His ambitions were soon realized. When Virginia seceded from the Union in 1861, after some "persuasion" from the Confederate military, the commander of the Navy Yard in Norfolk relinquished his control of the shipbuilding facility to the Confederates. This was important for the Confederate Army, which needed a shipbuilding facility.

Charles Williamson Flusser

The Union Army knew that by claiming the Norfolk shipyard, the Confederate Army would soon take the battle to the sea and into waterways, especially around and into North Carolina. North Carolina's Roanoke Island was considered to be of strategic importance; by seizing it, the Union Army could take control of the railroad connection between the North and the South. A plan unfolded to seize the island, take control of nearby New Bern, and either take or destroy the Wilmington and Weldon railways.

The stage was set for naval conflict, and in 1862 Flusser was given command of his own Union gunboat. He gained admiration from even seasoned naval officers for his handling of the USS *Commodore Perry* in the battles of Roanoke Island and Elizabeth City. Flusser was said to be so talented and crafty a seaman that he could float his seven-hundred-ton gunboat on either a "wet sponge or a heavy dew," traversing the most shallow waterways into North Carolina and routing out the enemy. He became known as Lion-hearted Flusser.

What makes this story remarkable is the craft Flusser used to wage his watery North Carolina campaign—a former Staten Island ferryboat. After testing its seaworthiness, Flusser regarded it with no small degree of disgust. "This steamer, though a very good one for river and sound work, has proved utterly unfit for service at sea," Flusser wrote to his mother. "I turned back yesterday . . . from a sea in which I should have felt perfectly secure in an ordinary ship boat or small rowboat."

With Flusser at the helm of the most unlikely warship and former ferry boat *Commodore Perry*, he proved himself beyond all doubt a capable naval officer. Later in the war he was put in charge of real gunboats and helped the Union Army make a successful invasion and conquest of coastal North Carolina. He died in the Battle of Plymouth, on April 19, 1864.

You can learn more about Flusser and the Civil War in general at the Museum of the New South in Charlotte. See "Virtual North Carolina" for website information.

The Gibraltar of the South

Known during the Civil War as "the Gibraltar of the South" because it was deemed unassailable, Fort Fisher was the largest earthwork fortification in the South and in a perfect spot to protect Confederate interests. Fort Fisher was built overlooking the Cape Fear River on one side and the Atlantic Ocean on the other, and it protected blockade runners who used the port of Wilmington. When all other ports were effectively cut off from the Confederacy, the last surviving port of Wilmington and its protector, Fort Fisher, became crucial. Union forces attacked Fort Fisher not once but twice, in late 1864 and early 1865, making the fort the target of the most extensive naval bombardment of the Civil War.

Six weeks after the fall of Fort Fisher and the subsequent surrender of Wilmington, General Robert E. Lee surrendered at the Appomattox Court-house. The Gibraltar of the South

Civil War reenactors line up for a meal at Fort Fisher State Historic Site. (Courtesy N. C. Division of Travel and Tourism)

had become another statistic of the Civil War.

After the Civil War, Fort Fisher was allowed to fall into disrepair and was left to the ravages of the sea. Several attempts were made to save it, as the beach continued to encroach and nature and time began to reclaim the area.

Finally, in 1958, what remained of Fort Fisher became a State Historic site. A visitors' center there contains interpretive exhibits and artifacts from sunken blockade runners in the area. Fort Fisher is now a peace-filled locale, with picnic areas, a public beach and hiking trails.

Just Can't Keep a Confederate Soldier Down

Captain Richard Keough was of Company H, Sixty-eighth Regiment, North Carolina Troops, which in April 1863 was holed up at "the Widow Gascon's house" at Poll's Fishery near the mouth of the Chowan River. Since March 1863, Keough had been wanted for the Edenton ambush of a member of the First Regiment of New York Mounted Rifles. Lieutenant Charles Flusser and his men captured Keough and other Confederate soldiers and took them to Plymouth to the Provost Marshal.

Amazingly, Keough was released after taking the Oath of Allegiance to the United States—then promptly found his way back to his own company, to fight again!

Fighting in the Buff

On more than one occasion, soldiers on both sides were obliged to go *au naturel*, such as when fording a deep creek. They'd roll their clothing around their guns and carry them

185

over their heads when crossing rivers. Other times they'd be without clothes when bathing in the rivers or trying to wash lice off their bodies. Sometimes they would use nudity as an unusual tactical element to surprise the enemy. Fighting unclad soldiers could be discombobulating enough to gain victory.

One such instance was on July 26, 1863, when Confederate General Matt W. Ransom gave the soldiers of the Twenty-fourth North Carolina permission to clean up in a millpond. Suddenly, several hundred soldiers in blue descended upon them, and Ransom's men were obliged to fend off their attackers despite being nude. The Union soldiers tried to rout the Confederates at Boone's Mill, but after a five-hour battle, gave up. E. M. McCook, a Union general, wrote in his journal about such battles "in the buff" as "certainly one of the funniest sights of the war."

DID YOU KNOW?

"Swoosh or "Sloosh" was an unusual campfire concoction made by Confederate soldiers: they ground corn with their rifle butts, mixed the corn with bacon drippings, molded it around their bayonets, and baked it in the campfire.

Hard Times in the Carolinas

During the Civil War, civilians as well as soldiers had to make do with what was on hand or come up with substitutions. What's amazing is that some of these remedies and recipes are still in use today.

Women made apple pie without apples by mixing any kind of sweetener, butter, and nutmeg with a bowl of moistened crackers (*that's* where that recipe came from!). Coffee substitute was made from roasted acorns and a small amount of bacon fat or lard, or dried sassafras leaves and ground okra seeds. Coffee drinkers in the Confederate states stretched that bean by adding wild chicory—and you can still find some brands of coffee-chicory blends on grocery shelves today.

Dysentery could be cured with salt and vinegar, boiled together. One grandmother remembers that old folks in her family used charcoal cooled from the fire, then pounded and mixed with milk and turpentine to treat scarlet fever and diphtheria.

When Even the Bravest Man Wept

General Braxton Bragg assigned Confederate Major Pollock B. Lee the emotionally-charged task of surrendering the city of Charlotte to Federal troops at the end of the war. Lee had always been a stalwart soldier, not given to emotional outbursts, but a comrade wrote of him that day, "It was the only time I ever saw him let fall a tear."

Sunken History

Of all the Civil War sites in the Tar Heel State, perhaps the most historically valuable is under water—three hundred feet of water. On New Year's Eve 1862, the Union's first ironclad ship, USS *Monitor*, sank along with many of her crew off the coast of Cape Hatteras.

The *Monitor* had recently battled the Confederate ironclad the *Merrimack* (also known as the *Virginia*), off the coast of

Hampton Roads, Virginia. The battle ended in a stalemate, and the *Monitor* set sail for Beaufort to help the Union blockade beat back the Confederate blockade runners.

The *Monitor* was not exactly a sleek, smoothly running vessel. She had been nicknamed "Cheesebox on a Raft" because of her poor maneuverability and how low and clumsily she rode in the water. She was being towed to Beaufort by the steamship *Rhode Island* when tragedy befell.

As can happen in the Outer Banks, stormy weather struck almost without warning. The unruly ocean took up where the *Merrimack* had left off. The *Monitor* began to take on water, foundering early in the evening. Around midnight, as the

USS Monitor (Wikipedia)

Rhode Island was attempting to rescue the *Monitor's* crew, she sank, taking sixteen men down with her.

No one knew the exact spot where the *Monitor* lay on the ocean floor, and for over one hundred years her whereabouts remained a mystery. Finally, in 1973, a Duke University research team discovered the vessel upside down, on the sandy bottom of the ocean floor, 240 feet below the surface and sixteen miles southeast of Cape Hatteras. Attempts to bring her up were unsuccessful, but in 1998 the U.S. Navy, the Mariners' Museum (based in Newport News, Virginia), and

NOAA (National Oceanic and Atmospheric Administration) began a five-year-long recovery effort.

Over four hundred artifacts (including the engine, the propeller, a 160-ton revolving gun turret, and two large Dahlgren cannons weighing 150 tons each) have been recovered and are now on display at the Mariners' Museum. Additionally, in March 2007, the Mariners' Museum, in conjunction with NOAA, opened its new USS Monitor Center. Built at a cost of $30 million, the 63,500 square foot center has exbibits, conservation labs, research facilities, and houses a full-scale replica of the original *Monitor*, constructed by their partners at Northrop Grumman, Newport News, Virginia.

The U.S. government placed the sunken *Monitor* remains on the National Register of Historic Places two years after she was discovered. In 1975 NOAA designated the *Monitor's* resting place on the ocean floor a National Marine Sanctuary—the first place in the United States to be so designated.

Another Ironclad Story

In April 2002, a replica of a Confederate ironclad, The CSS *Albemarle*, was launched on the Roanoke River in Plymouth as part of the celebrations of Plymouth's yearly Living History weekend. An exact replica of the original Civil War iron lady, she is now on display at the Port O' Plymouth Museum in Plymouth, Washington County. This museum has been listed as one of the "Top Ten Civil War Sites in the Carolinas." See "Virtual North Carolina" for website information.

The Near-Death Experience of Zebulon Vance

Asheville native Zebulon Vance was practicing law and serving as a congressman in Washington, D.C., when news arrived of the start of the Civil War. Vance had been a staunch Union supporter, but he was dismayed by Lincoln's call for volunteers after the firing on Fort Sumter, and realized his true loyalties lay with the Confederacy. Vance resigned his congressional seat, returned home to the mountains, and gathered his own set of volunteer soldiers, who became known as the Rough and Ready Guards. Later they became part of the Twenty-sixth North Carolina, and Vance became their colonel.

The Twenty-sixth North Carolina's "baptism by fire" was at the Battle of New Bern on March 14, 1862. Fighting against Burnside and his more than eleven thousand men, Vance's retreat to New Bern was cut off. The only avenue of escape was through Bryce's Creek.

Although Colonel Zebulon Vance became Governor after the war, he never lived down the story of his near death experience at the battle of New Bern. (Courtesy of N. C. Dept. of Cultural Resources)

It had rained heavily before the fighting, but Vance probably didn't take this into account, and still thought it was a wading creek. "Follow me, men!" he shouted to his frightened troops, as he and his steed plunged into the creek. But Vance didn't come up—weighed down with uniform, boots, ammunition, sword, and pistol, he sank like the proverbial stone. Some of his men saved him from drowning, and the soldiers crossed the creek in a boat, eighteen at a time.

Although Vance's Twenty-sixth North Carolina would go into history as having the most Confederate casualties at Gettysburg, and Vance would go on to become governor of North Carolina, the humorous story of Vance's near-death experience followed him throughout the rest of his political career.

The life and times of Zebulon Vance are commemorated at the home of his birth in Weaverville. The reconstructed 1830s-era Zebulon Vance Birthplace is open to the public.

The Economy and the Blockade Runners

As the Civil War continued much longer than either side had anticipated, Federal forces closed port after Southern port, and both civilian and soldiers alike felt the sting. The greatest impact was on the Confederate inflation rate: in May 1861 a one-dollar gold piece in Richmond was worth $1.10 in Confederate currency. By the end of the war, however, that same gold piece cost $60 in Confederate money.

As inflation rose, exacerbated by paper money with little gold to back it, so did the cost of precious goods. Rod Gragg wrote in *Planters, Pirates, and Patriots* (Nashville: Rutledge Hill Press, 1994) that basic commodities such as soap either disappeared or became prohibitively expensive. Even a sewing needle became a fiercely protected treasure.

Times were desperate, and to answer the need of the people for clothing, medicines, ammunition, and arms, a new breed of businessman arose: the blockade runner. The blockade runners and their ships largely saved the Army of Northern Virginia from starvation and kept the war going long after it was expected to end.

Their ships were built to run silently yet powerfully through Federal blockades as they headed toward commercial trade with foreign ports. They were two hundred feet long, weighing four hundred to eight hundred tons, with perhaps as many as three funnels. Their shallow draft (five to eleven feet) made them excellent at slipping in and out of the smaller inlets usually left unguarded by Federal gunboats. The vessels were fore-and-aft side wheelers (boats with four paddle wheels, two on each side, at opposite ends), which made them capable of sailing in a zigzag course to evade their enemy.

Although blockade running was extremely hazardous, many adventuresome sailors tried it, and by late 1862 blockade running had been elevated in Confederate eyes to a fine art. Blockade runners themselves were regarded as heroes as they fearlessly plied the waters with their vessels.

One such vessel, the *Fanny and Jenny,* was known as the Queen of the Blockade Runners. Like many others, however, the *Fanny and Jenny* met her fate at the hands of Federal blockaders. In February 1864, after returning with war contraband from Bermuda, she was in Wrightsville Beach, headed toward Wilmington, when not one but two blockaders discovered her. After the blockade-running captain refused to comply with a warning to "Heave to," the blockaders peppered the iron-hulled ship with cannon and gunfire. All surviving hands leaped to lifeboats while the Confederate vessel sank.

Shortly after the sinking of the *Fanny and Jenny*, the last Confederate port of Wilmington was effectively sealed off when Union soldiers took nearby Fort Fisher on January 15, 1865. This had been the last open port for blockade runners, and suddenly the Confederate Army, most notably in northern Virginia, faced critical shortages of food and ammunition. It was the beginning of the end for the Southern states.

The *Fanny and Jenny* is still under the waters of the Atlantic, and rumors of sunken treasure have drawn divers to her. At certain times and tides of the year, she can be seen from the beaches at Topsail Island.

The *Fanny and Jenny* carried one treasure to her watery grave: a gold sword, inscribed *To General Robert E. Lee, from his British Sympathisers,* that had been placed in care of the captain. Doug Medlin of Topsail Island, who runs a fishing and dive shop called East Coast Sports (and as of press time 2022, is serving his second term as Mayor of Surf City), hopes to find this and other treasures. "The *Fanny and Jenny* as well as many other blockade-running ships are right near shore," he says, "although some of them have migrated with the shifting of the sands, or because of storms." For years, Medlin has taken teams of divers to the sunken hulls of the blockade runners, including the *Fanny and Jenny*. "We salvaged some lead ingots off the ship, and I found an old padlock," he says, "but I never have found any of the gold said to be on board, or anything like a sword."

So that means there's treasure off the coast, just under the water, waiting to be discovered.

STRANGE... BUT TRUE!

A Coincidence Saved a Spy from Hanging

In the early days of the Civil War, a 16-year-old from Raleigh by the name of William Donald Carmichael served in the Confederate Army. He was with his unit in Virginia when he and a few other of his fellow soldiers went on a reconnaissance mission to check the size and position of a nearby Union encampment.

When Yankee scouts discovered the presence of Carmichael and his patrol, a skirmish ensued. Several Union soldiers were wounded or killed; all the Confederate soldiers were killed, except for Carmichael. He was immediately taken prisoner and set to be hanged as a spy the following Friday.

It was the Wednesday before his fateful day that Carmichael was sitting alone in his cell, pondering his brief life and its impending end, when a group of men walked down the corridor. One, a tall man with a beard, leaned in close to the bars: "Why are you in here, son?" he asked.

"They're going to hang me this coming Friday, sir," young Carmichael replied, his voice tremulous.

The bearded tall man turned to his companions. "Get me someone to transcribe a pardon for this young man," he said. "He's too young to know what he was doing, and therefore he's too young to hang. Let him go back to his home and his family."

In short order, the pardon was drawn up; Carmichael was later released in a prisoner exchange. He did go home to his family, and after the war was over, practiced law in Virginia. After this, he left for New York, where he presented the first Gilbert and Sullivan Opera performed at the Casino Theatre.

His grandson, William "Billy" Donald Carmichael, was comptroller of the University of North Carolina during the 1940s. Billy Carmichael often wondered about what brought President Abraham Lincoln down that particular prison corridor on that particular day in 1862, to pardon the young man who would become Billy's grandfather, saving him from the hangman's noose.

You can learn more about this and other stories at the North Carolina Museum of History in Raleigh. Their special exhibit, "North Carolina and the Civil War," was a traveling one at the time of this book's publication in 2022.

"Network to Freedom": Roanoke Island's Freedmen Colony

Many people don't know that the first Freedmen's colony was in the Tarheel State. On the grounds of Fort Raleigh National Historic Site, there is a monument attesting to this, that reads "The Freedmen's Colony of Roanoke Island 1862-1867." The other side of the monument has an artistic rendition of a man, looking across the water, and a woman (presumably his wife) on her knees, arms upraised in ecstasy, along with a small boy and his dog. The inscription beneath this reads: "Former slaves give thanks by the creek's edge at the sight of the island—'If you can cross the creek to Roanoke Island, you will find safe haven."

The story behind this monument goes something like this:

During the Civil War, in 1862 there was a battle over control of Roanoke Island. When the island fell to Union Forces, word spread throughout North Carolina that slaves could find "safe haven" there.

The first to be freed by Union soldiers were approximately 200 Black people who had been forced to work on the Fort. They were joined by others, in short order.

Freedmen's School, James Plantation, North Carolina (Wikipedia)

Recognizing the importance of education to their successful emancipation, they received their first teacher to the island in 1863. A man named Horace James of the Freedmen's Bureau introduced the concept of domestic manufacturing to the newly freed islanders. They set to work learning skills such as spinning and weaving, while also constructing their homes. Everyone who was able to do so, worked in some capacity for the betterment of all. Many of the men joined the Union effort and took up arms as soldiers.

After the Civil War and Andrew Johnson became President, in 1867 he issued a proclamation saying that land owned by whites prior to the Civil War was returned to them, so the island residents suddenly lost their properties. Many families left after this.

Today, you can learn more about the enslaved Blacks who came to Roanoak Island and discovered how to live as free people at the Fort Raleigh National Historic Site. Here you can find exhibits on the Algonquian settlers, early English explorers and settlers to the area, the Civil War Battle of Roanoke Island and the Freedmen's Colony. Here you will also find trails, earthworks, an amphitheater (where the drama "The Lost Colony" is performed) and more. See "Virtual North Carolina" for website information.

CIVIL WAR TRIVIA

Q. What battlefield was the site of the largest and bloodiest battle in North Carolina? (Hint: it's in Johnston County.)

A. Bentonville Battlefield.

Q. What percent of Southern casualties in the Civil War were North Carolinians?

A. An amazing 25 percent of all Southern Civil War casualties were North Carolinians.

Q. During the Civil War, nearly four hundred successful blockade runners obtained supplies for North Carolina by sailing to what port?

A. Nassau, Bahamas.

Q. What Fayetteville native was said to be the best blockade runner of them all?

A. J. N. Maffitt. As a lieutenant with the Confederate Navy, and at the helm of the CSS *Florida*, Maffitt boarded, pilfered and sank approximately 25 Union vessels during the course of the Civil War.

Q. How were Union troops occupying the grounds of the state capitol building in Raleigh informed that the war was over?

A. A signal, a kind of flare, was fired from the roof of the capitol building.

Q. What was the difference in monthly pay between a Confederate brigadier general and a Union one?

A. Fourteen dollars—Confederate generals earned $301 and Union generals $315.

Q. Where can you find the remains of the Confederate ram, the *Albemarle*, on display?

A. Her remains are on display at not one, but three, different places. One of her cannons is at the naval base in Norfolk, Virginia. Her smokestack is part of an exhibit at the Museum of the Albemarle in Elizabeth City, NC; and her bell can be seen at the Port-O-Plymouth Civil War Museum in Plymouth, NC.

Q. What fort was part of the Cape Fear line of defense and fell to Union soldiers in February 1865, allowing Wilmington to come under Union control?

A. Fort Anderson, nearly 90 percent intact and now a state historic site.

Q. What historical home in Hillsborough once served as headquarters for Confederate General Wade Hampton and is where General Joseph E. Johnston drafted the articles of surrender (papers) he later gave to General William T. Sherman in April 1865?

A. Alexander Dickson House.

Q. What was the name of the battle over the Dismal Swamp Canal?

A. The Battle of South Mills.

Q. Where was the first Freedmen's Colony established in America?

A. Manteo.

Q. Where was the first Provisional Government of the Civil War established?

A. Hatteras.

Q. Who was the physician at the famous Confederate prison in Salisbury?

A. Josephus Hall.

Q. What Union general made Josephus Hall's home his headquarters in April 1865?

A. General George Stoneman. (The Josephus Hall House in Salisbury is still intact, with tours offered by costumed guides.)

CHAPTER 10

FROM CIVIL WRONGS TO CIVIL RIGHTS

The Greensboro Sit-ins

On February 1, 1960, four Black college students made history when they entered the downtown Woolworth store in Greensboro and purchased school supplies. Then the four—Ezell Blair Jr., Franklin McCain, Joseph McNeil, and David Richmond—calmly took seats at the "Whites Only" lunch counter. The young men, all Tar Heel natives, sat there the whole day, waiting to be served. They probably didn't realize their actions that day would be the flashpoint behind the national Civil Rights movement.

The sit-in was a denouncement of segregation, a nonviolent assertion for African American people to receive the same treatment as white people. Although the young men didn't get served that first day, they determined to return every day to the lunch counter.

The Greensboro lunch counter sit-ins occurred every day for six days, with each successive day seeing a growing number of college students crowding the lunch counter, until Woolworth was forced to temporarily close its doors. The students then suspended their "sit-ins" to allow the merchants in the community time to desegregate their shops and restaurants.

When college students Ezell Blair Jr., Franklin McCain, Joseph McNeil and David Richmond sat down at the Woolworth lunch counter in Greensboro, they probably never imagined the impact their actions would have on the national civil rights movement. (© Greensboro News and Record, used with permission)

It was a painful and tumultuous time, and some people paid for their beliefs through violence and even death. The Greensboro lunch counter sit-ins, some of the first Civil Rights demonstrations in the United States, made history and caused America to reflect on injustices, eventually creating new laws to replace cruel and archaic ones.

Today, Greensboro is a thriving and cosmopolitan town that embraces diversity while remembering its past. You can see exhibits about the Woolworth sit-ins at the Greensboro Historical Museum. In addition, an International Civil Rights Center and Museum is now located in the old Woolworth building, and you can discover even more about local diversity at the Mattye Reed African Heritage Center, located on East Market Street. Incidentally, the latter Center houses the nation's "largest collection of African art and artifacts," according to their website. See "Virtual North Carolina" for website information.

North Carolina's Own Underground Railroad

Levi Coffin was born in New Garden. Quaker by birth and rearing, Coffin grew up to disdain slavery and all it entailed.

Coffin became an activist in helping runaway slaves to freedom. The New Garden area had a Quaker boarding school, and the woods behind the school are said to have harbored many runaway slaves. Eventually the woods became filled with hiding places such as dug-out pits covered with leaves and hollow logs large enough to hold a fleeing, frightened fugitive from slavery.

One night, a slave owner tracked a runaway to Coffin's door. Although Quakers are said to be teetotalers, Coffin just so happened to have some moonshine on hand, reportedly made by a neighbor. Coffin plied the man with the whiskey while the slave fled to another safe house. By the time the slave owner sobered up, he had forgotten why he had journeyed to New Garden—and the slave was on his way to freedom.

Levi Coffin (Wikipedia)

Historians surmise that over thirty years, thousands of slaves found their way to freedom via Guilford County's Quaker settlement. Although Coffin moved on, first to Indiana and later to Ohio, he was one of the key people responsible for organizing the Underground Railroad.

False Bottom to True Freedom

Quakers in North Carolina supported the abolitionist movement, but in keeping with the tenets of their faith, did so in nonviolent ways. Richard Mendenhall, a Quaker who lived in Jamestown in the High Point area, hid runaway slaves in a wagon with a false bottom, and transported many a fugitive to freedom. You can still see the wagons he used at his home at Mendenhall Plantation (also known as Mendenhall Homeplace) in High Point, which is open for tours.

Currently there are approximately thirty tour-able sites where you can learn more about the Underground Railroad in North Carolina. See "Virtual Carolina" at the back of this book.

The "Green Book" Project

It's amazing to me now that there ever was a time in American history where Black people weren't welcome everywhere, such as restaurants and hotels. It was so much of 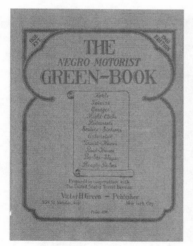 an issue that Black travelers were obliged to get copies of the so-called "Negro Motorist Green Book," which was published from the 1930s to 1966. This book was a guide to let Black travelers know where they could go and stay, have a meal, or even get their hair done while away from their hometown. I first read about this when Maya Angelou wrote about how her church's parishioners would welcome visitors from out of town into their private homes, because there were no hotels in Stamps, Arkansas that were open to Black travelers.

In North Carolina, there were 327 such places listed in the "Negro Motorist Green Book." The Green Book Project, created under the auspices of the North Carolina African American Heritage Commission, was part of a traveling exhibit in 2020 and 2021, and made possible through funding from the Institute of Museum and Library Services.

See "Virtual North Carolina" for website information relating to this project.

Charlotte Hawkins Brown: "Transforming the Lives of Black Youths"

Born in Henderson, North Carolina in 1883, the young Black girl was raised in Massachusetts. The granddaughter of former enslaved people, at age 18 young Charlotte felt compelled to return to the Tar Heel state and become an educator of rural Black children.

Charlotte Hawkins Brown

She founded the Palmer Memorial Institute the following year (1902) in Sedalia (named after Alice Freeman Palmer, an educator and Brown's mentor). As the years went by, Palmer achieved fame and acclaim across the entire United States as a nationally respected high school preparatory establishment. It is said that the school transformed thousands of young Black people during its 69-year-existence.

Palmer's graduates went on to stellar careers in government, education, various science fields and the arts.

Palmer closed its doors in 1971 but the campus is now a State Historical Site—the first such site in North Carolina to honor a female.

Today, visitors can tour the campus, the Charlotte Hawkins Brown Museum, and explore Brown's residence during the years she lived there (Canary Cottage). The Palmer Memorial Institute, the campus and museum are all overseen by Tanesha Anthony, Site Manager. They have a birthday event the Saturday closest to Brown's birthdate of June 11 and in December, a musical Christmas celebration with the town of Sedalia. See "Virtual North Carolina" for website information.

Princeville: First U.S. City Incorporated by African Americans

At the close of the Civil War, newly emancipated African Americans in Edgecombe County first sought help from Union soldiers still in the Tar Heel state. Once soldiers left the state, the freed Blacks settled in an area named Freedom Hill, not far from Tarboro. Incorporated in 1885, Freedom Hill's name was changed to Princeville, to honor Turner Prince, a Black man who was involved with building many of this unique community's homes.

The people of Princeville endured many injustices as they sought to improve their lives and those of their children. Princeville now stands today as a symbol of their perseverance and determination.

Princeville has been flooded several times, especially when Hurricane Floyd hit in 1999, and the townspeople saw themselves dealing with a 23-foot storm surge. President

Clinton visited and encouraged people to make donations to help the people of Princeville get back on their collective feet; the singer Prince donated $37,000 of disaster relief for the town.

Today, you can visit Princeville and see how far the city and its people have come. You can learn more about their determination and their history by visiting the Museum of Princeville. It's located on 310 Mutual Blvd. in Princeville. The gift shop has lots of things you can take home to learn more, such as DVDs and books.

The Middle Passage and North Carolina

Between the years 1560 to 1850, nearly 5 million kidnapped Africans were taken to such far-flung places as Brazil and the Caribbean. The "Middle Passage" was the transatlantic crossing where those kidnapped Africans were taken to the Americas.

Some of these survivors of the Middle Passage arrived and disembarked in various places in the United States. One of those destinations was Portsmouth Village, at what is now Cape Lookout National Seashore. Ranger Nate Toering of Chief Interpretive Services with the Park said that these people have now received the recognition they have long deserved: The fall of 2022 saw visitors and dignitaries at a ceremony to honor those who died during the Middle Passage, and the millions who survived and became enslaved people who helped build the New World.

Middle Passage Marker Sites have since been put in place in Beaufort and Wilmington. This project was the result of the Eastern Carolina Foundation for Equity and Equality.

Q&A

Q. What organization oversees the North Carolina Civil Rights Trail?

> A. The North Carolina African American Heritage Commission.

Q. What foundation supports this effort?

> A. The William G. Pomeroy Foundation based in Syracuse, NY.

Q. In 1951, what city was a high school walkout to protest the terrible conditions of the school and its inferior learning materials?

> A. Adkin High School in Kinston. As a result of the more than 700-student walkout, the school board modernized the facilities and improved instructional materials.

Q. What high school football team in North Carolina was among the first to integrate?

> A. Brevard High School, in the early 1960s. Incidentally, even with the hostile environment both on the field and in the stadiums, the team won co-championship that year, beating all predictions that they would lose every game. They got to take home the trophy, based on a coin toss with co-champion Reidsville High School.

Q. Two Black professionals (a doctor and a dentist), H. H. Creft and George Simkins, challenged the city of High Point to do away with their "whites only" policy of what sport?

> A. Golf.

Q. What North Carolina town witnessed a massive protest against unfair and inequitable voting rights in 1964?

A. Enfield. At that time, although Halifax County had more than 50 percent Blacks in its population, only 14 percent were registered to vote.

Q. What was the name of the landmark case in North Carolina which, in the judge's ruling, helped protect Black teachers from losing their jobs due to participation in the Civil Rights Movement?

A. Johnson versus Branch. Willa Cofield Johnson, a teacher at Thomas S. Inborden High School, was threatened with termination for her participation. She won!

Q. What town was forced to integrate their city recreational pool after protests by residents and members of the NAACP?

A. Monroe. The facility is known today as Monroe Country Club and Golf Course.

Q. What church in Ahoskie was a meeting place for city residents and NAACP members, to plan their peaceful protests in the mid-1960s?

A. New Ahoskie Baptist Church.

Q. What is the name of the first so-called "Haven for Blacks" on the coast of North Carolina, established in 1949?

A. Ocean City Beach Community.

CHAPTER 11

WHEELERS & DEALERS (ENTREPRENEURS)

Playing "Chicken" in Valle Crucis

In 1883 a general store was established in Valle Crucis, and now Boone, Waynesville, Hendersonville, Asheville (and Knoxville, TN) have similar emporiums. This store's original motto was "Goods for the living, coffins and caskets for the dead." It was established by Henry Taylor, who became partners with W. W. Mast and later sold him all interests to the store. It's now known as Mast General Store and offers "everything you need for life in the nineteenth century and most of this one."

Around 1909, a man named Farthing owned another general store down the street. Both stores bartered for goods, often taking chickens in trade. Some local boys saw that

211

At Mast General Store in Valla Crucis, you can see the original "chicken trapdoor" that was used to thwart pranksters. (Photo by J. D. Dooley. Used with permission)

Farthing put the chickens in a coop in his backyard. They came up with a devious plan, retrieving the chickens and taking them for trade, this time to Mast General Store.

No one knows how many times the same chickens were "rebartered," but Mast caught on to the trickery and installed a trapdoor inside his store. It led into the basement under the building, where the chickens were safe from youthful chicken "recyclers." Next time you're in Valle Crucis, ask anyone at Mast General Store to show you the chicken trapdoor.

All That Glitters… Makes a Good Doorstop

It was a beautiful day in the spring of 1799, and young Conrad Reed very much wanted to make a foray to the creek on his family's farm in Stanfield. "Please, Pa," he probably begged his German-born father, John Reed. It was Sunday, and Reed probably hesitated before allowing his young son some time to relax in the outdoors. Finally, he relented, and off young Conrad went with his siblings, who also were allowed to skip church that day.

Conrad wandered the woods on the Reed Farm in Cabarrus County, before coming to Little Meadow Creek. Near the creek banks, something yellow glinted in the water. Curious, Conrad took the seventeen-pound rock home to show his father.

John Reed, most likely born in Germany as Johannes Reith, had been a Hessian soldier who had left the ranks of the British Army at the end of the Revolutionary War. He had settled in Cabarrus County to be near his fellow Germans. Like most farmers in those days, Reed was semi-literate at best, and consumed by

Young Conrad Reed's discovery of a gleaming yellow rock in Little Meadow Creek led to America's first gold rush. (Pen and ink by Buck O'Donnell, (Courtesy Reed Gold Mine Historic Site)

practical matters such as his corn and wheat crops. The family decided that the rock would make a good doorstop, and there it sat on the floor, propping open a door, for three years.

A visitor explores the tunnels at Reed Gold Mine in Stanfield. (Courtesy of N. C. Division of Tourism, Film and Sports Development)

As time went on, John Reed became curious about the yellow stone, and in 1802 he took it to a jeweler in Fayetteville. Amazed to see a seventeen-pound stone of solid gold right there on his countertop, the jeweler sensed that the farmer didn't know much about the price of the precious metal. "How much do you want for it?" he asked.

Reed paused for a moment. It had been a good doorstop, but here was someone asking to buy it from him. He asked what he thought was a huge amount in those times—three dollars and fifty cents.

John Reed had just sold the first piece of gold ever documented as discovered in the United States—and it had a value of about $3,600. As word got out about gold in the lower Piedmont area, Reed must have realized his naïveté with the jeweler, and started learning what he could about the creek-mining process. The next year, he formed a partnership called Reed Gold Mine with men he knew and trusted: Frederick Kiser, Reverend James Love, and Martin Phifer Jr.

They continued with their farming and mined in the off-season, when the waters in the creek were at their lowest and the creek bed easiest to mine. The first year, Peter, one of Reed's slaves, discovered the biggest single nugget, weighing a whopping twenty-eight pounds.

Gold fever spread, and other people living in the Piedmont area explored their creek beds with pans and rockers. News of the gold discoveries went out around the world, attracting English miners. When in 1825 gold was also found in veins of white quartz rock, an interest in underground gold mining increased. Mining this way was much more expensive, and Reed and his partners didn't start underground mining until 1831.

But there was soon to be trouble in Paradise, even among the nouveau riche Reeds. A family quarrel broke out concerning the mine business, resulting in a court injunction that closed the mine for ten long years. After John Reed died a wealthy man in 1845, the mine was sold at public auction. It changed hands several times, but during the California Gold Rush of 1849 the mine fell into disuse.

Now in the hands of the state of North Carolina, the Reed Gold Mine is open to tourists who want to try their hand at panning for gold. The establishment also shows films highlighting the first gold discovery and tours of restored portions of the underground mining tunnels.

The Reed Gold Mine has found a new kind of treasure these days—tourism.

Strange But True!

Why do people think of California instead of North Carolina when they think of the first gold rush in America? One explanation has it that it was because of the technology called photography. It didn't exist when gold was first discovered in North Carolina; photography debuted just four years before the California Gold Rush. Thus, journalism and photography have left us a skewed sense of history when it comes to the discovery of gold in America.

Another "First" in North Carolina

Not only did the Tar Heel state beat out California in having the first gold rush, they had another first: according to the NC Department of Tourism, America's first grapevine was discovered on the North Carolina coast. That was in the year 1584.

Today, the Old North State boasts of approximately 200 wineries within its boundaries. And there are about as many wine festivals as there are wineries. Two stellar ones are the North Carolina Wine Festival, held every October in the town of Cary. Another is the Hinnant Festival and Grape Stomp, also held every October at the Hinnant Family Vineyards in Pine Level. In 2022, the latter festival celebrated their 50th anniversary of holding their celebration. I'm sure they love "raisin" the roof and have a stomping good time. See "Virtual North Carolina" for website information.

Gatling and His "Lifesaving" Gun

Born in Maney's Neck, Hertford County, Richard Gatling was a plantation owner's son who began fiddling around with farm machinery as a young boy. His interest in making machinery to increase efficiency on his father's farm led the young man to invent a cottonseed-sowing machine, a machine to thin cotton plants in the field, a screw propeller, and a rice-sowing machine, among others.

He was traveling by boat to Philadelphia when the boat became icebound; Gatling was stricken with smallpox, with no physician on board to care for him. After this trip, the industrious Gatling enrolled in medical school in Cincinnati, Ohio, so he would never again be helpless in a medical crisis.

After inventing a hemp-processing machine and a steam plow, Gatling turned his attention to military machines and invented a steam ram to be used by warships. Then he began thinking back to the rapid-sowing machines he had invented and thought, why not invent a similar machine—one that fired bullets?

The man who had taken the Hippocratic oath in Ohio had noble intentions in inventing such a weapon. A rapid-firing gun, he reasoned, could replace hundreds of soldiers on the battlefield, thereby saving lives. It could eliminate the need for large armies, and therefore large numbers of casualties.

On November 4, 1862, Gatling was awarded patent number 36,836 for his rapid-fire gun equipped with six rifle barrels, shooting approximately two hundred bullets a minute. Although one general used twelve of the guns in the James River campaign of May and June 1864 in the Civil War, he did so without proper military authorization. With typical government bureaucratic speed, by the time authorization was given for use, the war was over.

The Gatling Gun was further modified to ten barrels shooting three hundred shots per minute. It was used around the world in the Spanish-American War, the Franco-Prussian War, and the Russo-Japanese War.

Ironically, the gun invented by a man sworn to save lives, a gun developed to stop wars and mass human destruction, only expanded upon that theme.

The Battle of the Bureaus

The world's largest Duncan Phyfe chair can be seen in the city of Thomasville, built to acknowledge the large numbers of chairs made in the town's factories. This chair is made of steel and concrete, set in a 12-foot limestone base, and stands 18 feet tall. Of course, many visitors use it as a backdrop for a "photo-op."

Besides the huge Duncan Phyfe chair, two bureaus have been erected in the nearby town of High Point, called the "Home Furnishings Capital of the World." In 1920, a huge chest of drawers was built by the High Point

Furnitureland South (Wikimedia)

Chamber of Commerce as an eye-catching gadget. Originally 20 feet tall, the now-38-foot-tall Goddard-Townsend block front chest is complete, down to the "socks" dangling from one of its drawers.

Not to be outdone, Furnitureland South erected its own chest of drawers—standing more than 80 feet tall, near the Interstate.

DID YOU KNOW?

The Tar Heel State is a geologist's and rock-hound's dream. North Carolina is the only state that has produced all four of the major gemstones (diamonds, rubies, emeralds and sapphires). In addition, more than three hundred different minerals have been found in North Carolina. Mines located throughout the state will let you try your luck at gem mining. Castle McCulloch in Jamestown is a restored gold refinery, listed on the National Register of Historic Places (circa 1832), and this sure-enough castle (complete with stone walls three feet thick, a drawbridge, and a seventy-foot tower) offers tours and panning for gems.

A gold mill and museum are also on the premises; it's such a picturesque venue that people have reserved it for weddings and receptions. See "Virtual North Carolina" for website information.

Castle McCulloch in Jamestown, a restored gold refinery, offers tours and gem panning. (Courtesy Castle McCulloch, Photo by BG Photography)

Making Headlines: Josephus Daniels

Born in May 1862 in Washington, North Carolina, Josephus Daniels was the son of a Confederate shipbuilder. He lost his father before he was even a toddler, and his mother, Mary, struggled to make ends meet to provide for Josephus and his two brothers. Eventually the family moved to Wilson, where Mary became postmistress, and young Daniels found the calling for his life's work.

Josephus held down several odd jobs to help with the family income, but what intrigued him the most was working in a printing office. He became fascinated with newspaper publishing. At age sixteen, Josephus owned a newspaper, the *Cornucopia,* with his brother Charles, and Josephus edited another publication, *Our Free Blade*. By age eighteen, he bought out all interests supporting the newspaper, the *Advance,* covering four counties, and used the periodical as a platform to hold forth on political issues dear to his heart, such as temperance and trade.

In 1882 the brothers established the *Free Press* in Kinston. The young newspaper magnate campaigned for the Democratic Party and Grover Cleveland, using his latest newspaper as the pulpit for his editorial sermons. All this before entering college!

Daniels attended Wilson Collegiate Institute, then studied law in 1885 at the University of North Carolina at Chapel Hill and passed the bar the same year. Although he never practiced law, he combined his legal acumen with his business sense to purchase two newspapers in Raleigh, the *State Chronicle* and the *Farmer and Mechanic*, and merged them into one. The new *State Chronicle* served Daniels as a platform for his own politics, and he was elected printer to the state, an office he held from 1887 through 1893.

Buying and selling newspapers as suited his business and political interests, Daniels served in Washington, D.C., in the Department of the Interior. In 1894 he returned to Raleigh after purchasing the Raleigh-based newspaper, *News & Observer*.

Outspoken and inflammatory in his beliefs, Daniels held forth on topics ranging from Jim Crow laws, trusts, Southern railroad companies that ran politics in the South, and sensationalized crimes. Although his newspaper was given the derogatory nickname "Nuisance and Disturber," Daniels's belief that dullness was an editorial crime helped his newspaper to become the first in the world to have more subscribers than the population of the city in which it was headquartered. Even William Randolph Hearst offered to buy the *News & Observer* (he was turned down).

Josephus Daniels (Wikimedia)

In 1912 Daniels promoted Woodrow Wilson for president of the United States, and Wilson then appointed Daniels as Secretary of the Navy, a position he held from 1912 to 1921. Daniels, in turn, appointed a young man as his assistant secretary—Franklin Delano Roosevelt.

In 1932, although Daniels was encouraged to run for state governor, he turned his attention to promoting Roosevelt for the presidency. When Roosevelt won the office, Daniels was named Ambassador to Mexico.

His years there were tumultuous: the American Embassy was stoned upon his arrival because the people blamed Daniels for the bad luck they had experienced for nearly two decades. Under President Wilson, when Daniels was Secretary of the Navy, the Navy had bombarded the Mexican Naval Academy at Vera Cruz, then invaded Mexico and ousted its president, General Victoriano Huerta. These among other things were blamed on the fiery-penned newspaperman.

Despite this, Daniels worked to improve relations between Mexico and the United States, and during his tenure supported a plan for universal education in Mexico.

In 1941 his wife, Addie, became ill, and Daniels resigned and resumed his leadership at the newspaper, continuing his anything-but-dull editorial tradition. After his wife's death, the government commissioned the SS *Addie Daniels* in her honor in 1944.

Daniels penned four books about his military experiences, two relating to the navy and two on Woodrow Wilson. Daniels died in January 1948, but the *News & Observer* made him immortal—and a middle school in Raleigh bears his name today.

The Rub That Relieved Millions

In the 1890s a young pharmacist in Greensboro named Lunsford Richardson found himself facing the dilemma so many parents faced then: his son Smith had the croup, and anything used as a poultice irritated his baby's skin. What could he do?

Richardson decided to ask his brother-in-law to use his laboratory to do some experiments. The pharmacist finally hit on a mixture of a Japanese mint oil (menthol), camphor, and eucalyptus in a base of petroleum jelly, and found that it gave relief to croupy coughs. Body heat caused the rub to vaporize, and through inhalation and absorption of the medicines in the petroleum jelly, the patient found relief.

Successfully selling the rub locally, by 1905 Richardson invested his entire life savings in a laboratory, and his son went to work with him. They changed the name of the rub from Richardson's Croup and Pneumonia Cure Salve to honor the brother-in-law who had loaned his laboratory and set about on the first mass-mailing campaign in the United States. The salve was an instant hit both in the states and internationally, and during the flu epidemic of 1918, sales rose from $900,00 to $2.9 million. Richardson died in 1919 a wealthy man.

The brother-in-law's name was Dr. Joshua Vick. And the salve? You know it today as Vick's VapoRub. You can learn more about Vick's at an exhibit on display at the Greensboro History Museum. See "Virtual North Carolina" for website information.

The "Rose Buddies" of Elizabeth City

About thirty-five years ago, Elizabeth City had little to attract tourists to its small, quaint, and friendly town. The village seemed to be in need of something that would make it more than just a quiet town on the shores of the Pasquotank River in northeastern North Carolina.

Two long-time residents and friends, Fred Fearing and Joe Kramer, met after church one Sunday and discovered more than a dozen visiting yachtsmen docking at the newly completed Mariners' Wharf. The Pasquotank flows into the Atlantic Ocean, and the city had just finished building a wharf that allowed sailors a complimentary forty-eight-hour dockage.

Being of a social bent, the two Southern gentlemen serendipitously decided to throw a party for the wharf's first visitors, thinking it would be a nice way to say thank you. They rounded up wine, cheese, and all the accompaniments. Kramer went to his rose garden and clipped 17 roses for each of the wives, or "first mates," of these initial visiting sailors. From this first modest reception, something phenomenal resulted.

Inspired by the two self-made marketing men, the town began to host a reception every evening, April through November, for sailors visiting the waterfront city. On any of those nights, if someone sailed into port and docked at Mariners' Wharf they would be treated like a visiting dignitary. In 1981 Joe Kramer passed away, but his roses were transplanted to Mariners' Wharf and continue to bloom there. Fred Fearing took over the clipping and giving of the roses. At a certain time of year, though, he handed out something else. "When the weather gets too cool for roses, and the cotton is ready, I hand the ladies cotton bolls and tell them, 'Now you're a cotton-picking North Carolinian,'" said Fearing.

Elizabeth City and its growing number of "Rose Buddies" became internationally famous for their hospitality to the

Fred Fearing, one of the original "Rose Buddies," hands a rose to visitor Sarah Lacey. The people of Elizabeth City welcome visiting sailors with a fee-free pier and a reception, boosting the economy of this quaint town. (Photo by the Author)

boating community. Such notables as Walter Cronkite, Bill Friday (former president of the University of North Carolina), and NBC personality Willard Scott have been guests. Scott also gave the town its first "rose buddies" golf cart. Until Fearing passed away in 2007, people would often see him in the golf cart, greeting newcomers who arrived by sea looking for a welcoming port.

And they discover it in Elizabeth City—more bustling than it used to be, thanks to Fearing and the Kramer, but still just as friendly and charming. A post-script to this story is although, due to the Covid pandemic, much of the tradition of the "Rose Buddies" is no longer feasible, Elizabeth City is now known as the "Harbor of Hospitality" with its 14 boat slips at Mariners' Wharf, where sailors can dock free of charge. Visitors to Elizabeth City say they "feel at home in no time."

DID YOU KNOW?

Elizabeth City is home to the largest U.S. Coast Guard base in the United States

---

The Birthplace of Pepsi-Cola

In New Bern in the 1890s, a young pharmacist named Caleb Bradham kept experimenting with kola and coca extracts, trying to hit on a drink that would taste good and make people feel good, too. The young man affectionately known as "Doc" finally made the perfect concoction of sweeteners, flavorings, and carbonated water. Friends raved about the new soda and dubbed it "Brad's Drink," but Bradham kept looking for a name with more "oomph" to it. He found out about a registered name that was for sale by a New Jersey company and bought the rights to the name "Pep Kola" for a hundred dollars. This became Pepsi-Cola, and

© Pepsi Cola

within ten years Doc Bradham was a rich man, with the soda marketed in twenty-four states.

After World War I was declared, however, financial problems hit. Bradham had invested nearly everything he had in sugar stocks, thinking the price would go up because of the war. It dropped instead, and he declared bankruptcy in 1923.

After being owned by several holding companies, the Pepsi formula was bought by the Loft Candy Company of New York. Now there are more than seven hundred bottling facilities around the world.

Bradham's two drugstores still stand in New Bern. His first is on the corner of Pollock and Middle Streets with a banner that reads, "The Birthplace of Pepsi-Cola." This shop, known as "The Pepsi Store," is part old-timey soda shop, part museum and part souvenir store where you can purchase just about anything relating to Pepsi-Cola. The second, at the corner of Broad and Middle streets, has been renovated into a wonderful eatery called the Chelsea Restaurant. Although the rest of the building has been altered to serve the needs of restaurant patrons, the downstairs has kept the look and feel of Doc Bradham's turn-of-the-century drugstore, complete with pressed tin ceiling and mosaic tile floor. See "Virtual North Carolina" for website information.

The "Hole" Truth about Krispy Kreme

Winston-Salem is the home of the world-famous Krispy Kreme Doughnuts, established in 1937 by Vernon Rudolph. While Rudolph was operating a doughnut shop in Paducah, Kentucky, he got the now-famous doughnut recipe from a French chef from New Orleans. Taking the recipe with him, Rudolph set up shop in Winston-Salem.

The rest is entrepreneurial history: Krispy Kreme now produces collectively more than two *billion* doughnuts a day, with shops making anywhere from three thousand to twelve thousand doughnuts per hour (depending on the size of the shop). But there's more to the story than just numbers.

Krispy Kreme has developed a kind of following, and the doughnut that gave coffee the best break it ever had is a part of Southern culture. Shops have opened as far away as Los Angeles and New York City, and the Krispy Kreme phenomenon has been discussed on National Public Radio. There's a Krispy Kreme website (www.krispykreme.com), on which you can sign up to become a member of "Friends of Krispy Kreme," and order merchandise such as coffee cups, caps and clothing. Since *InStyle Magazine* mentioned Krispy Kreme doughnuts in their wedding issue (Spring 2002), wedding planners by the thousands have been calling their local doughnut shops, ordering doughnuts for receptions. Krispy Kreme is such a part of the culture, that when area residents in Raleigh petitioned the courts to have a local Krispy Kreme shop's sign made smaller and less gaudy, the doughnut company won the decision in court to keep the sign, and now the shop's sign at 549 Person Street has landmark status.

Hey, after all, it's not just a doughnut—it's the epitome of the American dream. Glazed.

Lost and Found: The Queen Anne's Revenge

The ship once sailed by Blackbeard may rejuvenate the area of North Carolina that the infamous pirate terrorized during his years of piracy. The *Queen Anne's Revenge* had been in the waters of the Atlantic since she ran aground in 1718.

Then in November 1996, Intersal Incorporated, a Florida-based diving and treasure-hunting company, found the wreckage in only twenty-five feet of water in Beaufort Inlet. Recovered items include a bronze bell from 1709, a cannonball weighing twenty-four pounds, and a sounding weight.

As artifacts from the *Queen Anne's Revenge* continue to be discovered in what are now protected waters, interest in the ship and its historical context have increased exponentially. The artifacts are on display at the North Carolina Maritime Museum in Beaufort, and twice a year, the *Queen Anne's Revenge* Project in cooperation with the museum holds an interactive dive called "DiveLive" for schoolchildren and other interested persons. In 2002 the Maritime Museum opened a repository for the *Queen Anne's Revenge* artifacts, with interactive displays, a diorama of the wreck site, a model of the ship, and more. The repository is about a mile from the museum on West Beaufort Road near the airport.

It seems that after more than three hundred years, the people of North Carolina may now be getting some of Blackbeard's treasure—in the form of scientific research, government grants, and tourist dollars.

DID *YOU KNOW?*

The oldest house in Beaufort is said to once have been the home of the infamous pirate Blackbeard. Now a private home known as Hammock House, although not open for tours visitors can view the home from the comfort of their cars or bicycles, read the informational sign posted on the front lawn, and see the historical sign posted by the front door. Going by Hammock House is listed as among the top ten things to see in Beaufort, according to TripAdvisor.

The Dukes of Durham

At the end of the Civil War, Washington Duke returned to his wife and three sons at their home in Durham and discovered that virtually everything of value had been taken or destroyed. One twenty-five-pound sack of raw tobacco leaves, however, had not been discovered in its hiding place.

Duke and his sons prepared the leaves and sold them for a surprisingly good price, as during the war soldiers on both sides had come to enjoy what they called "bright leaf" tobacco. (Today, virtually all coastal-plain tobacco is the bright leaf, flue-cured variety, which is used nearly exclusively for cigarettes.) From this nest egg, Duke became a tobacco manufacturer and started a factory, called W. Duke & Sons Tobacco Company, that prepared tobacco for market.

Washington Duke stands next to his first tobacco factory, which was actually a converted corncrib. Fifteen thousand pounds of smoking tobacco was produced in one year using this building. (Courtesy Duke Homestead State Historic Site, Durham, N. C.)

The living they made was adequate but modest. Then in 1884 Duke heard of a machine (invented by James Bonsack of Virginia) that would roll cigarettes. Immediately, he bought the patent rights for what others dismissed as a machine that probably wouldn't be profitable. Before long, Duke's tobacco company had something akin to a world-wide monopoly in the cigarette industry, and Durham became the tobacco capital of the world.

By 1907 the Duke tobacco estate was worth more than $300 million, and in 1924 Washington's son, Buck, decided to be philanthropic with some of the profits. He created a world-class university from the former Trinity College (previously moved to Durham), which was renamed Duke University that same year. Buck Duke then added more buildings, dormitories, and the magnificent Duke Chapel, surrounded by 20,000 lush acres.

At the Duke Homestead State Historic Site and Tobacco Museum, you can see where Washington Duke first came home to bad news—and learn how one family took "lemons" and made their own version of lemonade. See "Virtual North Carolina" for website information.

Strange... but true

An Accident that Led to a Billion-Dollar Industry

The method used for curing cigarette tobacco was developed by accident, according to Caswell County historian Sallie Anderson. It happened in 1839, Anderson said, that a slave named Stephen Slade was left in charge of a barn full of tobacco, owned by Abishai Slade. Young Stephen's job was to monitor the coals and not let them go out, as this was what "cured," or ripened, the tobacco, as it was hung suspended about four feet from the coals.

But, as young people are wont to do, Stephen fell asleep on the job. Horrified, he awoke to dead coals and a cool barn. He raced to a nearby blacksmith's shop and brought back fresh, hot coals, and spread them on the floor. This "accident" of lowering the heat, then raising it again, only served to improve the flavor and color of the tobacco. Stephen's accident led to improved curing techniques. You can learn more about this at several places: The Museum in Yanceyville, the Tobacco Museum in Durham, the Tobacco Farm Life Museum in Kenly, or The Tobacco Museum in Winston-Salem. See "Virtual North Carolina" for website information.

Sunken Treasure, Avast!

Near the town of Wilmington is a small fishing village called Carolina Beach, settled by a family whose last name was Winner. Their descendant, Captain Carl "Skippy" Winner, lives up to his family name—he's a diver who searches sunken ocean-going crafts for salvage. Winner has discovered sunken treasure, but not gems or gold: he makes a living salvaging wrecks and selling what he finds. For fifty years, Winner has been diving on blockade runners, looking for salvageable artifacts. Some of the artifacts he has recovered are on display at the Smithsonian in Washington, D.C.; the Naval Museum in Newport News, Virginia; and the North Carolina Museum of History in Raleigh.

Carolina Beach has an easygoing ambience that belies its history: this area has been more than once fraught with violence, as desperate soldiers and civilians alike found themselves caught up in the Civil War, and generations later,

Captain Skippy Winter stands aboard one of his boats, holding a bronze lug nut he dove for and salvaged from a sunken wreck – it may not look like treasure, but for him it is. (Photo by the Author)

World War II. The ports in the area were some of the last open to the Confederacy, explains Winner, and were used by increasingly desperate blockade runners transporting goods to civilians and soldiers—and many met their fate in these waters. (You can read more about blockade runners in Chapter 9.) Similarly, German U-boats made quite a few attempts to invade the United States via these same small ports. Many met the same fate as the blockade runners, and now lie on the ocean floor.

Winner became fascinated early on by the history that lies beneath the waves. As a teenager, he began diving the waters near his home, with a diving regulator he made himself. Realizing that much could be recovered from the ocean floor, he began salvaging in 1956 and eventually built up a salvage operation with a fleet of nine boats.

His fascination with history led him to read about the Civil War blockade runners and World War II German U-boats in the area. "You can look out over the waters around here," Winner told me when I first interviewed him in 2006, "and at low tide, see the top of sunken blockade runners' ships." An underwater salvager is a combination of historian, detective, and diver, Winner explained. He researched each wreck intensely, finding out details of the ship and its sinking, and the lay of the ocean floor.

One of his biggest salvage operations was in nine fathoms of water twenty-seven miles off the Masonboro Inlet, where a tanker named the *John D. Gill* was hit by a German torpedo and sank. It had been under water since 1941, but despite time, tides, waves, and a ten-foot tiger shark the divers named George, Winner and his crew salvaged much of the ship. The salvage job paid forty-nine cents a pound—in one year, Winner salvaged 190,000 pounds of brass, 17,000 pounds of copper, and 8,000 pounds of copper-nickel (you do the math!). Not a bad living at all, it seems, reaping the sunken treasure just beneath the waves.

Due to advanced years, Winner retired since this book's last publication, but there are many marine salvage business owners who will take you out to sea if you want to try your hand at finding valuable artifacts. Who knows what you may find? Here are just a few samples of Winner's sunken "treasures:"

❖ Prehistoric clam shells, oyster shells, and animal bones

❖ Foreign coins

❖ An anchor chain from a Spanish galleon

❖ Civil War–era bullets, knives, guns, shoes, and china

❖ A World War II–era cannon

❖ Human remains from a World War II German U-boat

❖ Porcelain toilets ("nothing grows on porcelain and they are a beautiful sight")

❖ A completely made bunk bed and a wooden footlocker full of clothes from the American World War II tanker *John D. Gill*

What All the Buzz is About: Burt's Bees

Burt's Bees began in the early 1980s with a stray beehive that Burt Shavitz found. He left his photojournalist business in Manhattan behind and moved to Maine. He believed in living simply and made his home out of a 300-square-foot turkey coop. While in Maine, he met artist Roxanne Quimby and the two, as they say, "hit it off." The pair expanded Burt's beekeeping business and also added merchandise to their product line, starting with beeswax candles and lip balm.

They relocated again, this time to their permanent location in Durham, North Carolina. Now Burt's Bees is a multi-million-dollar operation, but the company continues to focus on sustainable, low-impact living and production. Burt passed away a few years ago, and his 300-square-foot cabin was moved from Maine to the new headquarters in Durham. Today, visitors love to tour the headquarters, which includes the largest observation hive in the state, and see the products lab, using ingredients from nature's bounty. Their headquarters, built inside a former tobacco building, is open to the public. The outside of the building has a mural painted on it by famous artist Matthew Willey, who is devoted to painting 50,000 bees in murals around the world. See "Virtual North Carolina" at the back of this book for website information.

The Wild West in North Carolina: Love Valley

You'll find a real-life cowboy town in the Tar Heel State in Love Valley, which has as one of its monikers "Cowboy Capital." Andy Barker began this small community (current population is approximately 150) and wanted to make a re-creation of the Western towns from his childhood days, watching Westerns on TV. Although he has since passed away, his vision of a real-life Western town is what is today Love Valley, said to be the only such Western town in the entire Eastern United States.

When you first come into the town, you will find (near Andy's old Hardware Store) a list of rules which includes "No Loose Horses." The main street is also closed to motor vehicles—it's only open to pedestrians and horses.

In the town, there's even a "Miss Kitty's," which is a bed & breakfast. The main street looks much like what you would see on a re-run of "Gunsmoke."

The rest of the town includes a saloon, a marshall's office, a couple of cafes, a blacksmith shop and a few other shops which sell anything from lace to leather goods. The entire Main Street has hitching posts in place, for visitors to tie up their horses while they go inside.

For those who wish to saddle up, but are without a mount of their own, there are various numbers of places that rent horses, and some of them offer guide services. The trails in and around Love Valley offer riders and their horses all kinds of views—more than 2,000 acres of land to explore.

There are various events the town holds throughout the year, including a rodeo, so hoof it on over! See "Virtual North Carolina" for website information.

WHEELERS & DEALERS TRIVIA

Q. What was the name of R. J. and Katherine Reynolds's home, located outside Winston-Salem?

A. Reynolda. It is now used as an art museum.

Q. Before the Civil War, what city in North Carolina was the site of a U.S. mint?

A. Charlotte.

Q. What town on the Pasquotank River gets its name from its main business of building small commercial sea-going vessels?

A. Shipyard.

Q. What does the seated figure on the North Carolina State Seal symbolize?

A. Plenty.

Q. What town has a museum called Mill Village Museum, depicting life in a company-owned mill town?

A. Cooleemee, Davie County.

Q. Where is the famous blacksmith shop owned by Mike and Bea Hensley, artisans who have created works for the Smithsonian and for well-known people?

A. Spruce Pine.

Q. What town in North Carolina manufactures the most denim in the world?

A. Erwin.

Q. In what city in North Carolina can you attend the world's largest furniture show?

A. High Point.

Q. By what produce is the town of Mount Olive known (it's not olives!)?

A. Its nickname is "Pickle Town, USA."

Q. What is the *Fayetteville Observer*'s claim to fame?

A. It is North Carolina's oldest newspaper; it began publishing in 1816.

Q. Where can you find a museum featuring the history of the Carolina Freight Company and the story of its founder, C. Grier Beam?

A. In Cherryville. The museum is named the C. Grier Beam Truck Museum.

Q. What artist and furniture crafter helped put the town of Lexington on the map?

A. Bob Timberlake.

Q. What town is famous for its hand-crafted pottery?

A. Seagrove.

Q. Where was the first Hardee's Hamburgers established, and in what year?

A. In Rocky Mount, 1960.

Q. What innovative yacht building company, established in the early 1960s, set out to build yachts to withstand the treacherous waters of Cape Hatteras?

A. Hatteras Yachts. They are based in the town of New Bern and welcome people who want to live "life without limits."

CHAPTER 12

FILM, MUSIC & DRAMA

Hollywood in North Carolina

After New York and California, more movies, documentaries, and TV shows are filmed in North Carolina than any other state. Since 1980, more than five hundred movies, several thousand commercials, and more than a half-dozen TV series have used the Tar Heel State as their setting. The state has been so popular for moviemaking that Wilmington is home to Screen Gems Studio, whose president is Frank Capra Jr. Outside Hollywood, there's no larger full-service studio and sound stage

Jodie Foster plays her role in The Dangerous Lives of Alter Boys (Courtesy N.C. Film Commission)

production facility. North Carolina also has a half-dozen other production facilities, offering twenty-seven sound stages in addition to those at Screen Gems. One noteworthy studio is Hollywood East in Shelby, with the largest cyclorama stage in the world.

Collie Khouri directs the filming of the Divine Secrets of the Ya-Ya Sisterhood in Wilmington. (Courtesy N.C. Film Commission)

Why has North Carolina become the eastern version of Hollywood? Climate is a draw, as are the scenic and geographical diversity—not to mention the friendly people.

Here's just a sample of the hundreds of films made in North Carolina:

❖ *The Color Purple* (1985)

❖ *Dirty Dancing* (1987)

❖ *Bull Durham* (1988)

- ❖ *The Ryan White Story* (1989)

- ❖ *The Hunt for Red* October and Days *of Thunder* (both 1990)

- ❖ *The Last of the Mohicans* (1992)

- ❖ *The Fugitive* (1993)

- ❖ *Nell* (1994)

- ❖ *Richie Rich* (1994)

- ❖ *Forrest Gump* (1994)

- ❖ *Patch Adams* (1998)

- ❖ *The Green Mile* and *The Rage: Carrie 2* (both 1999)

- ❖ *The Original Kings of Comedy* (2000)

- ❖ *Hannibal* (2001)

- ❖ *Shallow Hal* (2001)

- ❖ *Divine Secrets of the Ya-Ya Sisterhood* (2002)

- ❖ *A Walk to Remember* (2002)

- ❖ *Chicks 101 (2004)*

- ❖ *Talladega Nights: The Ballad of Ricky Bobby (2006)*

- ❖ **Leathernecks (2008)*

From Mill Village to Abandoned Town to Movie Star

Back in the early 1900s, in Hickory, North Carolina, two families partnered to create the Henry River Mill Manufacturing Company, which opened its doors in 1905 as a cotton yarn manufacturer. The company built 35 houses for the workers and their families, along with a boarding house, a bridge, a company store, a dam (for hydroelectricity) and a brick mill factory.

By 1963 the company had tripled its production from the early days, but overseas companies were increasingly producing more yarn for less expense, and the mill shut down. The last resident moved from the mill town around the late 1990s or early 2000s. There the mill village lay, abandoned and falling into a state of disrepair.

In 1977, a private owner purchased the mill town, but upon his death in 2015, the unimproved village became the property of his estate.

In 2017, two families, Reyes and Namour, approached the estate with an offer to purchase the entire village. They repaired the property, restored an initial mill home, and made many other improvements. It was shortly after this that the Henry River Mill Village became a kind of movie star.

This restored mill village was the setting for the sci-fi dystopian movie "Hunger Games" (District 12). Today, the Henry River Mill Village is open for tours, weddings, photography sessions, reunions, and more. People love to be able to experience what life might have been like in the early 1900s and explore the town that became a kind of movie star on its own. If you like, you can even stay overnight in one of the renovated mill homes. See "Virtual North Carolina" for website information.

Hurrah! The Old North State Forever!

William Gaston wrote "The Old North State" (the town of Gastonia was named after him) and Mrs. E. E. Rudolph collected and arranged the music. In 1927 the General Assembly officially adopted this as the state song of North Carolina. Here are the words, so you can sing along!

The Old North State

Carolina! Carolina! Heaven's blessings attend her!

While we live we will cherish, protect, and defend her;

Tho' the scorner may sneer at and witlings defame her,

Still our hearts swell with gladness whenever we name her.

(Chorus): Hurrah! Hurrah! The Old North State forever!

Hurrah! Hurrah! the good Old North State!

Tho' she envies not others, their merited glory,

Say whose name stands the foremost, in liberty's story,

Tho' too true to herself e'er to crouch to oppression,

Who can yield to just rule a more loyal submission.

(Repeat chorus)

Then let all those who love us, love the land that we live in,

As happy a region as on this side of heaven,

Where plenty and peace, love and joy smile before us,

Raise aloud, raise together the heart thrilling chorus.

(Repeat chorus)

The Story of the "Songcatcher"

In 1908 a woman named Olive Dame Campbell accompanied her minister husband to the Appalachian Mountains. While his work was to save souls, she herself became a "songcatcher," a term used to describe someone who collects songs.

Stunned by the beauty of the mountaineers' songs and their talents when it came to crafts, Campbell began collecting the ancient ballads and studying and recording how handcrafts were made. In 1925 she founded the John C. Campbell Folk School in Brasstown, named for her husband, to record and teach traditional Appalachian Mountain ways. What the "songcatcher" began is now the oldest folk school in the United States; the folk school offers classes in mountain musical and craft traditions.

The Song of the "Chanteymen"

In the coastal area around Beaufort as late as the 1940s and 1950s, a group of local African-American fishermen sang as they plied their trade in the waters. These were traditional work songs that went back generations. "The songs were sung so that all the men pulling on the nets would be in synchronicity," Connie Mason, Beaufort historian, explains, and these fishermen were called the Chanteymen. Unfortunately, mechanization brought an end to the Chanteymen in the 1950s when hydraulic blocks were used to pull up nets, eliminating the need for large crews to haul the nets.

Although the era of the singing fishermen is past, the songs of the Chanteymen have been preserved in recordings in the

North Carolina Maritime Museum in Beaufort. Here are the words to a few stanzas of one such song, author unknown, provided by Connie Mason.

I'm Gonna Roll Here

I'm gonna roll here / Roll here a few days longer (pull)

I'm gonna roll here / Roll here a few days longer (pull)

Then I'm going home, boys / Lord, Lord, I'm going home (pull)

I left my baby / Standing in the backdoor crying (pull)

I left my baby / Standing in the backdoor crying (pull)

Saying, Daddy don't you go / Lord, Lord, Daddy don't you go (pull)

The Night Elvis Came to Town

It was the year 1956. A sold-out crowd of 5,000 people at the local YMCA in the city of Lexington waited to hear a young man perform his music that, until this night, they had only heard on the radio. The young man, relatively new to the entertainment industry, likely waited a bit nervously backstage as he heard the crowd grow in size and volume.

Then he stepped on stage with his guitar and began singing, while dancing with moves that some audiences thought were a bit suggestive.

For this young man was Elvis Presley. He "wowed the crowd" so much that they wanted more.

Sixty years later (in 2016), Lexington hosted a sold-out performance of Elvis Presley's Broadway-style show, "Elvis

56," commemorating that first year when "the King" came to the Tar Heel state. The crowd loved the show and thus another show, "Elvis Back in Lexington," was performed at the local Civic Center.

Finally, the Lexington Tourism Authority decided to have a Tribute Festival to the King and make it an annual event. The first such Festival was in 2022.

The festival includes two competitions (main and youth), with an entry fee and cash prizes.

You think you can sing and dance like the King? Why not try out for this year's festival? See "Virtual North Carolina" for website information.

"Saint" John Coltrane

Acknowledged as one of the more prolific as well as versatile players in jazz, John William Coltrane has left a legacy that transcends the world of music. He died in 1967, but his life and music continue to shape the lives of others.

Coltrane was born in 1926 in the town of Hamlet to John R. and Alice Blair Coltrane. His father was a tailor but also an amateur musician, and his grandfather a presiding elder in the African Methodist Episcopal Zion Church in High Point, where Coltrane was raised.

When Coltrane was still a young boy, his father, grandparents, and an uncle died, leaving his mother obliged to find work as a domestic to support herself and her son.

Coltrane played first the clarinet and horn, then the alto saxophone when he joined the high school band. After he graduated from high school, the family moved to Philadelphia, where the young sax player began playing in local clubs. In 1945, when he was drafted into the navy and stationed in Hawaii, Coltrane played with other sailor-musicians, and in 1946 he made his first release, with singer Tadd Dameron (*Hot House,* Rhino Records).

Once out of the navy, Coltrane moved back to Philadelphia, switched from alto to tenor sax, and played with several bands. The high point was playing with Dizzy Gillespie, and his first solo during a performance of "We Love to Boogie."

That was in 1951. Coltrane had fallen victim to a heroin habit, and his addiction made him unreliable. Coltrane was fired by Johnny Hodges and then hired by Miles Davis, a former drug addict himself. Davis apparently saw the promise and potential in Coltrane's style, and worked to help the saxophone player kick the heroin habit.

Coltrane's performance at the Newport Jazz Festival in 1955 resulted in a recording contract with Columbia Records, and the New Miles Davis Quintet debuted with Prestige Records in 1956 before coming out with "Round About Midnight" for Columbia in 1957. Davis and Coltrane played together until April 1957, when Davis fired Coltrane because of his persistent and recurring heroin problem. Being fired may have been a wake-up call for Coltrane, who finally succeeded in kicking the heroin habit for good.

Coltrane played and recorded with Lee Morgan, Kenny Drew, and fellow North Carolinian Thelonious Monk, among others. His style became increasingly radical and experimental, and he became known not only for his prolific recordings (seven different labels carry his work), but also his

John William Coltrane (Wikimedia)

commitment to jazz. One of his biggest commercial hits was his adaptation of Rodgers and Hammerstein's "My Favorite Things," the improvisation for which he is probably best known.

Coltrane's light was too soon extinguished, however, when he died of liver cancer in 1967. He is still regarded as one of the most influential jazz musicians ever and received many music awards. In 1992 Coltrane was posthumously awarded the Grammy Lifetime Achievement Award.

The city of Hamlet honors him with the annual John Coltrane "Edutainment" Jazz Festival held the first Saturday in October (directed by another musician, Gerard Morrison) and Coltrane's birthplace has been restored and made into a museum (called the Coltrane Blueroom), recognizing the musician's life and achievements.

But Coltrane's legacy transcends music—and state borders.

In 1965, in a nightclub in San Francisco, a hairdresser named Franzo Wayne King heard Coltrane and remarked that the experience was "a baptism in sound . . . a very serious and earnest journey to seek out God." Following this musical "baptism," King founded the Saint John Coltrane African Orthodox Church in San Francisco, using music as a way of touching people's souls. Now known to the members as Archbishop King, he leads his flock in three-hour church services that are influenced by Coltrane's music and are part worship and part jam session (like Coltrane, King also plays saxophone). The church celebrated its 50th anniversary in 2019.

Coltrane once said he hoped to show people the "divine in a musical language that transcends words, to speak to their soul." Now, decades after his death, the North Carolina jazz great is helping people find God through music. For websites relating to all things John Coltrane, see "Virtual North Carolina" at the back of this book.

Other Famous Music Folk Born in North Carolina

- **Clyde Edric Barron Bernhardt:** blues trombonist, Gold Hill.

- **Joseph Leonard "Joe" Bonner:** pianist and composer, Rocky Mount.

- **Margie Bowes:** country singer, Roxboro.

- **Carol Brice:** contralto, Sedalia.

- **Alden ("Allen") Bunn:** blues guitarist, near Wilson.

- **J. C. Burris:** harmonica player, King's Mountain.

- **Shirley Caesar:** known as "Baby Shirley, the Gospel Singer," started with the Charity Singers, Durham.

- **George Clinton:** R&B songwriter, singer, bandleader, Kannapolis.

- **Floyd ("Dipper Boy") Council:** nicknamed "Devil's Daddy-in-Law," blues guitarist and mandolin player, Chapel Hill.

- **Mary Cardwell Dawson,** opera director, Meridian.

- **Donna Fargo:** country music singer, best known for *Happiest Girl in the Whole U.S.A.* and *Funny Face,* Mount Airy.

- **"Blind Boy" Fuller** (born Fulton Allen): blues man, Wadesboro.

- **Don Gibson:** singer, best known for hit song "Oh, Lonesome Me," Shelby.

- **George Hamilton IV:** country singer, Winston-Salem.

251

- **Kay Kyser:** famous bandleader of the 1940s, Rocky Mount.

- **Weston Wilbur Little:** singer and bass musician, Parmele.

- **John D. Loudermilk:** country musician who had his own radio program at age eleven, Durham.

- **Clyde McPhatter:** R&B singer, Durham.

- **Charlie Poole:** bluegrass banjo picker, who played with the North Carolina Ramblers, Randolph County.

- **Del Reeves:** country music singer, best known for "Be Quiet Mind" in 1961, Sparta.

- **Woody Shaw:** trumpet player, Laurinburg.

- **Nina Simone** (born Eunice Waymon): soul singer, pianist, arranger, Tryon.

- **William "Billy" Taylor:** pianist, composer, educator and musical director, Greeneville.

- **Eva Narcissus Boyd**, better known as "Little Eva," found fame with her song "The Locomotion." This Belhaven native passed away in 2003.

- **Snuffy Jenkins**—Harris native, was a pioneer of the 3-finger style of banjo playing and influenced such musicians as Earl Scruggs and Homer "Pappy" Sherill.

- **Arthel "Doc" Watson**—Born in Stoney Fork Township and blind since birth, this musician played harmonica, banjo and guitar. His best-known song is probably "When the Roses Bloom in Dixieland."

- **Billy "Crash" Craddock**—got his nickname from playing football. The best-known songs from this Greensboro native include "Knock Three Times" and the 2021 hit, "Paint Your Toes."

- **James Taylor**—this long-time resident of Chapel Hill, married for a time to Carly Simon, is best known for "You've Got a Friend."

- **Kate Smith**—this Raleigh-born native's best-loved song is "God Bless America."

- **Stonewall Jackson**—This native of Tabor City, best known for his country music song "Waterloo," is the first entertainer to join the Grand Ole Opry without a recording contract.

- **Ronnie Milsap**—best known for his hit song "Smoky Mountain Rain," this Robbinsville native won the Country Music Association's Entertainer of the Year Award in 1977.

- **Earl Scruggs and the Earl Scruggs Review**—this Cleveland-born bluegrass guitarist played with Lester Flatt for the banjo-duet theme song "Theme from the Beverly Hillbillies."

- **Charlie Daniels and the Charlie Daniels Band**—this Wilmington-born native is best known for his hit country song, "The Devil Went Down to Georgia."

- **Thelonious Monk**—This Rocky Mount native is a jazz pianist and developed the style of music known as "bebop."

- **Roberta Flack**—this singer from Farmville started out as an English teacher but is best known and loved for her songs, "Killing Me Softly," and "The First Time Ever I Saw Your Face."

- **Randy Travis**—born as Randy Traywick in Marshville, this musician and actor was inducted into the Country Music Hall of Fame in 2016, has won 10 AMA Awards, 9 ACM Awards, 8 Dove Awards, 6 Grammies and 6 CMA Awards, as of 2022. He's probably best known for his songs "Forever and Ever, Amen," and "On the Other Hand."

- **Ben E. King**—from Henderson, the late R&B musician is best-known for his songs "Save the Last Dance for Me" and "Stand By Me."

- **John Boy and Billy**—known throughout the radio-tuned-in world for their weekday morning "Big Show" out of Charlotte.

Helping Musicians, Preserving Music

Outside the town of Hillsborough is an old farmhouse that has been converted into a recording studio and administrative offices. This quiet place is the result of a vision shared by Timothy and Denise Duffy. Their mission is to give a hand to musicians living in poverty, while preserving little-known yet unique music before it's gone forever.

The Duffys' organization is called Music Maker Relief Foundation, and benefits musicians whose style is rooted in a Southern musical tradition, are fifty-five or older, and earn less than $18,000 annually. It began in the 1980s, when Timothy began booking blues musicians from nearby Winston-Salem and Greensboro. From those proceeds, he started a foundation to help musicians in dire need with the most basic of necessities—such as a pair of new shoes.

Now more than a hundred musical artists are being helped with food, affordable housing, medical care, and other basic needs. Most have an average income of only six thousand dollars a year, and some are as far away as Canada and California.

The Duffys also preserve these musicians' works. While Denise handles the administrative end, Timothy travels to meet with musicians. He has recorded musicians' work in tumbledown shacks and fields, as well as in the Hillsborough studio. Many of these musicians, most of whom have been making music for fifty years or more, have never previously had their music recorded. The Duffys are also working to make sure that the music of Chicago, Memphis, Nashville, and the Mississippi Delta are not forgotten. As musician Taj Majal said of Duffys' work, "Music Makers clearly dispels the notion that real blues musicians are long gone." Working with the musicians and artists they refer to as "partners," Tim and Denise Duffy are preserving history, culture and music that would otherwise be lost forever.

If you ever drive by their farm in Hillsborough, roll down your windows and listen. You just might hear something you have never heard before, being recorded for posterity in the Duffy studio.

Although the Hillsborough studio is not currently open for tours, their website has information relating to their partners' musical and artistic events, CDs and YouTube videos. See "Virtual North Carolina" for website information and links to this important work.

There's No Place Like Home, Unless You're Here!

America's only Wizard of Oz theme park, Land of Oz, opened in 1970 but closed to the public about 10 years later. Every fall, during three weekends in September, the Land of Oz opens for people of all ages to visit with characters from the movie and book. People delight in getting to walk the yellow brick road, have their picture taken with Glinda, the good witch, or even with one of the repulsive flying monkeys. The festival, called Autumn at Oz, is held in Beech Mountain. Visitors are encouraged to dress as their favorite character. See "Virtual North Carolina" for website information.

When Waynesville Goes International

Since 1984 the city of Waynesville has hosted a music and dance festival unlike anything else in the state. Every July the

Dancers from Sicily perform at Folkmoot, an international Folk Festival in Waynesville. (Courtesy Folkmoot, USA)

townspeople celebrate the heritage of music and dance with an international folk festival called Folkmoot (an old English term meaning "a gathering of the people"). The North Carolina Folk Festival brings in dancers from nearby Cherokee, North Carolina and such far-flung places as Togo, the Czech Republic, Mongolia, Paraguay, and more. Not only is Folkmoot a celebration of international cultures, but also a cultural exchange. Dancers entertain in several surrounding counties during their visit and stay in hostel-like quarters in a refurbished school, the Folkmoot Friendship Center.

For four days every July, the town of Waynesville does more than showcase dancers from the world over—the people there become international diplomats of sorts, in the mountains of the Tar Heel State.

Libba Cotten: Upside-down Music

Libba (Elizabeth) Cotten was born in Chapel Hill around 1892, but her music didn't hit it big until she was past her sixtieth birthday. Mostly she played for family until she made her professional debut in 1959 with Mike Seeger at a concert in Pennsylvania. From then on, she was regarded as a professional folk artist. Her best-known song is "Freight Train," which she wrote when she was twelve and was first recorded by several other groups, including Peter, Paul, and Mary.

When Cotten was a little girl, she desperately wanted to learn to play a musical instrument. Her brother had a banjo, and when Cotten asked if she could try her hand at it, he said no, as most siblings would. But the little girl was determined.

When her brother left the house, Libba would sneak into his room, where he kept his banjo under the bed. The problem was that Libba was left-handed, and the banjo was strung for a right-handed player. She couldn't change the way the strings were, because her brother would know she'd gotten to the instrument—so she played it upside down. When in later years Libba bought a guitar, she couldn't play it or tune it until she reversed the strings and played the only way she knew.

The left-handed, two-fingered picking style of Libba Cotten worked—in 1972 she won the National Folk Association's Burl Ives Award for her lifelong contribution to folk music. Her last album, *Elizabeth Cotten Live,* won a Grammy for best traditional folk music, two years before her death in 1987.

A Flair for the Dramatic

North Carolina is awash with annual dramatic performances, many of which are performed outdoors. Here's a partial list of plays and where they are performed.

- *The Amistad Saga* (Raleigh)
- *Blackbeard's Revenge* (Swansboro)
- *Cape Fear Shakespeare Festival* (Wilmington)
- *First for Freedom* (Halifax)
- *From This Day Forward* (Valdese)
- *Horn in the West* (Boone)
- *The Legend of Tom Dooley* (Wilkesboro)
- *The Liberty Cart: A Duplin Story* (Kenansville)

- *Listen and Remember* (Waxhaw)

- *The Lost Colony* (Roanoke Island)

- *The Rising Splendor* (New Bern)

- *Strike at the Wind* (Pembroke)

- *The Sword of Peace* (Snow Camp)

- *Unto These Hills* (Cherokee)

- *Worthy Is the Lamb* (Swansboro)

- *Blackbeard: Knight of the Black Flag (Bath)*

From *The Notebook* to *Kindred Spirit Mailbox*

Fellow author Nicholas Sparks and I once had a book-signing together at a table we shared during a literary festival in Greensboro. Sparks, who makes his home in New Bern, writes his books with their settings in different parts of the Tar Heel state. His novel, *Every Breath* (2018), features something unique.

On a reserve adjacent to Sunset Beach on Bird Island (part of the Brunswick Islands), there is a mailbox, but it's not just any mailbox: this one has a name, the Kindred Spirit mailbox. In this mailbox, anyone may write just about anything. It can be a note of advice to those who come after, or a letter to a long-lost or unrequited love.

The Kindred Spirit mailbox has been through many coastal storms and other types of inclement weather, but locals and visiting tourists help take care of it. Since the Kindred Spirit mailbox was placed on this island, more than 100,000 people have visited this unique mailbox. It seems to carry an aura of mystery and romance.

Only a writer like Nicholas Sparks would see the potential and romantic lure of a simple mailbox.

Behind the Mystery of the Kindred Spirits Mailbox

In reading about this mysterious mailbox, I did a little digging to find out more as to who first put it there and why. In 2014, CBS Evening News Anchor Chip Reid did a segment about this, and here's the gist of it.

A local man named Frank Nesmith placed the first Kindred Spirits mailbox about a mile and a half from the parking lot in Sunset Beach (Bird Island). That was back in 1979 (other sources say 1981). Nesmith left a blank notebook inside the mailbox in the hopes that people visiting this uninhabited island would come by and be intrigued enough to leave a written message.

Copyright Our State Magazine

The KS mailbox "project" exceeded Nesmith's hopes. Over the years, more than a hundred thousand people have come to the beach and the mailbox there and have shared their innermost thoughts, dreams and life experiences, written down either in the notebook or in a single letter.

The messages cover all kinds of thoughts and emotions and uncover secret hopes, dreams and tender or even painful memories. One, read aloud by Reid, was a love letter from a widower to his recently deceased wife.

Writing messages for the mailbox has now covered several generations, with family members adding messages of their own in what has now become a time-honored tradition.

Local volunteers help monitor the mailbox. These letters and messages have a final home in the North Carolina Archives Collection, at the University of North Carolina in Wilmington (at the William Madison Randall Library). The full journals at last count numbered more than 500.

Who knows what you will write, when you get the chance?

"The Hills Are Alive"

In North Carolina, the hills and valleys are alive with the sound of young male voices, raised together in perfect harmony, as they carry on a centuries-old tradition of all-boy choirs.

In 1971 Bill Graham (no relation to Billy Graham) arrived in Durham to become full-time director of music at the local First Presbyterian Church. "We had sort of a large music ministry back then, with separate choirs for boys and girls," he says. Apparently, Graham's work with the choir was noticed, as people began to come to his church to ask to sing with the choirs. Someone suggested a community boys' choir.

It started with about a dozen of the church's best singers, called the Durham Boys' Choir. Seemingly overnight, the choir grew to more than forty boys. "We didn't even guess the scope of what the choir would become," Graham says. "And someone told us that if we could last five years, we'd be really doing something, and by then we should go on the road."

By 1975 Ben Smith, choral director at Duke University, called with a proposal. Duke was planning a Noah's Ark production that required three singing sons of Noah and forty-two singing animals. The problem was, it was spring, and school was almost out. Then one of the mothers suggested a week of camp for the choir, while the boys did the play.

After the three performances, suddenly the Durham Boys' Choir was a success. (Every year since, the group has made the choir camp a tradition, making a trek to Summer Music Camp in Black Mountain.) That led to Leonard Bernstein's *Mass* at Duke, and Duke gave the choir red robes that they still wear. In 1983 Graham got a call from the North Carolina Symphony to join in Benjamin Britten's *War Requiem*.

The group incorporated and became the North Carolina Boys' Choir. In 1991 the choir added a chamber choir composed of former choir boys, singing tenor and bass. Graham also has a training choir to prepare boys for the concert choir, and they tour a different part of the country each year.

The choir performs at Duke University and usually does one Christmas performance each year. In 2011, they added a Girls' Choir, which sometimes performs with the Boys' Choir.

Both choirs have toured nationally and internationally. In 2014, the Choirs sang in Carnegie Hall in New York City. The Choirs are funded by parents, gifts, fundraisers, grants, and concert ticket sales. The headquarters of the North Carolina Boys' and Girls' Choirs is a block away from the University of North Carolina at Chapel Hill, in the Old St. Thomas More Catholic Church building.

Unlike most choirs, the Choir rehearsals are often open, so if ever you're in the area, stop in and give 'em a listen.

FILM, MUSIC AND DRAMA TRIVIA

Q. Lena Wilson, Vaudeville performer and jazz singer, was born in what North Carolina town?

A. Charlotte.

Q. What Winston-Salem actress had a starring role in *Kiss Me, Kate* and *Showboat*?

A. Kathryn Grayson.

Q. What Winston-Salem actress starred in *Beyond the Valley of the Dolls?*

A. Pam Grier.

Q. What producer and screenwriter, whose greatest films include *The Greatest Story Ever Told* and *The Cheyenne Social Club*, was born in 1929 in Charlotte?

A. James Lee Barrett.

Q. What was the last movie for Salisbury-born character actor Sidney Blackmer?

A. *Rosemary's Baby.*

Q. Where in Asheville was Peter Sellers's last movie, *Being There*, filmed?

A. The Biltmore House.

Q. What movie starring John Wayne was filmed in part in North Carolina?

A. *The Green Berets.*

Q. What Stephen King movie features more than a dozen eighteen-wheeler trucks running rampant through Wilmington?

A. *Maximum Overdrive.*

Q. What play was the first-ever outdoor drama in the United States?

A. Paul Green's play *The Lost Colony,* first performed in Roanoke Island in 1937.

Q. What actor born in Roanoke Rapids is most famous for his roles in movies such as *From the Terrace, Advise and Consent,* and *Happy Birthday, Wanda June?*

A. George Grizzard.

Q. Who played the leading role in *Thunder Road,* filmed in North Carolina in 1958?

A. Robert Mitchum.

Q. What historic home in Southport was the setting for the movie *Firestarter?*

A. Orton Plantation.

Q. What famous director was born in Washington, North Carolina?

A. Cecil B. DeMille.

Q. What musical theater company based in Winston-Salem and composed of volunteers from the Triad area and students from the North Carolina School of Arts has been performing since 1978 and giving performances twice a year since 1984?

A. The Piedmont Opera Theatre.

CHAPTER 13

FLORA, FAUNA AND NATURAL PHENOMENA

Move Over, Rover—Guide Horses Are Here!

Janet and Donald Burleson in Kittrell have started the only school of its kind in the world: they train guide horses for sight-impaired people.

The Burlesons founded the nonprofit Guide Horse Foundation in 1999 as an alternative to guide dogs. Horses live longer than dogs, they point out, and thus have a longer service life.

"We were inspired by a little horse we had as a pet, Twinkie," Janet explains. "She made us start thinking how small horses like her could be used as service animals to help people." Janet says that pygmy horses, which usually grow to a height of two feet, are bred all over the country. The horses

A guide horse assists a blind person on the New York subway.
(Courtesy Janet and Donald Burleson, Guide Horse Foundation)

are donated to the foundation, and usually a dozen horses are training at a time. The Burlesons also have about twenty-five of their own horses, both miniature and Arabian.

How do they transport the horses? Janet explains that they flew Delta with a horse named Cuddles in March 2000—the first time a horse had ever flown in the passenger cabin of an airliner. "Delta was very cooperative and let us come out to the airport and train the horse on the plane before the actual flight," says Janet.

The Burlesons say the pygmy horses are "amazingly simple" to train, and theirs have successfully learned more than twenty-three commands, including "load up," when boarding a taxi or automobile. Wearing a harness and leash, the tiny horses lead their masters in a manner similar to that of a guide dog. The Burlesons' first client was Dan Shaw of Ellsworth, Maine, and they now have a waiting list of people wanting their own version of Cuddles.

This Place Is the Cat's Meow

On fifty-five acres outside the town of Pittsboro, you will find an unusual place: the Carnivore Preservation Trust (CPT). It was established in 1981 by Michael Bleyman, Ph.D., a genetics professor at the University of North Carolina in Chapel Hill, who wanted a facility to breed endangered and threatened species that are vital to their ecosystems.

The animals he chose were primarily rodent killers, pollinators, or seed dispersers, whose roles are crucial to the environment. Species included caracals, servals, ocelots, and binturongs (also known as Asian bear cats, a little-known carnivore from southeast Asia). Dr. Bleyman also rescued many big cats, such as tigers and leopards, from horrible living conditions and provided them with a safe, comfortable home.

Dr. Bleyman died in 1997, and the current board of directors adopted a new mission: to provide sanctuary for endangered animals, primarily carnivores, and to promote education about their conservation. Today CPT houses around 160 threatened and endangered carnivores from ten different exotic species, including those mentioned above. The organization also finds homes for animals, placing them in other sanctuaries and zoos around the country. CPT recently obtained licensure from the U.S. Department of Agriculture and has applied for accreditation with the Association of Sanctuaries.

CPT is funded by private donations and is a volunteer-based organization. Volunteers are encouraged to come and lend a hand. As of press time (2022), CPT was open for school field trips and tours, but such tours fill up quickly. They also have a gift shop, the proceeds of which help support the work of the CPT. See "Virtual North Carolina" for website information and links.

The Wild Horses of Currituck Sound

Most towns have leash laws for pets—but in the coastal village of Corolla, the wild horses are pretty much free to roam. The horses are descended from what Southerners call "Old Family" and have been here longer than any human family in North Carolina.

Early in the 1500s, horse breeders on the Barbary Coast of northern Africa began to breed a special stock of horse that was above average in stamina. Impervious to heat and comfortable on sand, the animals also had an easy gait and an equally mild temperament. These horses became known as "Barb" horses, and Spanish explorers took them in their galleons as they explored the New World.

Eventually, because of shipwrecks or other reasons, some of these horses were left here. Because their genes had given them the amazing ability to withstand and even thrive under the extreme environmental conditions of the Outer Banks, by the eighteenth century they were firmly established in Corolla.

Today, the horses are still relatively free, but with the coming of civilization, issues involving the free-roaming animals had to be addressed. The horses are now cared for through donations to the recently incorporated Corolla Wild Horse Fund, Inc., a nonprofit organization that works with the Currituck County officials, the North Carolina National Estuarine Research Reserve, the Currituck National Wildlife Refuge, and private landowners.

Former Horse Fund director Lloyd Childers has been pleased with how the horses and people live together. The new plan, she said, keeps the horses out of the developed areas, lets them be periodically counted and evaluated, and ensures the protection of other plants and animals. She added that with significant grants from the William H. Donner Foundation of New York and under the new Chief Operating Officer, Jo Lanagone, people and wild horses will continue to live in harmony.

The Corolla herd has been linked to Spanish origins, Childers said. "DNA studies confirmed their ancestry, and they have been recognized by the state of North Carolina as a significant historical and cultural resource. Now they're part of the scenery and culture of the Currituck Beach and Currituck Lighthouse which includes glimpses of free-roaming horses, with their genetic roots in the Old World."

The Corolla Wild Horse Fund has a lovely museum (also in Corolla) and a gift shop, which also sells items online. Check out "Virtual North Carolina" for website information and links.

If ever you want to see the wild horses of Currituck County, there are currently approximately seven guide groups who will take you to see them. Just remember that you "herd" about them here first.

270

The Wild Banker Ponies

Hundreds of years ago, a Spanish galleon shipwrecked off the coast of Ocracoke Island, and a handful of Spanish mustang ponies were left stranded there. Early settlers first employed the ponies to pull carts of fish and goods delivered by boat. Later, the U.S. Lifesaving Service used the ponies for patrolling the beaches, looking for shipwrecks. During World War II, the U.S. Coast Guard used the ponies to help them patrol the beaches in search of German U-boats that might be lurking nearby. During the 1950s the local chapter of Boy Scouts used the ponies (making this troop the only mounted Boy Scout troop in the country).

As Ocracoke Island continued to grow in human population, people became concerned for the ponies' well-being and protection. In 1959, the Banker Ponies' permanent home is on 188 acres of corralled beach and marsh; they are under the care of the National Park Service. Visitors are welcome to come see the ponies at the Ocracoke Pony Pens off Highway 12.

DID YOU KNOW?

The Great Dismal Swamp in northeastern North Carolina, which also reaches into Virginia, covers 750 square miles of the Tar Heel state. It is an area of incredible biodiversity, created when the continental shelf made its last significant shift.

In Spring a Tar Heel's Fancy Turns to Turtles

Every year, beginning around the middle of May and lasting through August, a fascinating phenomenon occurs along the coast of North Carolina. By dark of night, huge female loggerhead sea turtles, each weighing three to five hundred pounds, lumber up the beaches where they themselves were hatched. Once there, they dig holes in the sand and lay their eggs—usually just over a hundred—and cover them with sand. After returning to the ocean, the mother loggerheads may return to their nesting spot to lay more eggs, usually at fourteen-day intervals for the entire nesting season.

As this occurs, hundreds of volunteers from North Carolina coastal communities walk the beaches. These volunteers, part of the Sea Turtle Conservation Project, protect the hatchling turtles as they emerge from their shells and struggle to get to the ocean.

Jean Beasley, who runs the Karen Beasley Sea Turtle Rescue and Rehabilitation Center in Topsail Island (KBSTRRCTI), explains that volunteers first look for the tracks of the mother turtle—which look like bulldozer tracks on the beach. Volunteers then rope the nesting areas off so no one disturbs them. All nest sites, eggs, hatchlings, and sea turtles are protected under the Endangered and Threatened Species Act.

Dangers to baby turtles include raccoons, foxes, feral cats, and dogs. "The most common predatory danger for the hatchlings are ghost crabs," Beasley says. "They will wait outside the nest and attack the turtles as they emerge from their shells and struggle to cross the sand and get to the ocean." Once the turtles reach the ocean, they face sharks and predatory fish, as well as gulls and other birds that fly out over the water.

The job of the volunteer "turtle patrols" is limited to keeping predators away from the baby turtles as they struggle to get to the sea. "We have people come here, year after year, to help protect the hatchlings," Beasley says. "They plan their vacations around when the turtles hatch."

Like most places in the world, the Rehabilitation Center itself, which cares for injured or sick turtles, had to be closed due to the pandemic. As of press time (2022), the turtle hospital has come out of its shell (pun intended) and is open for scheduled tours. See "Virtual North Carolina" for website information.

Now the project is international in scope, with sea turtle conservationists working all over the globe to protect this wide-ranging species.

No Match for Mother Nature!

In 1915 developers in Hyde County had an ambition for Mattamuskeet Lake—they wanted to drain it and then farm and build upon the land. They didn't realize they were dealing with a very stubborn Mother Nature.

Developers forged ahead with the plan; a town called New Holland sprang up near the lake site, and the world's largest pumping station was built. The lake was drained, all right, and for a few years it was farmed successfully—but then heavy rains and nature had their say. The land again filled with water, and Lake Mattamuskeet returned.

At least the developers knew when they were beaten and decided to make the best of things. With the help of the

Civilian Conservation Corps, in 1934 the world's largest pumping station became Mattamuskeet Lodge, and in 1981 it was placed on the National Register of Historic Places. The lake itself, North Carolina's largest natural lake, was named Mattamuskeet National Wildlife Refuge.

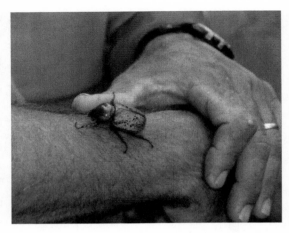

A naturalist counts beetles at the Great Smoky Mountains National Park. Over 9,200 species of flora and fauna have been recorded in the park so far. (Photo by the Author)

The Refuge is open for hiking, picnicking, birdwatching and fishing and it is under the management of the department of the U.S. Fish and Wildlife Service, Department of the Interior. As of press time (2022), the Lodge was closed due to the need for extensive renovation. It does, however, make for a great photo from the outside.

The Amazing Great Smoky Mountains National Park

The Great Smoky Mountains National Park (GSMNP) is one of the most unusual and beautiful places in the world. This 520,000-acre preserve ranges from wetlands to mountains and is one of the most biologically diverse places on earth. More than 10,200 species of living things have been recorded there, but scientists say this represents only a small percentage; every year more species are recorded, adding to the already impressive list.

Here are just a few of the features that make the Great Smokies so great; some of these features are pointed out by guidebook author Jeff Bradley [*The Tennessee Handbook: Including Nashville, Memphis, the Great Smoky Mountains, and Nutbush* (Chico, California: Moon Publications, 1999)].

❖ Home to at least sixteen native mammals

❖ The largest black bear habitat in the eastern United States

❖ Habitat for about two hundred species of birds, including the scissor-tailed flycatcher, western kingbird, cliff swallow, tanager, and finch

❖ The only habitat for Cain's reed-bent grass, Rugel's ragwort, and Jordan's red-cheeked salamander

❖ Home to more than three hundred varieties of trees, more species than in all of Europe

❖ Home to nine hundred varieties of wildflowers—more species than in any other place except Central China

Currently the park sees more than twenty million visitors a year!

About one-fourth of the acreage has never been disturbed; 95 percent of the park is forested, and there are more than seven hundred miles of streams. The park also preserves a unique collection of log buildings and maintains seventy-five historic structures depicting various aspects of pioneer life. It's an amazing place to visit!

Twenty million people can't be wrong.

Elk in the GSMNP

Most people probably don't think of elk when they think about a visit to GSMNP. Elk used to be indigenous to this part of the Tar Heel State, but according to the park's website, due to loss of habitat and over-hunting, the elk disappeared from North Carolina, with the last wild elk killed in the 18th century.

But this changed several years ago, with the introduction of elk in 2001. The park brought in an experimental herd of 25, then in 2002, they brought in another 27. As of last count, the elk population is approximately 200 head. All elk are monitored via radio-collars. Some of the best places to view elk are in the Cataloochee area (often called North Carolina's Cades Cove). Visitors are often warned to view the animals from the relative safety of their vehicles, especially during mating season in the fall. It is during this time that the males call out in what is known as "bugling," to warn other males away while attracting the females. See "Virtual North Carolina" for several websites pertaining to this fascinating creature.

Want to be Amazed by Monarchs? Here's your chance

The Monarch Butterfly is one of those creatures that is a source of fascination for many naturalists. Each fall, the colorful and huge winged insects migrate more than two thousand miles from the northeast portion of the U.S. to Mexico. It's around the months of September and October that the Monarchs make their winged appearance in the Asheville area. With the many wildflowers along the Blue

Ridge Parkway, there is plenty of food to keep them going as they migrate. See "Virtual North Carolina" for website information about this fascinating winged visitor to the Tar Heel State.

Love Nature? They've Got a Celebration for It in North Carolina!

For those folks who love to get close-up and personal with all things Mother Nature, just about anyplace in the Tar Heel State has a festival to celebrate it.

Hardy souls who love cold water can take part in the Polar Plunge, which is one activity held every January as part of the Winterfest held in Blowing Rock.

Every April, the town of Fayetteville has their Dogwood Festival, featuring carnival rides, live music and food vendors serving a variety of culinary concoctions. Local chefs hold a one-day Cork & Fork during the festival, where they serve up some of their best cuisine paired with a delightful array of wines.

Every December, flower-lovers will delight in going to "Christmas at Biltmore," in Asheville.

The Cradle of Forestry

As a young boy growing up in Connecticut, Gifford Pinchot was encouraged by his father to become a forester, although it was not a profession in America at that time. Pinchot went on to study forestry in France (the United States had no forestry school), and in 1892 he came to the mountains of North Carolina to work on George Vanderbilt's Biltmore Forest Estate.

Next he became involved with the National Forest Commission, and in 1898 he was named chief of the Division of Forestry (later to become the Bureau of Forestry and, still later, the Forest Service). At the time, the Department of the Interior controlled Forest Reserve lands. Pinchot and others worked diligently to have the Forest Reserves moved to the Department of Agriculture; this occurred in 1905, when the Forest Service was created. Pinchot became chief of this new Forest Service. Pinchot also founded the Society of American Foresters, which first convened at his residence in Washington, D.C., in November 1900.

The class of 1905 at the Biltmore Forest School, the Nation's first school of forestry, poses for a picture. (Courtesy Forest History Society, Durham)

Under Pinchot, by 1910 national forests grew from 56 million acres to 172 million acres, and forestry was elevated to a true profession. Sharing his philosophy of the "greatest good for the greatest number," he taught his foresters to look at the long-term effects of their decisions.

Today Pinchot is regarded as the father of American conservation because of his great and unrelenting concern for the protection of American forests and the environment. He popularized the concept of conservation of our natural resources.

What is amazing is the tremendous difference Pinchot made at a time when timberlands were thought to be virtually endless. At that time, anyone who took up the cause of the forest was thought a few branches shy of a complete tree. The concept of protecting a forest was a new one—people thought natural resources were meant to be used and could never be used *up*.

Pinchot's successor, Carl Alwin Schenck, began America's first school of forestry in 1898, then called the Biltmore Forest School. The campus has since been reconstructed and the land deeded to become part of the Pisgah National Forest. The original buildings are now part of a museum and educational center called the Cradle of Forestry in America. The Cradle property is open to visitors, with trails and guided hikes, a tour of their seven historical buildings, a ride aboard the Climax steam train, lunch in the Cradle Café and more. They have events throughout the year, including history re-enactors, a creepy trail hike called "The Legend of Tommy Hodges" (more on that in the chapter on Ghosts), and a Forest Festival, which includes a lumberjack competition, an archery contest and an axe-throwing competition. See "Virtual North Carolina" for websites, links and more.

DID YOU KNOW?

The Forest History Society, a nonprofit research and educational organization established in 1946, is an international association based in Durham. This society is the international leader in forest and conservation history and the primary contact for inquiries from around the world. Its library and archives contain the most comprehensive collection about forest and conservation history anywhere. Researchers, scientists, students, teachers and journalists from around the world use this information for their work. It is a truly unique resource.

The Kudzu Culture and Alternative Medicine

One "naturalized" North Carolina plant arrived in the United States as a vine used to shade the Japanese pavilion during the 1876 Centennial Exposition in Philadelphia. Americans hailed the kudzu as a "miracle" plant that would help prevent erosion and provide inexpensive feed for livestock. During the 1930s and 1940s, it was embraced as a farmers' and conservationists' panacea and planted throughout the Southern states, where it took a liking to the weather and environment.

Now North Carolina and neighboring states are draped with kudzu. It covers old barns, obliterates the words on roadside fences, and adorns interstate signs and anything moving too slowly to avoid its tendrils. It grows a foot a day in good conditions, so you can't just cut it back and think you're done. A hard frost stops it for a spell, but it never really goes away.

North Carolinians have just about given up fighting it and have embraced it as part of their culture. Realizing that herbicides and mowing are either too expensive, harmful to the environment or just don't work, the people of the Tar Heel state have found uses for the plant. Take seventy-three-year-old Edith Edwards, the self-proclaimed Kudzu Queen. She eats kudzu, adding it to such everyday dishes as casseroles, and attributes her longevity to this. She also makes hats and even Christmas trees out of the vines. Her husband, Henry, has started a business called Kudzu Cow Farm, where he produces more than 1,000 bales of kudzu every year for use as a nutritious food for cattle.

Kudzu has also found a use in alternative medicine—some medical researchers have found it can help fight alcoholism. Maybe it'll become another of North Carolina's cash crops. "Alternative medicine," of course, isn't new at all to the people of the Tar Heel state. In the old days, when you needed medicine, you just went out into the yard or the nearby woods to find the plant that would provide the cure.

Straight from a Sci-fi Flick

The small, greenish plant is about half a foot tall, with small white flowers and leaves ending in a blade-like form divided into two halves. The deceptively delicious-looking plant exudes a sweet-smelling fluid.

This can attract a fly, which in turn can attract a small frog, which soon becomes a meal for the plant. When the frog touches the outer portion of the leaves, the two halves snap shut, triggered by sensorial hairs. Long, sharp spines along the leaves' margins keep the frog from escaping. Inside the plant, sensors detect nitrogen in the frog's body, and digestive juices begin to dissolve the frog. Once digestion is complete, the innocent-looking leaves open again.

This plant is *Dionaea muscipula,* or Venus flytrap. Common to the Carolinas, the plant is often found around Carolina Beach State Park and other boggy places within a two-hundred-mile radius of Wilmington.

The Venus Flytrap, a carnivorous plant, can be found around Carolina Beach State Park and in other boggy places. (Courtesy N. C. State Museum of Natural History)

North Carolinians are proud of the plant that makes this state its home. Fascination abounds for the plant, and with good reason. It's one of a kind. "The Venus flytrap is the only plant I know that has two lobes that close over prey," said Jaime Amoroso, botanist with the North Carolina Natural Heritage Program. "There are places where you can't walk without stepping on them, but the overall range has been shrinking due to habitat loss."

When you see the Venus flytrap in the wild, remember that it's a protected plant, so don't disturb it.

DID YOU KNOW?

Wilmington holds its North Carolina Azalea Festival every April, and they celebrate one of their favorite blooming shrubs in the South with musical concerts, fireworks, home garden tours and the crowning of their Azalea Queen. Take your best "buds" with you when you go.

Love Marine Life? North Carolina's Awash with Aquariums!

North Carolina is home to not one but four wonderful aquariums, and they are all different. They are located at Roanoke Island, Fort Fisher, Pine Knoll Shores, and Nag's Head. The last one at Nag's Head, Jeanette's Pier, is my personal favorite. Its 3,000 gallon aquarium inside holds all sorts of marine life, like moray eels and clownfish, but outside you just might catch a glimpse of humpback and right whales during their migratory season (roughly November through April).

You "Otter" Check Out These Places!

Discovery Place is a whole network of fascinating museums in North Carolina. Two are in Charlotte (Discovery Place Nature and Discovery Place Science); one is in Huntersville and another is in Rockingham (these last two are both Discovery Place Kids). The year 2022 marked the organization's 75th anniversary.

"The two in Charlotte are connected by a trail which takes visitors along Little Sugar Creek," Elliot Provance, Senior Director of Collections, told me. "Discovery Place Nature is right along this trail and Discovery Place Science is just a few blocks away, in the heart of the city's center. " As of press time (fall 2022), plans were underway for a brand-new Discovery Place Nature, which will have as its highlight of its "Living Collections," North American River Otters.

Provance added, "Discovery Place Science features a 41-year-old Rainforest Exhibit that is home to a variety of flora and fauna. This exhibit is home to one of only a few dozen Great Blue Turacos [*Corythaeola criststa*] in the United States. This large blue bird from the depths of the African rainforest is impressive to see and hear. This collection plan is focused on pan-tropical species and shows our visitors how our own home is connected to places far away."

Every Dog Has His (Work) Day

Patti Moran, president of Pet Sitters International based in King, had to "paws" one day when an idea came upon her. She knew about Take Your Daughters to Work Day. What about a Take Your Dog to Work Day?

The more Moran thought about it, the more she realized she wasn't barking up the wrong tree. In June 1999 the first such day was held. It has grown in popularity and now more than five thousand participants (and their pooches) from both the United States and Canada have at least *one* good day at the office each year. The goal, Moran says, is to call attention to the benefits dogs offer as pets, and "encourage adoptions from animal shelters, humane societies, and rescue clubs." The project enjoys the sponsorship of Iams Dog Food and Loews Hotel, among others.

Moran says everyone has a tail-wagging good time.

Mildred, the Mother Bear of Grandfather Mountain

Less than a hundred miles northeast of Asheville is the town of Linville, home to the only private park in the world designated by the United Nations as an International Biosphere Reserve. It's known as Grandfather Mountain because, in profile, it resembles an old man's face.

To be designated as an International Biosphere Reserve, an area must be home to a certain number of endangered plants and wildlife. (The exclusive list includes the Niagara Escarpment in Canada and the African Serengeti.) Grandfather Mountain and its environs support forty-two rare and endangered species, including about a dozen that are globally endangered. At last count there were 149 species of birds in the park. The United Nations periodically sends scientists to do studies of the endangered plants and wildlife, to learn how to preserve them for posterity.

Another amazing thing about Grandfather Mountain is one of the most colorful characters ever to come out of the woods—Mildred the Bear.

Mildred was brought from the Atlanta Zoo to Grandfather Mountain in 1968 and set free there by the Wildlife Commission to procreate, as the number of black bears in the area was diminishing rapidly. Mildred immediately set to work trying to charm the people of Linville—after all, she had been a "pet" of the Atlanta Zoo secretaries and was not your typical wild black bear.

Over the years, Mildred had ten cubs of her own, and people were amazed at how gentle she was—she not only allowed humans near her cubs (generally a very dangerous undertaking), but also appeared to enjoy the many photos tourists took of her and her offspring. Then something happened that astonished the lay and scientific community alike.

Someone brought Mildred an abandoned cub named Hobo, hoping she might raise it, even

Mildred the bear lives on in her statue at the Grandfather Mountain Nature Museum – and in the many bears she has raised, who still reside in the forests nearby (Reproduced with permission from Hugh Morton, photographer)

though wild bears usually reject motherless cubs. Mildred, affectionate bear that she was, took the cub as one of her own. Next, she adopted another abandoned cub named Punkin, then two siblings, Elizabeth and Walter.

Mildred became so popular that she was probably the most photographed bear in the world. She appeared in magazines such as *National Geographic, Outdoor Life,* and *Northwoods,* and in publications by the U.S. Forest Service.

286

Mildred lived longer than most bears in the wild and died in her sleep as she dozed on January 1, 1993. She was just a few weeks shy of her twenty-seventh birthday and was buried near an orchard on the mountain.

Mildred lives on in her descendants, the black bears of Grandfather Mountain, and in the museum. Thanks to talented sculptor Johnpaul Harris, you can see a bronze statue of Mildred and two of her cubs standing in the lobby of the Grandfather Mountain Nature Museum. Her three-acre former home, called Mildred the Bear Environmental Habitat, is accessible by foot. The founder of Grandfather Mountain, Hugh Morton, also recently passed away; his dream, and Mildred's legacy, live on in what they left behind for us.

You Couldn't "Bear" It If You Missed Seeing This Place!

Did you know the largest black bears on Earth and the highest concentration of these animals (*Euarctos Americanus*) is on the Albemarle-Pamlico Peninsula in eastern North Carolina?

The town of Plymouth has a museum you should "paws" in your travels and go see. It's the Bear-Ology Black Bear Museum. This museum showcases and celebrates the magnificent furry animal and many of the exhibits are interactive. Kids especially love to have their picture taken after they step inside a life-size black bear model with its face cut out.

The first Saturday in June, which is also National Black Bear Day, the town holds a celebration called the NC Black Bear Festival, or simply "Bear Fest." Begun in 2015 under the direction of Tom Harrison, the Bear Fest has been one of North Carolina's best events and has won awards every year.

This year's Bear Fest included a "B'Air Show" with a Bear Drop of 300 parachuting stuffed bears, the Army Golden Knights elite skydiving team demonstration, a flight formation demonstration, helicopter rides, bi-plane rides and hot-air balloon rides, as well as wild bear tours and more than 30 other activities. See "Virtual North Carolina" for website information.

FLORA, FAUNA & NATURAL PHENOMENA TRIVIA

Q. What is the name of the first cultivated wine grape, found in North Carolina?

A. The scuppernong.

Q. Who first recorded his findings of the scuppernong grape in his logbook in 1524?

A. Florentine navigator Giovanni da Verrazano.

Q. When was the first commercial vineyard established in the state?

A. Medoc Vineyard was founded in Halifax County in 1835.

Q. How many commercial vineyards did North Carolina have in 2000?

A. More than two hundred and fifty.

Q. What world-class botanical garden of 450 acres was established in Belmont in 1991?

A. Daniel Stowe Botanical Garden.

Q. Approximately how many miles of rivers and streams lie within North Carolina's borders?

A. About forty thousand.

Q. What is the name of the museum in Ocean Isle Beach that was founded by Charlotte native Stuart Ingram and that features exhibits of not only the different kinds of fish to be found in the waters of inland and coastal North Carolina, but also has exhibits of wildlife such as waterfowl and deer, and where you can also see stars?

A. It's the Museum of Coastal Carolina and Ingram Planetarium.

Q. What zoo spearheaded a national crusade to help save the beleaguered animals in Afghanistan's Kabul Zoo during the war there?

A. The North Carolina Zoological Park (pictured above) in Asheboro. (Courtesy of N.C. Division of Tourism, Film, and Sports Development)

CHAPTER 14

LIGHTHOUSE AND COASTAL TALES

The Mercurial Nature of the Outer Banks

Along North Carolina's coast, the Grim Reaper has been busy for hundreds of years, giving the treacherous waters its name, the "Graveyard of the Atlantic." The ocean has claimed several thousand oceangoing vessels since explorers and settlers first arrived on U.S. shores, and the North Carolina shoreline has always had a reputation for being extraordinarily dangerous, striking fear in even the most seasoned and intrepid crew.

Part of the reason for the extreme danger of these waters is the combination of current and wind. Prevailing North Atlantic winds are westerly but change direction quickly and with an exasperating lack of predictability. In the early days of sailing, ships traveling from Europe to America invited disaster if they sailed anytime between January through the end of March, when the winds were worse and even more unpredictable.

Then there's the hydrography (water flow and underwater landforms) to be considered. The hydrography of the area around Cape Hatteras called Diamond Shoals is mercurial. As a matter of fact, nautical topographers do not chart the hydrography of Diamond Shoals, due to the extremely changeable nature of the ocean floor.

There's a plethora of places where you can go and see and learn more about this remarkable body of water. One is the Museum of the Sea in Buxton, which is a two-minute walk from the Cape Hatteras Lighthouse, and the North Carolina Maritime Museum in Hatteras. See "Virtual North Carolina" for websites and useful links.

The Ghost Ship of the "Graveyard of the Atlantic"

Over the years, hundreds of ships have been lost to the area around Cape Hatteras and the treacherous waters of Diamond Shoals. One story in particular still haunts the seafaring history annals of North Carolina.

In the bitterly cold February winds of 1921, coast guardsmen saw in the dawning light a five-masted schooner under full sail. Run aground, her prow was deep in the sandy beach. The previous night's watchman at Cape Hatteras had told the incoming watchman it had been quiet, with no storm and nothing unusual. There was the ship, however, run firmly aground. No crew was visible, and no signs gave a clue about what could have caused the ship to run upon the shore and into the beach with such apparent force.

The ship was the *Carroll M. Deering*. Her lifeboats were gone, and a ladder swung from her side. No answering calls responded to the guardsmen's distress whistles. When the seas calmed and low tide came in, the coast guardsmen boarded the *Carroll M. Deering* and discovered that a cat was the only living thing aboard.

Equally disturbing was the fact that, except for missing nautical papers, destroyed steering apparatus, and the rudder being left to swing freely, everything appeared as though the crew had just that moment stepped into their berths or up on deck. The table was set with food, which had been partially eaten. The salon's lights still shone and the crew's bunks were all in order.

The mysteriously derelict schooner Carroll A. Deering, as seen from the Cape Lookout lightship on 28 January 1921. (Wikimedia)

The ship had last been under the command of William B. Wormell, who had taken the vessel on a run to Rio de Janeiro, Brazil. Some rumors said that his crew had made mutinous plans and planned to do away with Wormell on the return voyage, while others said Wormell had been popular with his crew. Some speculated that pirates had taken the ship—but since it was returning with no goods aboard, what could they have possibly wanted?

By the time each story was investigated and each lead followed to a dead end, six departments of the U.S. government, from the Navy to the Department of Commerce, had become involved. None had an answer about what had happened to the ship's crew.

Eventually, one of Cape Hatteras's inevitable storms came up, destroying what remained of the once-proud ship. No one knows what happened to her between South America and the cape, and the mystery of the *Carroll M. Deering* and her crew will forever remain just that—a mystery.

The Surfmen and Fonzie the Lifesaving Dog

In 1873 Congress established the U.S. Lifesaving Service. Its purpose was to set up lifesaving stations along the coast, and to employ people to staff the stations, especially surfmen (men who patrolled the coast on foot or horseback, looking for ships in distress). Ultimately, seven such stations were built at approximately seven-mile intervals along the coast of the area known as Chicamacomico.

There is one such station still intact today. In the village of Rodanthe on Hatteras Island, you will find the Chicamacomico Lifesaving Station, which was one of the first stations to be built on the coastline of the Tar Heel State. The buildings on the site constitute the most complete surviving U.S. Lifesaving Service/Coast Guard station complex in the country, and the grounds have been made into a museum open to the public. But there's more to the story than that. This is a family tale—the heartwarming kind with a dog in it.

For lots of folks on the coast, lifesaving, patrolling the shore, and taking care of beacons and lighthouses were a family tradition. Take Levene Midgett, who took over the Chicamacomico Lifesaving Station around 1911, shortly after the death of the previous keeper—his cousin, who was known as Captain Ban Midgett. The Midgett family held a sort of monopoly on lifesaving stations in the area. In fact, it was difficult around Chicamacomico *not* to hire someone whose last name was Midgett. In 1970 the U.S. Census showed that 103 of the 266 inhabitants of the three villages of Chicamacomico were Midgetts.

In the early 1940s Levene had a dog named Fonzie, a black Labrador retriever who was noted and loved for being a "surf-dog." When Levene hoisted the U.S. flag at the station every morning, Fonzie would stand up tall (locals say "as close to standing at attention as a dog could get") and then put his paws on the surfmen's line-throwing equipment, ready to go to work. Historian Robert Huggett says, "The dog always did as he was told; it got to be where the surfmen thought Fonzie was a surfman—and so did Fonzie. During World War II he was taken on patrols of the beaches, looking for beached mines and anything that might have come from a ship."

Fonzie died of old age around 1952. He's buried in the Midgett family cemetery, about 150 yards from the lifesaving station. Fonzie was given a military burial with full honors of the Coast Guard. (Huggett says, "He was probably the only dog on the island to be given a military funeral.") His grave, which you can still see today, is marked with a decommissioned mine. Next time you're visiting the lifesaving station, "paws" by Fonzie's grave.

Beacons of Light and Life

For sailors everywhere, but especially around the shoreline of the North Atlantic and North Carolina in particular, lighthouses are a beacon of hope and life, especially when extreme danger is imminent. Before the appearance of lighthouses, bonfires on shore illuminated the way for some of the first sailors.

For nearly two hundred years after North Carolina was settled, its shores had no lighthouses. Finally, after losing hundreds of ships and countless lives to the "Graveyard of the Atlantic," the U.S. government, still in its fledgling stages, passed legislation to build lighthouses in 1793.

The first was the Bald Head Lighthouse in 1795, followed by Ocracoke in 1795 and Cape Hatteras in 1802. After the Civil War, Congress established the Lighthouse Board, which oversaw construction of new lighthouses every forty miles along the coast. (The Lighthouse Board later became the Lighthouse Service and is now a part of the U.S. Coast Guard.)

For those whose feet never leave dry land, lighthouses continue to capture the imagination. Originally fueled by kerosene and now equipped with sophisticated technology, lenses, and radar equipment, six lighthouses now illuminate the shoreline along the Tar Heel State, from Bald Head Island in the south to Currituck in the north.

If lighthouses could speak, what tales they would tell! Here's a brief list of the lighthouses:

Cape Hatteras Lighthouse was built in 1870. It stands 193 feet tall, making it the tallest in the United States. Long considered the guardian of the treacherous Diamond Shoals, the area around Cape Hatteras and its lighthouse is now a National Seashore. For some years, the lighthouse was threatened by the waters over which it stood guard. Waves pounded away at the foundation of this 4,800-ton giant of granite, brick, marble, iron, brass, and bronze. Finally, the shoreline was only one hundred and twenty feet away from the base of the old lighthouse. One major hurricane and the old landmark could be doomed.

The National Park Service had been reinforcing the beachfront with sandbags, but in early 1999 it began preparing to follow the recommendation of the National Academy of Sciences that the tower be loaded up and rolled to a new site up the beach where the lighthouse could guard the cape in safety.

Workers first separated the lighthouse from its foundation using a heavy-duty diamond-wire saw. It was then raised on one hundred hydraulic jacks and steel beams slid underneath. Seven additional steel beams fitted with roller dollies supported lighthouse and frame. Five hydraulic rams nudged the lighthouse down a track, as the monolith made its way to its new home a half-mile up the beach.

Workers moved the lighthouse at a top speed of one foot per minute, with engineers using computers to constantly check the proper placement of the jacks to keep the structure level. Workers lubricated the travel tracks with bars of Ivory soap—which, like lard, is a time-honored nautical tool for instances such as this.

Finally, the lighthouse arrived at its new location on July 9, 1999, two weeks ahead of schedule and without even so much as the hint of a crack in the mortar. Thanks to professional lighthouse movers of local and national renown, the most famous lighthouse in America had arrived at its new home, where you can see it today.

The red-brick Currituck Beach Lighthouse is visited by more than eighty-three thousand people each year. (Courtesy of N. C. Division of Tourism, Film and Sports Development)

Currituck Beach Lighthouse, sometimes referred to as Whalehead, is located at the village of Corolla, north of Kitty Hawk. Standing 158 feet tall, the lighthouse was built in 1875 to light the last remaining dark forty-mile stretch of the south Atlantic coastline between Cape Henry Lighthouse in Virginia and Bodie Island Lighthouse. There's a special reason for the popularity of this red-brick lighthouse: in and around the grounds you can see and hear the wild horses of Corolla, which enhance the romantic feeling of the area. More than eighty-three thousand people visit Currituck Beach Lighthouse annually.

Bald Head Lighthouse, built in 1817, is the oldest lighthouse in North Carolina. "Old Baldy," as it is affectionately called, is an octagon-shaped structure on Bald Island, and has long been used to guide ships around the treacherous Cape Fear and Frying Pan Shoals. A previous version of the lighthouse, built in 1796, was torn down and replaced with the existing lighthouse. Deactivated in 1935, it still stands proudly at its original ninety feet and is now a museum. A rewarding panoramic view awaits those who brave the 112 wooden steps to the top of the lighthouse. You can gain access to Smith Island and Old Baldy Lighthouse by boat.

Oak Island Lighthouse, 169 feet tall, is on the lower southeastern coast and is the newest addition to the lighthouses lining the Maryland, Virginia, and North Carolina coastline. Built in the 1950s, it is also the brightest lighthouse in the United States and the second brightest in the world (the first is in Calais, France), with its beam of light visible for 19 miles. Oak Island replaced the previous Cape Fear Lighthouse in 1958; it is accessible by a bridge connecting the island to the nearby city of Southport. When Oak Island opened with a lighting ceremony, the old caretaker of the Cape Fear Lighthouse, Charlie Swan, who had maintained that beacon for fifty-five years, threw the switch.

Price's Creek Lighthouse, built around 1848 as one of a string of beacons along a twenty-five-mile stretch of the Cape Fear River, lies abandoned and unused about two miles from Southport. It lies on land now owned by Archer Daniel Midland (ADM), a chemical company making citric acid. Although you can't tour the lighthouse, plans are underway to turn the beacon over to the city of

Southport, so tours may be possible in the future. In the meantime, you can see the twenty-foot-tall lighthouse tower from the ferry as it crosses the Cape Fear River between Southport and Fort Fisher. During the Civil War, this lighthouse was a signal station for the Confederates and the only means of communication across the Cape Fear River. Confederate soldiers rendered Price's Creek inoperable after the second battle of Fort Fisher in 1865 (but the current property owner repaired the cannon damage and decay), when they had lost control of the Cape Fear River.

Ocracoke Lighthouse, built in 1823, stands in the fishing village of Ocracoke Island, an area once frequented by the notorious pirate Blackbeard. It's one of the oldest continually operating lighthouses in the country. The adjacent lighthouse keeper's house was built to withstand inclement coastal weather, with sixteen-inch brick walls covered with whitewashed mortar. The seventy-six-foot lighthouse still is whitewashed, using a recipe recommended by the U.S. Lighthouse Board: Take unslaked lime, and add boiling water, salt, powdered Spanish whiting, and ground rice. Add more boiling water and clear glue. Mix until smooth and apply while hot.

Bodie Island Lighthouse represents the third attempt to place a lighthouse on Bodie Island (pronounced "body," one legend says because of so many bodies that washed up on shore), north of Hatteras Island at Oregon Inlet. The first lighthouse, standing at the rocky shore of the island, leaned so much that it was irreparably out of alignment. The second was blown up by Confederate soldiers (rather than let it fall into Union hands). The third and existing structure stands at 150 feet; construction began in 1871 and was completed in 1872. Although the lighthouse itself is not open, the lighthouse keeper's quarters have been converted into a visitors' center and museum under the management of Cape Hatteras National Seashore. The beautiful lighthouse with its distinctive black-and-white bands is popular with tourists, historians, and naturalists, and accessible by a bridge to the island.

Cape Lookout Lighthouse, built in 1859 on the Core Banks east of Beaufort, has helped sailors navigate the treacherous ten-mile stretch of waters known as Lookout Shoals. On the lands of the Core Banks in the nineteenth century, a small village called Diamond City thrived, with an economy based on the whaling industry. Fierce storms and raging tides drove the settlers to move west to nearby Shackleford Banks, but historians write of human skeletons found in the area, exposed by the constantly shifting sand. The 169-foot-tall lighthouse can be reached by boat from Harkers Island, Beaufort, or Morehead City. It is painted in a distinctive black-and-white diamond pattern. Although the lighthouse is not open to the public, the lighthouse keeper's home is open for tours.

Roanoke River Lighthouse –there have actually been one lightship and two lighthouses here. The existing Roanoke River Lighthouse was constructed in 1886, the third screw-pile lighthouse to occupy the mouth of the Roanoke River where it meets the Albemarle Sound. The Roanoke River lightship was built in 1835, but then the Civil War broke out in the 1860s. As Union soldiers advanced, CSA soldiers scuttled the lightship.

In 1886, the second lighthouse was built but it was decommissioned in 1941 by the Coast Guard. The lighthouse was sold to a private individual (Emmett

Wiggins) in 1955 and it was moved to his private property on Pembroke Creek. The passage of years saw the lighthouse fall into disrepair.

After Wiggins' death, the Edenton Historical Commission purchased the lighthouse from his heirs in 2007. Erienne Dickman, Tourism Director for Chowan County, said, "They purchased the lighthouse, donated it to the state, and the state restored it as part of the Historic Edenton State Historic Site." After lovingly restoring the grand lady, she was moved to Edenton Harbor in 2012. This lovely lighthouse is now open for tours. The Edenton State Historic Site on Broad Street, Edenton, is the entity that schedules tours.

See "Virtual North Carolina" for websites and/or links to these lighthouses.

Portsmouth Island: Mecca for Solitude and Shelling

First settled in 1753, this island was one of the largest established villages along the Outer Banks. At one time a bustling settlement, when ships changed their routes and then, later, the Civil War happened, followed by a downturn in the economy, many people began leaving the island. The last remaining residents of the island left in the early 1970s. Deserted, it was taken over by the National Park Service. Friends of Portsmouth Island volunteered to help renovate some of the significant buildings on the island.

Today, it's listed on the National Register of Historic Places. Visitors can get a sense of island life as it was "back in the day," and explore such buildings as the post office, the church, the schoolhouse and Coast Guard station. The buildings' interiors look as though someone just left for a while. One house was restored and became the island Visitor

Center; it contains exhibits about the history of Portsmouth Island.

The beach itself is a great place for finding shells and fishing. Portsmouth Island offers guided tours.

Preserving Maritime Culture: Ocracoke's Working Watermen's Exhibit

For hundreds of years, people of the coast have made their livelihood on the water. From shrimping to tonging for oysters to fishing, this maritime culture has been passed down through the generations.

Then in 2006, the last fish house on the island went up for sale. For the many families who made their living from the sea, this meant they would not have access to bulk ice (to keep their catches cold) and no outlet to sell what they caught.

The watermen banded together to help ensure their collective future, and once again the maritime culture is a thriving one. Today, you can go learn more about it at the Ocracoke Working Watermen's Exhibit located in the former Willis Store & Fish House. Here, through exhibits, videos and special events, the public is made more aware of the maritime culture and its contributions to North Carolina's history and economy.

North Carolina: International Diving Mecca

Most people might think of Florida or Coastal California when they think of places to go SCUBA-dive or spearfish. But maybe it's time to re-think that, and consider North Carolina, especially the area of Morehead City, as an international diving destination.

Thousands of people come from all over the world to free-dive, SCUBA and spearfish off the coast of Morehead City. Dottie Benjamin, Charter and Sales Manager of Olympus Dive Center will be quick to tell you why: "Divers come from Asia, all over Europe, Canada and all parts of the U.S. to dive our many shipwrecks and have encounters with sand tiger sharks," she said. The coast off Morehead City, as has been mentioned in other sections of this book, has long been known as "The Graveyard of the Atlantic," as thousands of ships have sunk in those waters. One of the most popular wrecks on which to dive is the famous U352, a German U-boat that was sunk in 1942 by the Coast Guard Cutter, Icarus.

The sunken shipwrecks are underwater history, but the wrecks also eventually become home to a variety of marine life, including all types of coral, sponges, and sand tiger sharks.

Perfect Storm, Perfect Heroes

On October 25, 1991, the ninety-five-foot schooner *Anne Kristine* set sail from New York for Bermuda. The 123-year-old ship was the oldest continuously used sailing vessel in the world, launched from Norway in 1868. None of the crew had a premonition that, in less than thirty-six hours, their lives would be in grave danger.

The day after their departure, the crew of seven men and two women, including the ship's new owners, Norman and Mary Ann Baker, was alerted to the storm brewing about five hundred miles southeast. Captain Joey Gelband turned the ship's bow west to try and sail around the storm (which was to become Hurricane Grace). But a second storm was coming toward the *Anne Kristine*: the nor'easter that Sebastian Junger wrote about in *The Perfect Storm*, which was later made into a movie. The two storm systems were heading toward each other, with no escape for the ship and her crew. By October 29 the storm had peaked, and the crew was in a desperate situation.

DID YOU KNOW?

Lighthouses are often painted with different designs and colors and even built in various shapes to increase their visibility and to help sailors determine their own location as they sail along the coast. The most favored colors are highly contrasting black and white, sometimes in a band, diamonds, or even a spiral candy-cane design. Each lighthouse also has a different type of beacon, with assigned its own character of light, called a code. Each lighthouses beacon has variations in intensity, color, beacon elevation and frequency of the flash.

The crew had changed course to head inland, but ever-increasing waves pounded the *Anne Kristine* and washed over her decks, and her pumps could not keep up. As she began taking on water, the captain called his first "Mayday." Elizabeth City's Coast Guard Station sent out a C-130 (a military air transport aircraft) with dewatering pumps, followed by two new Jayhawk helicopters. The pumps would be dropped so the crew could use them to try to keep the vessel from sinking, and then the helicopters would pick up the crew.

This was no ordinary rescue, even for such a seasoned helicopter pilot as Lieutenant Commander Paul Lange. He ran low on fuel and was forced to refuel on the heaving decks of the USS *America*, in thirty-foot seas and fifty-mile-per-hour winds, off the coast of Cape Henry, Virginia, a feat in itself.

Arriving at the crippled and pounded *Anne Kristine*, Lange discovered that the pumps carried by the C-130 had all missed their mark, and the second rescue helicopter had not arrived. It was up to him and his crew to rescue the nine people, in fifty-foot seas and winds gusting at eighty miles an hour.

Dropping down to lower his rescue basket, Lange had to be ready to gain altitude rapidly to escape the rushing waves. Often the waves missed the bottom of the helicopter by inches, and the spray from one rogue wave washed into the open doorway.

Incredibly, Lange and his crew managed to rescue all nine crew members. As they pulled Helband into the helicopter, the *Anne Kristine* foundered, rolled on her side, and slipped under the waves. As Lange and his loaded helicopter returned home, he met the missing helicopter and they flew back to base together.

Lange and his crew, David Morgan, Duane Jones, and John A. Julian, received several awards for their bravery, including the 1991 Helicopter Heroism Award. Lange also received the Distinguished Flying Cross.

In one of the most monstrous storms ever to hit the eastern seaboard, Lange and his crew had flown nearly three hundred miles offshore to affect a rescue. Their work that night, in the "storm of the century," exemplifies what it is to be a hero.

LIGHTHOUSE AND COASTAL TRIVIA

Q. Who was the first commissioner of the U.S. Bureau of Lighthouses?

A. George R. Putnam.

Q. When was the Lighthouse Bureau abolished, and by what presidential act?

A. In 1939 the Presidential Reorganizational Act abolished the Lighthouse Bureau and made the U.S. Coast Guard the lighthouse authorities.

Q. What is the oldest lifesaving station in North Carolina?

A. The Coast Guard Station in Oregon Inlet.

Q. What county and military base were dubbed the first "storm-ready community" by the National Weather Service in 2000?

A. Onslow County and Camp Lejeune, the Marine Corps base located there.

Q. Who was the force behind the creation of the Marine Revenue Cutter Service, the precursor to the Coast Guard, on August 4, 1790?

A. Alexander Hamilton.

Q. What retirement home was created for sailors in the town of Sealevel?

A. Snug Harbor. Although the home also opened its doors to "landlubbers," it is still predominantly made up of "old salts," both male and female.

Q. What memorial on Ocracoke Island is dedicated to what was the precursor to the Navy SEALS?

A. It's the U.S. Navy Beach Jumpers Memorial. Located just north of Howard's Pub, the World War II-era Beach Jumpers used equipment made especially to confuse and distract the enemy. For example, they could simulate a very large amphibious landing using a small number of personnel.

CHAPTER 15

SPEECH, FOOD AND FASCINATING CULTURAL TIDBITS

The Way Things Are Said

From the mountains of west North Carolina to the Piedmont or heartland to the coast, the speech patterns of the residents are downright fascinating.

The coastal residents have accents reflecting their roots as well as their geography. On Harker's Island, for instance, people have retained speech patterns and accents reminiscent of the jolly old English of the Elizabethan era, especially noticeable when they say things such as "high tide" (which they pronounce *hoigh toyed*).

In the mountains, people have descended from folks who were educated in Shakespearean English—you may hear this referred to as Appalachian English or mountain English. Speech patterns in these relatively isolated pockets came from the early settlers from the British Isles in the late seventeenth and early eighteenth centuries, and people retained their linguistic roots because of the isolation, despite the passage of time. You can still hear these speech patterns today, double negatives and all—but rather than reflecting a lack of education, these speech patterns reflect a long history.

Mountain English uses *hit* for "it" and *we-uns* as another form of "us." The word "done" occurs often, as in "They done got married," or "That pig's done gone and got tangled up in the barbed wire." Other examples are using *a* as a prefix, as in "I was a-fixing to go to the store," or saying "I knowed it" instead of "I knew it." Just keep in mind that this usage is not evidence of ignorance, or you might find yourself a-fixing to get in a fight.

In the Piedmont area, due to an influx of people with varied ethnic and linguistic backgrounds, you will hear a little bit of everything. The further south you go, the more likely you will be to hear speech with a drawl, and the severity of the drawl does not seem to depend on how other members of the family speak.

Family is important to Tar Heel natives. The further back you can trace your family roots, the better. A native might say proudly that he is "fourteenth-generation Tidewater aristocracy," and that sort of attention to familial roots is part of the Tar Heel tradition and culture.

Wherever you ramble in North Carolina, be assured that in very few places on this planet will you find warmer, friendlier, more accommodating folks—who are also wonderful cooks! That combination has served to inspire many folks to set up permanent housekeeping in the Tar Heel State.

First of Its Kind: The North Carolina Museum of Art

It was back in 1956 that this museum in Raleigh first opened its doors. It was the first art museum in the nation to be established through state legislation and funding. As of 2022, this amazing art museum is home to 41 galleries (including its newest, The People's Collection, which opened in October of 2022), an outdoor amphitheater, a 164-acre park and more. It seems every month, the museum staff is planning another event such as a music venue, yoga in the park or special art exhibit.

The Vilest-Smelling, Sweetest-Tasting Weed

Every first Sunday in May, the American Legion of Haywood County (Waynesville) has its annual Ramp Festival. The ramp is a wild plant of the allium family (similar to an onion), which grows only in the Appalachian Mountains. In the spring the mountain people dig up the ramps, clean them, and cook them in all sorts of dishes.

For North Carolinians, the fact that the ramp grows only in this limited area makes it special enough to celebrate, with craft shows, lots of live bluegrass and country music, and of course plenty of ramps to eat (and they're in just about everything except maybe the ice cream).

American Legion member Mark Leopard says that ramps taste "real good" in meatloaf. Here's Mark's recipe, in his words:

Mark Leopard's Meatloaf with Ramps

You take the ramps, wash 'em real good, dice 'em up, and use 'em instead of the onions called for in your meatloaf recipe. You can even use the ramp tops. Mix 'em up with your other meatloaf ingredients and bake it as you usually would. They add a little bit of an onion-garlic taste to it.

Can't Win? Try This Contest!

Ayden has an Annual Collard Festival every September. This includes a parade, a juried art show, the crowning of the Collard Queen and a Collard Green Eating Contest. This two-day event is open to anyone with an appetite.

The contest rules are simple: the person who eats the most collard greens in thirty minutes (without throwing up) wins. The winning record, set a few years ago, is seven and three-quarter pounds. That record was broken in 2022 at nine and a half pounds. Herbie Carson, current Collard Festival chair, says, "That guy walked away like he hadn't eaten anything!"

"Nectar of the Tar Heels": Cheerwine

It was during World War I and the U.S. was in the midst of all kinds of rationing. One thing being rationed was sugar. They say invention is the mother of necessity, and with the sugar shortage, a Salisbury native named L. D. Peeler began mixing concoctions in his basement, trying to make a soft drink that would taste sweet without much sugar. He hit upon a unique soda, deep burgundy in color with a wild cherry taste and more carbonation than other beverages.

The drink he named Cheerwine became an instant hit in North Carolina (named Cheerwine because of its color and flavor, the soda is actually nonalcoholic). Today, the people of Salisbury celebrate this invention with their annual Cheerwine Festival. The festival features barbecue cooked in the cherry-flavored soda, music, arts and crafts, and sales of the drink they dubbed "Nectar of the Tar Heels."

One-of-a-kind Festivals

The Tar Heel State boasts many unusual festivals and contests—too many to mention them all. But here's a sampling to whet your curiosity:

- ❖ Lizard Lick started an annual event featuring lizard races to gain some recognition.

- ❖ Spring Hope wasn't content with simply having a Pumpkin Festival; it has an annual National Pumpkin Festival (guess it's the gardener's version of the World Series).

- ❖ Newport has its annual Pig Cooking Contest, said to be the largest such cooking contest anywhere in the world.

- ❖ Banner Elk doesn't have an "elk" contest, but every October it does have a Woolly Worm Festival.

- ❖ Saluda has a Coon Dog Day (which includes a barking contest, dogs only, please) every July.

❖ Spivey's Corner has a National Hollerin' Contest, which attracted so much attention that contestants have appeared on *The Tonight Show*.

❖ Oriental, on the coast, has an annual Croaker Queen contest. (A croaker is a fish—and they really do croak!)

❖ Clinton hosts the Eastern North Carolina Ugly Pickup Truck Contest.

❖ Beech Mountain has its annual Garbage Day to celebrate the purchase of the town's first garbage truck (in 1982).

❖ Holden Beach has its "Carolina Elvis" celebration every June. Don a dark wig and a white, sequined skin-tight suit and see if you can fool 'em.

❖ Ocean Isle Beach holds its annual "North Carolina Oyster Festival" every October. This two-day festival includes games and activities for the kids, live music, all kinds of food, and their signature Oyster Shucking Contest. Ask the more serious shucking contestant about the fastest way to shuck an oyster, and they might—what else? clam up.

❖ Winston-Salem holds its annual "Texas Pete Spirits of Summer" Festival, to celebrate the creation of one of the best-selling hot sauces on the market. The sauce was invented in the kitchen by Thad Garner, whose father owned a barbecue stand back in the 1920s. He named it "Texas," to give people an idea of its spiciness, and "Pete," the nickname of his little brother Harold.

❖ In the town of Mt. Olive, the Mt. Olive Pickle Company celebrates its best-selling brined cucumber with their annual North Carolina Pickle Festival. Every New Year's Eve, the townspeople drop a giant, three-foot-long pickle into a pickle tank to celebrate the ushering out of Father Time.

❖ The town of Marion hosts its Livermush Festival every June. The dish, which is comprised mostly of pig liver, cornmeal and other binding ingredients, is spiced with pepper and sage. Although locals say it reminds them of sausage, it tastes to me a lot like liverwurst. A manufacturer of the dish (Hunter's Livermush) is based in Marion, so why not celebrate it? The celebration is complete with food truck chef competitions, a kid's fun zone, a livermush eating contest and all kinds of musical performances. And no pork-based celebration would be complete without a hog-calling contest!

❖ If you can't get to Marion in June, in May they hold their Bigfoot Festival, celebrating all things relating to the legendary creature. See "Virtual NC" for website information.

A Seasonal Delicacy of the Finned Variety

Every year, from January through April, river herring surge from the Atlantic Ocean and up the Roanoke, Chowan, Tar-Pamlico, and other rivers in eastern North Carolina to spawn in those quiet and relatively protected waters. This seasonal occurrence sees a burst of human activity, as thousands of folks catch herring and cook them in makeshift "cook-up shacks" thrown up alongside riverbanks. Rivers Edge is a restaurant that grew out of this tradition; located in the tiny, two-red-light town of Jamesville, this establishment has cooked and served up herring to generations of diners.

Rivers Edge is closed in the summertime, and their busiest season is when the herring are running. Traditionally a Swedish specialty, the fried herring is usually served with an onion sauce.

You can have your herring fried a number of ways. 'Sunny-side-up' is barely fried. If you like your fish cooked until it's a deep golden brown, you would ask for it to be 'cremated.'

The herring are a part of the culture around here and serve as a seasonal reminder to old-timers who, in poorer times, lived off fish and collard greens. Now you can taste what life was like back then—only now, the herring are served up with freshly brewed iced tea and lots of homemade pie for dessert.

Corn, One of the Four Food Groups

Corn is one of the most abundant crops grown for human consumption in the Tar Heel State, and everyone, it seems, has a specific way to cook it. Diane and John Fitzgerald are transplants from New York, living just outside Canton. John went to a fancy chef's school up north, and when he came to his senses and moved to North Carolina, he brought with him the perfect way to boil corn. Here is his tried-and-true, always-delicious recipe:

John Fitzgerald's Boiled Corn

Pick the corn yourself just before you plan to shuck it, or buy it from a farmer so you know it's freshly picked. Start a big pan of water boiling, enough to cover the ears, then shuck the corn. When the water is at a rolling boil, put the ears in. Bring it to a boil again, then cover it and turn it off.

It can sit like this in the water, and it's important that you don't drain it until you're ready to eat the corn. It doesn't overcook; it stays juicy and fresh tasting. You can even leave it in the water overnight and have some cold boiled corn for breakfast. It hardly needs butter at all.

An Eagle's Nest—for Humans

In lovely New Bern, just a stone's throw from the Tryon Palace, is an old bed and breakfast known as the Aerie. An aerie is an eagle's nest, and this is about the most comfortable and inviting "nest" in North Carolina. Besides running a top-notch establishment, John and Beth Blackwelder are excellent cooks. Because of the great climate and fertile soil, herbs grow like proverbial weeds in North Carolina, and the hosts often cook dishes for their guests using herbs from their own garden. Here's a recipe using some traditional North Carolina herbs they grow.

Italian Herbed Eggs

2 to 3 eggs

Fresh oregano, chopped

Fresh basil, chopped

Parmesan or Romano cheese, grated

Fresh chives, chopped

Mix equal amounts of basil and oregano in a small bowl. Put a pinch of the blended herbs in a bowl. Add eggs and scramble. Sprinkle in cheese to taste and cook the eggs in a frying pan as usual. Garnish with the chives. Serve hot. Makes 1 serving—increase amounts for more servings.

The Seafood Capital of the World

Residents of the town of Calabash and the surrounding area have been cooking seafood since the introduction of the fishhook and net. They have a long-standing tradition of outdoor oyster roasts, which moved indoors as the years passed. They pride themselves on a secret style of frying seafood, referred to as "Calabash-style cooking."

One Chamber of Commerce staff member tried to describe what sets this place's style of seafood cooking apart. "The taste of Calabash cooking isn't so much about the flavor or spices," she says. "It's the way the seafood is prepared. It's lightly battered and quickly fried, which gives it a special taste that's not heavy." Calabash, known as "the Seafood Capital of the World," has a population of around two hundred and is known for its extraordinary number of restaurants—at least one for every ten people. You won't go hungry here, that's for sure.

Brunswick County resident Geneva Crawford has put together a cookbook called *Savory Treasures from the Sea and Beyond* (Ocean Isle Beach, N.C.: Savory Treasures, Out My Kitchen Window, Inc., 1999) with more than 150 recipes from families old and new to the area. Here are two that she thought reflected the taste of Calabash in particular and coastal North Carolina in general.

Slick Vic's Carolina Crab Cakes

(Contributed by Vic Gillespie, Holden Beach)

1 pound lump crabmeat

2 tablespoons mayonnaise

1 small onion, finely chopped

10 saltines, crushed

1 teaspoon mustard

1 to 2 dashes Texas Pete Hot Sauce

1 egg

$\frac{1}{2}$ stick butter

Mix all the ingredients except the butter, and form into 8 crab cakes. Melt half the butter in a heavy frying pan. Fry 4 crab cakes until golden brown. Repeat with the remaining crab cakes. Serve the crab cakes with coleslaw and fried potatoes, and perhaps a glass of white wine. Makes 8 crab cakes.

Shrimp Curry

(Contributed by Gigi Hutcherson, Calabash)

3 tablespoons oil

1 large onion, finely chopped

1 teaspoon fresh garlic, finely chopped

1 teaspoon chopped fresh gingerroot

$1/4$ teaspoon ground black pepper

1 teaspoon curry powder

$1/2$ teaspoon cumin

1 teaspoon cayenne

1 large tomato, peeled and diced

1 teaspoon salt

2 tablespoons vinegar

1 pound shrimp, peeled and deveined

Heat the oil in a saucepan. Sauté the onion, garlic, and ginger until soft and brown. Add the pepper, curry powder, cumin, and cayenne, and cook for 4 minutes. Add the tomato, salt, and vinegar. Cover and simmer until the tomato is reduced to pulp. Add the shrimp and stir well. Cover and simmer until the shrimp are done, about 5 to 10 minutes. Serve with white rice. Makes approximately 6 servings.

Roasted Oysters, Tar Heel Style

Marilyn Coleman Howarth, a granddaughter of Lucy Coleman, is one of a long line of seafood cooks. Back when I first interviewed her in 2007, she said that when growing up, she and other children earned tips by shucking oysters for the customers at her grandmother's restaurant. "We would shuck the oysters right at the table using a wooden-handled knife to pull the oysters out and put them in a bowl for the customers," she told me. Sometimes they had oyster-shucking contests.

Here is how she described the classic way to roast oysters:

Lucy Coleman's Classic Roast Oysters

First wash the oysters to make sure there's no sand or mud on them, then line the bottom of a flat pan with them. Cover the pan with a little water, maybe half a cup, just enough to keep the oysters from burning. Cover it with either a lid or a dishcloth to keep the steam on the inside. Steam them on medium heat; they open as they get done. If they cook too much, they'll dry. Some people like 'em juicy and some like their oysters drier. You serve the oysters with cocktail sauce, drawn butter, and hot sauce. Some people mix their own combinations using horseradish, ketchup and hot sauce—whatever your taste buds tell you. You always have a cold drink like iced tea or cola with it. And saltine crackers, too.

DID YOU KNOW?

Morehead City is the site for the annual North Carolina Seafood Festival, held in late September. This weekend-long celebration features live music, amusement park rides, a sailing regatta, seafood of all kinds, and an oyster-shucking competition. Attending this festival just might get you out of your shell!

Time Travelling in the Tar Heel State

If you'd really like to go back—way back—in time, there's no better place to do it than in the village of Huntersville, at their annual Renaissance Festival. This celebration runs from early October through the last weekend in November, and features music to comedy acts, jousting, artisan demonstrations and more. You'll get a glimpse of life as it might have been in a 16th-century open-air English village.

The Center of the (Barbecue) Universe

In Lexington in the 1920s, four men—Jesse Swicegood, Sid Weaver, Will Johnson, and Warner Stamey—noticed that when court was in session, the crowds were enough to support an eating establishment or two. They thought immediately of barbecue, and every day court was in session, the four set up their tents around the courthouse and cooked barbecue over makeshift cinder block pits.

Barbeque is served with red slaw and hush puppies at the Lexington Barbecue Festival. (Courtesy of N. C. Division of Tourism, Film and Sports Development)

The particular style of barbecuing eventually became famous and is known as Lexington-style barbecue. This is different than in eastern North Carolina, where the pig is cooked whole and served with white or yellow slaw. In the Piedmont area of Lexington, chefs cook shoulders and serve the barbecue with red slaw and hush puppies. Many of these chefs eschew electricity and gas and cook the pork over hickory coals.

Those tents are gone, but Lexington has become known around the world for its barbecue and has more barbecue houses per capita than anyplace else (at last count, sixteen for a population of about sixteen thousand). And, yes, they still cook with hickory coals.

Since Lexington is considered the Barbecue Capital of the World, it's only natural that they hold the Barbecue Festival every October. This two-day event features live music, all kinds of sides to accompany the barbecue, a pig race and fireworks at the end of the celebration.

Want to Try Making It Yourself?

Here's a slaw recipe from Wayne "Honey" Monk, owner of one of the oldest such family-owned barbecue restaurants in Lexington.

Wayne "Honey" Monk's Famous Slaw

10 pounds sugar

8 ounces salt

8 ounces black pepper

$\frac{1}{4}$ teaspoon cayenne

100 pounds medium-chopped cabbage

6 quarts ketchup

$\frac{1}{2}$ gallon vinegar

Mix the sugar, salt, black pepper, and cayenne into the chopped cabbage. Let sit for 20 minutes. Add the ketchup and vinegar and mix well. Refrigerate as long as possible before serving. (*Note:* This recipe is intended for a very large, restaurant-sized crowd. You may want to cut it down a bit when making this slaw for your own dinner table!)

Two Festivals Celebrating North Carolina's Best Foods

Did you know that the Tar Heel state is the largest producer of turkey, pork and yams? To celebrate these, there are two festivals that you might want to check out.

Raeford pulls out all the feathers—er, stops—to celebrate all things turkey with their Fall Festival, held in October. They have a parade, music, a golf tournament, a juried art exhibit, and all kinds of food, including turkey with all the trimmings.

Smithfield's Ham and Yam Festival is held the first Saturday in May and besides the food and arts and crafts, attendees have a squealing good time watching the piglet races.

Who Gives a Fig? Ocracoke Islanders Do!

Until I visited Ocracoke Island, I never realized that there are about 700 different varieties of fig trees in the world—and that NINE of them are in North Carolina (Ocracoke Island in particular). On Ocracoke Island, you'll find varieties like pound, brown, sugar, Portsmouth, Celeste, turkey, blue, late and lemon figs. To celebrate this, in 2014 the islanders began what is now their annual Ocracoke Fig Festival.

The Fig Festival includes a kick-off seafood dinner followed by several types of fig competitions. Here you'll find cooks who are proud competitors of their homemade fig preserves and fig cakes. There's also a kid's competition for young chefs. The year 2022 saw a new category called "Fish 'N Figs." That year's winner, Austin Daniel, created a fish dish using cobia (fish) with caramelized fig, palm sugar and fish sauce.

North Carolina's First, Biggest, and Most

Here are some North Carolina features that give Tar Heels bragging rights:

❖ **World's only gourd museum:** the Marvin and Mary Johnson Gourd Museum in the municipal building in the town of Angier. Some of the gourd art includes a Grinch face, musical instruments made with gourds, and a rendition of the "Last Supper." The town holds their annual Gourd Arts and Crafts Festival every November—and this may well be the only such festival in the world.

❖ **Highest swinging footbridge in the United States:** on Grandfather Mountain in Linville, more than a mile above sea level. Note: this is not for the faint of heart or those with a fear of heights (such as myself. My daughter Sarah made me cross it with her!). The footbridge sways with the wind.

❖ **Largest unsupported dome in North America:** the elliptical dome of the Basilica of St. Lawrence Church in Asheville. Made entirely of tiles, it measures eighty-two by fifty-eight feet and is a beautiful, awe-inspiring sight.

❖ **Rockfish Capital of the World:** the city of Weldon, where the rockfish spawn upriver every spring in the Roanoke River, and anglers from all over come to try their luck.

❖ **Largest open-face granite quarry in the world:** outside Mount Airy in Surry County; it measures one mile long and 1,800 feet wide.

❖ **Only Southeast museum devoted to the study of world cultures:** The Museum of Anthropology at Wake Forest University.

❖ **Largest ammunitions depot in the United States:** Point Military Ocean Depot, near Southport.

❖ **Oldest active military reservation:** Fort Johnston, in Southport, dating back to (pre-Revolutionary War) 1750.

❖ **World's largest Ten Commandments:** in Murphy, it's part of a Biblical theme park called Field of the Woods. The Commandments are carved into the side of a mountain and measure three hundred feet wide.

❖ **Christmas tree capital of the world:** Avery County, which produces more Christmas trees of every kind than anywhere else.

❖ **First national military park at a Revolutionary War site:** the Guilford County Courthouse National Military Park in Greensboro.

❖ **First planetarium at a university:** Morehead Planetarium (part of the University of North Carolina at Chapel Hill).

❖ **Only rural doctor museum in America:** the Country Doctor Museum in Bailey, dedicated to the life of the rural medical practitioner in the 1800s.

❖ **Largest unincorporated U.S. city:** Kannapolis, population thirty-five thousand. It's also the 16th largest city in the state.

❖ **Largest U.S. university-related research park:** Research Triangle Park in Durham, also home to many companies engaged in advanced scientific research and development.

❖ **Second-oldest river in the world:** the New River, which flows in North Carolina and West Virginia, and is about one billion years old (only the Nile is older). Mapmakers didn't discover it until they had already completed their cartography of the region.

❖ **World's largest frying pan:** in Rose Hill. The pan measures fifteen feet in diameter and is used during the town's Fall Jamboree Festival, and reportedly can hold more than 250 chickens at one time. Although there's another pan (in Long Beach, California) claiming this, that pan is made of fiberglass and therefore isn't a *real* frying pan.

❖ **Highest waterfall in the eastern United States:** Whitewater Falls in Sapphire. Although it's much narrower than Niagara, it beats it in height by 200 feet, with a total drop of 411 feet.

❖ **Largest collection of mugs in the world:** would have to be The House of Mugs (also known as The Cup House) in Collettsville. Owner Avery Sisk said in the year 2000 when he retired, his wife Doris insisted he begin a hobby. "I started nailing mugs to the front fence," he said, "and just couldn't stop." The entire fence, the house itself, and even the ceiling of the front porch are all covered in mugs. Sisk estimates he may have as many as 30,000 mugs. You can find the house along Old John's River Road, or a local will be happy to help you find it.

The world's only fossil of an Acrocanthesaurus (right) makes its home at the North Carolina Museum of Natural Science. (Courtesy of N. C. Museum of Natural Science)

CULTURAL TRIVIA

Q. Where was North Carolina's first newspaper established?

A. New Bern.

Q. What North Carolina community with a huge holiday lighting display has become known as Christmas Town?

A. McAdenville.

Q. What town is called the Smithsonian of the South and why?

A. Raleigh, because of its many free and family-friendly things to do.

Q. Where is the first public boarding school for mathematically and scientifically gifted high school students?

A. Durham, known as the North Carolina School of Science and Mathematics.

Q. New York drops a ball on New Year's Eve. What similar event happens in Raleigh? (Hint: it is known as the City of Oaks.)

A. At midnight a huge copper acorn is dropped in the middle of Moore Square, downtown.

Q. What is the name of the mythical maverick steer that makes an appearance during the celebration in Rodanthe called Old Christmas?

A. Ol' Buck.

CHAPTER 16

UNUSUAL GRAVE, GHOST AND BURIAL-SITE TALES

They Really Danced on His Grave!

In the town of Wilson is a lovely burial ground called Maplewood Cemetery. The stones and funerary art alone are worth a visit, and local historian Lu-Ann Monson supplied this tidbit behind one of its more intriguing graves.

Near the front of the cemetery you'll find a tombstone marking the remains of a high diver named Professor Antoine Danton. His act included leaping from a high tower into a small container of water on the ground below.

When he and his circus troupe came to Wilson to perform, he fell in love with a young local girl. His traveling lifestyle apparently did not suit her stay-at-home tastes, so his love was unrequited.

He grieved for his lost-love-that-never-was, and one night before performing in Goldsboro, he became inebriated. It was in this state of intoxication that he took his final and fatal dive. According to one historian, Danton was aiming for his target of a flaming hoop that marked the pool of water below, but the wind blew out the fire and he missed.

Conscious but mortally wounded, Danton asked his circus friends to see that he was buried in Wilson, his beloved's hometown, in Maplewood Cemetery. His fellow performers not only honored his request, but on their occasional return trips to Wilson, visited his grave, where they danced and performed at his burial site.

His tombstone reads:

Professor A. Danton

Died May 13, 1904

The intrepid high diver leaped from life into eternity at Goldsboro, NC, the night of May 13, 1904. Erected by the J.J. Jones Carnival Co. of which organization deceased was, at the time of his fatal leap, a member.

The Haunting Mystery of the Murder of Nell Cropsey

In the town of Elizabeth City, you will find charming vistas of the Pasquotank River, lush greenery, and enthralling architecture. If you stay long enough, you're bound to hear the tale of an unsolved murder and of a beautiful, feminine ghost who maintains a presence in a private home on Riverside Avenue (which was the Cropsey family home back in the 1900s). Residents there say they often see her or sense her presence, and that objects in rooms are frequently moved from where the owners left them.

The murder happened in 1901, but the mystery surrounding the murder of Nell Cropsey continues to intrigue not only the citizens of Elizabeth City, but paranormal researchers and other "ghost-busters" as well. Her legend has grown and endured over the years so much that, in 2021, the theme of the annual Elizabeth City History Ghost Walk was about her untimely death, and the continuing mystery surrounding it.

You can read the complete story about Nell Cropsey in chapter 1. See "Virtual North Carolina" for websites pertaining to this mysterious and haunting tale.

DID YOU KNOW?

Raleigh's Oakwood Cemetery, adjacent to the Victorian-era neighborhood of Historic Oakwood, contains more than forty thousand graves, including twenty-eight hundred Confederate soldiers, several US Senators, five Civil War generals, and seven governors.

The Old Burying Ground in Beaufort

In the lovely coastal town of Beaufort lies an ancient cemetery which dates back to the early 1700s. It holds the remains of many people, some with unusual tales behind their interment. One grave contains the body of a young girl, buried in a rather unusual "coffin."

Docents with the Beaufort Historical Sites lead tours of the Old Burying Ground (but now, there is an app known as UniGuide you can download, which will lead you on a narrated self-guided tour). One docent, Shirley Pleace, volunteered this tale.

In the 1700s, a family from England with the last name of Sloo settled in Beaufort with their infant daughter. When she was a little older, she asked to go visit relatives across the ocean. The father was agreeable and wanted to take his little girl to visit the family in England, but her mother would have none of that—she feared for her daughter's safe return.

After some persuasion, however, the mother relented. She made the father promise that he would return their daughter to her in Beaufort.

The mother's intuition turned out to be correct, and the little girl died on the return voyage from London. Through his grief, the father remembered his promise that he would return their daughter to Beaufort.

To do that, her body would have to be preserved. The father purchased a keg of rum from the captain and immersed his daughter's body in it to preserve her. This was how she returned home to her mother. The little girl's body, in fact, was buried in the cemetery, still in the keg of rum. Her grave is marked by a flat stone slab, a wooden marker, and a juniper tree.

Now the tale is related to everyone who takes the Old Burying Ground tour. School children often leave small items such as shells and pennies on the young girl's grave.

Another Old Burying Ground story tells of a Revolutionary War-era unknown but loyal British officer who fell grievously ill while stationed on his ship at anchor in the port of Beaufort. Before he died, he requested he be buried in full uniform, standing up, and facing England, with his right hand raised in a final salute to King George III. His inscription reads:

Resting 'neath a foreign ground,

Here stands a sailor of Man George's crown

Name unknown, and all alone,

Standing the Rebel's Ground.

A Piece of England in North Carolina

It was in World War II that German U-boats cruised the waters off Ocracoke Island. To help defend the U.S. coastline, in 1942 the British Royal Navy sent two dozen armed trawlers in addition to what the U.S. Navy had in place.

In May 1942, a German U-boat torpedoed the British Royal Navy's trawler, the *HMT Bedfordshire*. All 37 sailors, members of the Canadian and the British Royal Navies, were killed. Only four bodies were recovered as they washed ashore on the island. The people of Ocracoke Island donated a small plot of land and dedicated it to England. That is where they laid to rest the four sailors.

Every May, representatives from the U.S. Navy, British Royal Navy, U.S. Coast Guard and Canadian Royal Navy take part in a ceremony they hold at The British Cemetery to honor those who gave their lives aboard the *HMT Bedfordshire*. The ceremony includes the playing of bagpipes, a reading of the crew's names and a 21-gun salute.

The British Cemetery flies the national flag of the United Kingdom. The tiny graveyard is located at 234 British Cemetery Road, Ocracoke Island. This may be the only real estate in the U.S. dedicated to be "forever England."

The Culture of Death in the South

Southerners in general respond to deaths in a way that sets the region apart from the rest of the country. When someone passes away in the South, everyone gets to cooking, especially in traditional Tar Heel homes. You don't arrive empty-handed at a wake. You are expected to come with a covered dish, preferably something you made yourself (no fast-food fried chicken, no sir). If the body is on view at a funeral home, then the table is set up at the home of the nearest relative, to be laden with everything from chicken and dumplings to barbecue and coleslaw, corn bread, and always lots of desserts. Most often, the foods brought are dishes that the deceased would have enjoyed—a quaint way to pay respects to the dead.

James Villas and Martha Pearl Villas were a famous mother-and-son team from an "old family" hailing from Charlotte. I interviewed them for the first edition of this book in 2007, and I'm glad I did, for James' mother passed away in 2009.

Together, the Villas produced a number of cookbooks reflecting the flavors of the South, most notably *My Mother's Southern Desserts* (New York: William Morrow & Co., 1998). James is the editor of *Town & Country* magazine, and although he now lives in New York State and cooks with "Yankee flour" (flour made from wheat grown in Yankee country), he's still a Tar Heel at heart.

The following recipes are what Martha Pearl Villas refered to as "bereavement dishes." Try them for your next "bereavement" and see what a comfort they can bring.

335

Bereavement Chocolate Bread Pudding

2 cups finely grated stale white bread

2 cups milk, scalded (see note below)

²⁄₃ cup granulated sugar

2 ounces unsweetened baking chocolate, melted

1 teaspoon pure vanilla extract

¹⁄₂ cup chopped pecans or walnuts

1 cup heavy cream, whipped to stiff peaks

In a large mixing bowl, combine the grated bread and scalded milk and let stand for 15 minutes. Preheat the oven to 350 degrees. Grease a 1-quart baking dish.

Add the sugar, chocolate, vanilla, and nuts to the bread mixture and stir until well blended. Scrape the mixture into the prepared baking dish and bake until a cake tester or toothpick inserted in the center comes out clean, about 1 hour. Serve the pudding hot in dessert bowls with the whipped cream on top. Makes 6 servings.

Note: When scalding milk in a saucepan, stir continuously over moderate heat to prevent a film from forming. Never allow the milk to come to a boil and remove the pan from the heat the moment steam begins to rise.

Funereal Angel Bavarian

2 envelopes unflavored gelatin

¹⁄₂ cup cold water

2 cups milk

4 large eggs, separated

1 cup granulated sugar

2 tablespoons all-purpose flour

1/4 teaspoon salt

Grated rind of 1 large orange

1/4 cup fresh orange juice

1 pint heavy cream

1 10-inch angel food cake

Grated coconut from 1 small coconut

In a small bowl, sprinkle the gelatin over the water to soften, and set aside.

In a large, heavy saucepan, whisk the milk, egg yolks, sugar, flour, and salt until well blended. Cook over moderate heat, stirring constantly, until the mixture thickens. Remove from the heat, whisk in the gelatin mixture, and let cool completely, stirring several times. Add the orange rind and orange juice and stir until well blended.

In a medium-sized bowl, beat half the cream with an electric mixer until stiff peaks form, and fold into the cooled custard. Wash and dry the beaters. In a large mixing bowl, beat the egg whites until stiff but not dry peaks form, and gently fold them into the custard.

Break the angel food cake into small pieces and line the bottom of a large tube pan with half the pieces. Cover with half of the custard, then repeat the procedure with the remaining cake and custard, ending with custard. Cover with plastic wrap and let stand overnight in the refrigerator.

Turn the cake out onto a cake plate. In a medium-sized mixing bowl, beat the remaining cup of cream with an electric mixer until stiff peaks form and spread over the top of the cake. Sprinkle the coconut all over the top. Makes 12 to 14 servings.

When Is a Headstone a Footstone?

Just north of Charlotte in the pleasant town of Salisbury, a train running the railroad line of the Richmond and Danville Railroad on one November night in 1893 caught a man unaware (or others say inebriated) and ran over him — at least, part of him.

The train left James Reid with a severed foot. Although Reid eventually recovered, he wanted to do something special for his foot. So he buried his foot with what the *Salisbury Post* described as "appropriate ceremony," and a proper headstone was erected with this inscription:

The headstone (or footstone?) of James Reid can be seen in the cemetery of Trading Ford Baptist Church. (Courtesy Sheelah Donaldson)

Foot of

James A. Reid

Severed By a

Freight Train on

November 25, 1893

When Reid died in 1920 at age ninety-five, he was buried in the cemetery of Trading Ford Baptist Church, six miles away from his "other" headstone.

Today, many people come to visit these two old graveyards on account of what James Reid did with his bodily parts.

The Bodies above the Tunnel

To build the Dillsboro-Murphy rail line, the Danville Railroad Company (which succeeded the Western North Carolina and Norfolk Southern Railroad companies) had to cut a tunnel through a mountain of nearly solid granite along a bend in the Tuckasegee River near Dillsboro. As was customary in those days, the railroad used prison inmates for this arduous task. Every workday, the convicts were ferried across the Tuckasegee River to the tunnel site, where they labored with pickaxes, cutting and chipping away at the mountain.

Eventually the convicts finished carving out the 186-foot passageway, known now as the Cowee Tunnel. Unfortunately, not all of the prisoners survived the tunnel construction project. The story goes that several of the convicts were on the ferry, crossing a particularly treacherous stretch of the Tuckasegee. The ferry was a flatboat, moved across the river by cables. The convicts were shackled together, and when their boat capsized, all nineteen of the poor fellows drowned in the raging waters of the Tuckasegee. Their bodies were recovered and buried on top of the tunnel.

Today this line is used for the Great Smoky Mountains Railroad, and passengers are temporarily plunged into near-total darkness in a section of the tunnel with a sixteen-degree curve. Some people say you can hear the screams of the convicts and even see them, as you ride in the dark tunnel, directly underneath their burial site.

Wilmington's Oakdale Cemetery

If ever you visit Wilmington, be sure to take an afternoon tour of the Oakdale Cemetery. Besides viewing its beautiful funerary art and moss-covered mausoleums, you may learn of tales both tragic and mysterious.

The cemetery was established in the 1800s because the city ran out of room in its local churchyard cemeteries after Wilmington was ravaged by epidemics of yellow fever, diphtheria, and typhoid. A sixty-five-acre site east of Burnt Mill Creek was chosen, and Armand J. de Rosset, a prominent local doctor, became the first president of the board of directors of Oakdale Cemetery. Shortly after this, de Rosset's own six-year-old daughter, Annie, fell ill and died, and was the first interred in the new cemetery. Visitors can see Annie's grave today—it's an upright marker with a little lamb on top of the stone.

Walking around the cemetery, you'll also find a stone with a sculpted image of a dog and the words "Faithful Unto Death." The story goes that in 1880, riverboat captain William

A. Ellerbrook was caught under a flaming timber when helping to fight a fire downtown. His dog, Boss, rushed into the flames to try to retrieve his master. Unfortunately, Boss was overcome by smoke and died along with Ellerbrook. Later, the body of the heroic Boss was found with bits of his master's coat in his teeth. Some locals say that Boss still patrols the grounds of Oakdale Cemetery, watching out for his master.

The cemetery is also the final resting place of hundreds of Confederate soldiers in unmarked graves. Some local people say the cemetery is haunted with the wandering spirits of these brave men.

Poetic Immortality

About fifteen miles outside Robbinsville lies a beautiful forest of tulip poplar, hemlock, and cedar trees, with rich dark soil and an abundance of wildflowers and birds. The forest of nearly eighteen thousand acres has trees that tower as high as one hundred feet, many as big around as twenty feet. This forest is a protected area, named in memory of someone who was not a native of the Tar Heel State.

Alfred Joyce Kilmer was born in New Jersey in 1886, and after graduating from Columbia University in 1908, worked as an editor for the Funk and Wagnall Dictionary Company. His love of words led him to poetry. By the time America and Germany were embroiled in war, Kilmer was married with five children, and he enlisted in the New York National Guard. Once in France, although his primary job was intelligence gathering, Kilmer wanted to help fight. On July 30, 1918, he died in the Battle of Ourcq.

His name would not be memorable had it not been for his poetry, especially his most famous poem, "Trees." Published in 1914, this poem became a part of virtually every student's introduction to poetry, and Kilmer was assured immortality.

In 1935 a forester noted that Graham County held "one of the very few remaining tracts of virgin hardwood in the Appalachians." He recommended that the area be purchased to preserve some of the last remaining original forest growth in the mountainous area. When the Veterans of Foreign Wars found out about the setting aside of more than thirteen thousand acres, they asked the American government to make it a memorial to Kilmer. Thus from New Jersey to France to North Carolina, the story came full circle, and a memorial forest is forever preserved in the name of Joyce Kilmer.

Visitors to Joyce Kilmer Memorial Forest can enjoy the trees that inspired his famous poem. (Courtesy of N. C. Division of Tourism, Film and Sports Development)

You can hike the trails and footbridges of Joyce Kilmer Memorial Forest, take in its peace, marvel at its varied and huge trees and breathe in the fresh aroma of hemlock trees. Halfway on the trail is a bronze plaque with a brief biography of Kilmer. At the base of the trail under a protected stand is the poem for which Kilmer will be forever remembered.

Trees

I think that I shall never see

A poem lovely as a tree.

A tree whose hungry mouth is prest

Against the earth's sweet flowing breast;

A tree that looks at God all day,

And lifts her leafy arms to pray;

A tree that may in summer wear

A nest of robins in her hair;

Upon whose bosom snow has lain;

Who intimately lives with rain.

Poems are made by fools like me,

But only God can make a tree.

The Mysterious Disappearance of Peter Dromgoole

One of the most pleasant views of the Piedmont area of North Carolina is from the summit of Piney Prospect at the University of North Carolina in Chapel Hill. One of the mysteries of North Carolina is here, a huge boulder with slight reddish hues. The boulder and the red stain unaffected by weather provide the setting for a local legend.

The boulder, near the famous Gimghoul Castle, was once a meeting spot between a young university student, Peter Dromgoole, and his sweetheart, Fanny. It was 1831, so the story goes, and they were desperately in love. Here, sitting on this boulder, Peter and Fanny shared stolen moments with the view of the valley below and the burbling of a spring nearby.

But another young man desired Fanny's affections; he was mad with jealousy at the thought of Peter and Fanny together. Finally, the rejected suitor challenged Peter to a duel. Unbeknownst to Fanny, Peter accepted. He and the rejected suitor chose their seconds and met one night at the boulder under a full moon. Peter was killed in the duel, and the witnesses and the rejected lover buried Peter under the boulder, which was stained with his blood.

Upon learning of her lover's death, Fanny's health began to decline. She wept, sitting or lying prostrate on the boulder under which her Peter lay. Eventually, Fanny died of a broken heart. It is said that she, too, is buried underneath the boulder near the castle.

The boulder that legend says is Peter's burial site is now called Dromgoole Rock, and the spring nearby has been named Fanny's Spring. Locals also say that the boulder and castle are haunted, and on rainy nights, the water off the boulder runs red, as though awash in Peter's blood.

A Mysterious Burial Ground

At the Tennessee-North Carolina border town of Bryson City lies a place the Cherokee call Kituhwa (gah-DOO-ah). It is revered by the Cherokee as the birthplace of the People, where the Great Mystery handed down the laws by which they would live. It is also said to be the first earthly home of fire sent by God to his People.

This area has been inhabited for at least nine thousand years. British traders who arrived during the seventeenth century took Cherokee women for their wives and brought European crops to blend with the native ones.

Such activity made Kituhwa the largest and most important village in the valley. In 1720 its population swelled to nearly two hundred. By 1750 Kituhwa contained more than sixty houses, complete with gardens of corn and squash. But a friendly relationship with the British soured as more white men arrived, and in 1761 British troops attacked. With their broadswords, they slashed hundreds of acres of corn and other crops and burned the village to the ground.

On this site in the summer of 2001, archaeologists arrived with scientific equipment, searching for the magnetic "signature" left behind by burned earth. Using gradiometers to measure differences in magnetism in the soil, archaeologists traced a grid-like pattern across the fields of Kituhwa. The scientists were looking for a pattern of burnt earth, like that made by a house burning down.

What they found were the traces of stockade-like walls, the remains of burned houses, and a mound, measuring five feet high and forty-five feet wide. The most dramatic area is in two arcs, which might be from stockade walls or burned houses. Then the researchers found the long mound, the octagonally shaped townhouse that was Kituhwa's center for civil and spiritual fellowship. In its heart had burned the coals from the original Sacred Fire. Near this mound are as many as a thousand graves inside the old settlement, with more than a dozen outside the settlement itself.

The site was further researched in 2006, when a team of anthropologists from the University of Tennessee arrived to explore the area. They conducted their research using non-invasive, culturally-sensitive materials and devices, which measure electric pulses, radar and magnetic fields, to outline the underground remains of structures that were above ground and intact hundreds or even thousands of years ago.

Kituhwa Mounds. (Wikipedia)

Once under the auspices of the Great Smoky Mountains National Park Service, this birthplace of Cherokee culture has been returned to the descendants of those who lost it during the Trail of Tears nearly two hundred years ago. "The majority of the people want to see this area preserved," said

Brian Burgess of the Tribal Historic Preservation Office at the Eastern Band of the Cherokee's Tribal Offices when I first interviewed him in 2007. Burgess himself participated in the dig of 2001 and the research. "If there is any kind of development, it will be culturally sensitive—something that might accent the integrity of the tradition."

The site is significant because it is the "Mother Town" from which all the belief systems and culture of the Cherokee People originated. Burgess says the site is sacred. "Some of those graves are hundreds, even thousands, of years old."

Since the returning of Kituhwa to its People, every year the Cherokee gather together to break bread and celebrate this cultural and historic event.

Intriguing Epitaphs

Here are some tombstone inscriptions from burial sites around the state. These beautiful cemeteries are loaded with history, symbolism, and local lore.

From St. James Churchyard in Wilmington:

Slave to no sect,

No private path he trod,

But looked through Nature

Up to Nature's God.

—from the grave of Cornelius Harnett

How loved, how valued once

347

Avails thee not;

To whom related or by whom begot.

A lump of dust alone remains of thee

It's all thou art and the proud shall be.

—from an unidentified grave

From a small cemetery near Winston and Connor dormitories in Chapel Hill, this tombstone contains words from the UNC fight song:

I was a Tar Heel born

I was a Tar Heel bred

Here I lie

A Tar Heel dead

—from an unidentified grave

From the Honeycutt Family Cemetery in Stanley County:

Whitley, William "Uncle Billy"

December 17, 1775–April 4, 1890.

He cut a full third set of teeth.

The epitaph on Tom Wolfe's tombstone in Asheville Riverside Cemetery is one of the most poignant in the state. (Photo by the Author)

In case you were wondering, the dates on Uncle Billy's epitaph are correct. According to newspapers of the time, he lived to be 115 years old, giving him plenty of time to cut all those teeth.

The Haunting Story of Jump Off Rock

Just about five miles outside Hendersonville is Jump Off Rock, which offers beautiful views of the Blue Ridge Mountains. Local lore says this rock is haunted, and here is one variation of the legend.

Hundreds of years ago, perhaps even before the arrival of white settlers, a youthful and handsome Cherokee chief fell in love with a young and beautiful maiden who lived with her family in his village. They often met on top of this rock and would look out over the valley as they professed their enduring love for each other.

Then the chief was called to war; the young maiden promised to wait for his safe return. Some time after he left for battle, she got word from other returning warriors: her love had fallen in battle and she would never see him again.

Grief overcame the young maiden. That evening, near dusk, she climbed to the edge of their rock and jumped to her death below.

Some people say that, on moonlit nights, you can see her ghost at the rock ledge. Jumping Off Rock is at the end of Laurel Park Highway and there are several hiking trails there—just watch your step.

The Mysterious Legend of Tommy Hodges

You have probably read the story about The Cradle of Forestry in the chapter on Flora, Fauna and Natural Phenomena. There's a mystery about something that happened in the early days of the forestry school: Back in 1906, a young student of the Biltmore Forest School disappeared under mysterious circumstances. Being of a mischievous bent, Tommy Hodges' disappearance was at first considered to be a trick of his own doing. As days passed with no Tommy Hodges, though, his fellow students and teachers began to try and find him.

Tommy Hodges was never found; his remains and his fate are both buried beneath the years, but many continue to speculate as to what really happened to him.

Every year since about 2000, The Cradle of Forestry commemorates The Legend of Tommy Hodges with an outdoor drama (currently it is under the direction of Clay Wooldridge, Education Director for the School of Forestry). Usually held near the end of October, audiences are transported back to 1906 by actors who dress in period costume and speak from the point of view of someone they're re-enacting. For example, as the audience walks the trail, they will meet Mr. Jenny, who was the storekeeper for the Biltmore Forest School's commissary, and the school's founder, Mr. Schenk. Other actors represent some of Tommy Hodges' classmates.

The play changes every year, with each drama adding a different perspective to the story.

What really happened to Tommy Hodges? No one will ever know, but the outdoor drama is sure to give you chills!

GHOST, GRAVE & BURIAL TRIVIA

Q. What cemetery is said to be the most haunted in North Carolina?

A. This infamous title would probably have to go to Oakwood Cemetery in Raleigh. The hauntings there are said to be aggressive, where visitors are punched or scratched. Investigating the cemetery one warm summer night, paranormal researchers recorded "cold sports" of about 47 degrees in some places.

Q. What cemetery contains the remains of Charles F. Fisher (for whom Fort Fisher is named)?

A. The Old Lutheran Cemetery in Salisbury.

Q. What cemetery contains the mass graves of 11,700 Union soldiers who died as prisoners of war?

A. Salisbury National Cemetery.

Q. What was the nickname of the Italian carnival worker killed in 1911 in Laurinburg, whose real name was Forenzio Concippio and whose body was mummified and displayed for over sixty years at McDougal's Funeral Home until protests caused his body to be buried properly?

A. Spaghetti—because no one could pronounce his real name!

Q. Who is buried in Franklin County inside a large granite boulder covered with a marble slab?

A. William Jeffreys, who was a state senator from 1844 to 1845.

AMAZING NC, CHAPTER LINKS

<u>Author's Note:</u> Due to the fluid nature of the Internet, not all websites may be accessible or may have changed since press time. For major cities, simply Google in the city, state and any pertinent information you may be seeking.

<u>Chapter 1</u>

- Chang and Eng Bunker:
  http://www.surryarts.org/agmuseum/
- Caswell County Jail:
  https://sites.rootsweb.com/~ncccha/memoranda/caswellcountyjail.html
- The Devil's Tramping Ground:
  https://www.ncpedia.org/devils-tramping-ground
- The Country Doctor Museum:
  https://www.countrydoctormuseum.org/
- Town of Littleton Cryptozoology & Paranormal Museum: https://crypto-para.org/
- Blackbeard
  - NC Maritime Museum:
    https://ncmaritimemuseumbeaufort.com/
  - Graveyard of The Atlantic Museum:
    https://graveyardoftheatlantic.com/
  - NC Maritime Museum, Southport:
    https://ncmaritimemuseumsouthport.com/
- Caswell County Courthouse:
  https://nccha.org/memoranda/courthouse.html
- Museum of the Bizarre:
  https://www.museumbizarre.com/

Chapter 2

- Abraham Lincoln/Lincoln Hill Trail: https://blueridgeheritagetrail.com/explore-a-trail-of-heritage-treasures/bostic-lincoln-center/
- Museum of the Waxhaws: https://museumofthewaxhaws.org/
- Andrew Johnson Birthplace https://raleighnc.gov/mordecai-historic-park
- "Nolichucky Jack" , NC Museum of history: https://www.ncmuseumofhistory.org/
- Executive Mansion: https://www.ncdcr.gov/things-do/history/triangletriad/north-carolina-executive-mansion

Chapter 3

- Wright Brothers Memorial: https://www.nps.gov/wrbr/index.htm
- Agriculture and Transportation Museum https://www.tn.gov/agmuseum.html
- NC Maritime Museum https://ncmaritimemuseumbeaufort.com/
- Missiles and More Museum https://missilesandmoremuseum.org/
- Great Smoky Mtn Railroad https://www.gsmr.com/
- National Railroad Museum Hall of Fame https://hamlethistoricdepot.org/
- Tweetsie Railroad https://tweetsie.com/
- Kiwanis Club Wagon Train Event http://www.wncwagontrainnc.com/

Chapter 4

- Charlotte Museum of History
  https://www.charlottemuseum.org/
- The First "Tea Party," Penelope Barker Home
  https://ehcnc.org/
- "The Tale of The Overmountain Men" ,
  - ➢ Rocky Mount Museum
    https://www.rockymountmuseum.com/
  - ➢ NC Museum
    https://www.ncmuseumofhistory.org/
  - ➢ Overmountain Victory National Historic Trail
    https://www.nps.gov/ovvi/index.htm
  - ➢ Overmountain Victory Trail Association
    https://ovta.org/
- Guilford Courthouse National Military Park
  https://www.nps.gov/guco/index.htm
- The Lumbee Tribe Page:
  https://www.lumbeetribe.com/
- Greensboro Historical Museum
  https://greensborohistory.org/
- Museum of The Cherokee Indian https://mci.org/
- Tyrannosaurus, Asheville Museum of Science,
  https://ashevillescience.org/
  - ➢ Aurora Fossil Museum
    https://aurorafossilmuseum.org/
  - ➢ Pettigrew State Park
    https://www.ncparks.gov/state-parks/pettigrew-state-park

Chapter 5

- Ava Gardner Museum
  https://www.johnstoncountync.org/ava-gardner/
- Greensboro Historical Museum
  https://greensborohistory.org/
- Thomas Wolfe Memorial http://wolfememorial.com/
- Greensboro Historical Museum
  https://greensborohistory.org/
- Battleship North Carolina
  https://www.battleshipnc.com/
- Charles B Aycock Birthplace
  https://historicsites.nc.gov/all-sites/governor-charles-b-aycock-birthplace
- Andy Griffith Museum
  https://www.surryarts.org/agmuseum/
- Mt. Airy Mayberry
  https://www.visitmayberry.com/attractions/category/mayberry/
- NC Museum of History
  https://www.ncmuseumofhistory.org/

Chapter 6

- Mt. Mitchell State Park:
  https://www.ncparks.gov/state-parks/mount-mitchell-state-park
- Carolina Climbers Coalition
  https://carolinaclimbers.org/climbing-areas/sauratown.html
- Biltmore House https://www.biltmore.com/
- NC Museum of History
  https://www.ncmuseumofhistory.org/

Oconaluftee Indian Village,
https://cherokeehistorical.org/oconaluftee-indian-village/

- Museum of the Cherokee Indian https://mci.org/
- **"A Moonshine Story" Appalachian Cultural Museum Permanently Closed https://www.npr.org/2011/04/16/135442423/in-shuttered-museum-appalachian-history-boxed-up)**
- Carl Sandberg Home
  https://www.nps.gov/carl/index.htm
  Allison-Deaver House
  http://www.transylvaniaheritage.org/content/allison-deaver-house

Chapter 7

- Town of Bath Website: https://townofbathnc.com/
- "Mystery of Roanoke," FCF Website:
  http://ncroyalrangers.com/fcf/
- Hot Springs Welcome Center:
  https://www.hotspringsnc.org/about/welcome-center/
- Moravian Settlement, Bethabara Park:
  https://historicbethabara.org/
- Fontana Village Resort: https://fontanavillage.com/
- Scottish Heritage Center:
  https://www.visitnc.com/listing/fzpY/scottish-heritage-center
- Crossnore Communities for Children:
  https://www.crossnore.org/
- Billy Graham Evangelistic Association:
  https://billygraham.org/
  Billy Graham Training Center: https://thecove.org/

Chapter 8

- NASCAR Hall of Fame: https://www.nascarhall.com/,
  Petty Museum:
  https://www.richardpettymuseum.com/
  Camp Victory Junction:
  https://victoryjunction.org/camp-2/
  NC Auto Racing Hall of Fame: https://ncarhof.com/
  Rockingham Dragway:
  https://www.rockinghamdragway.com/

Chapter 9

- Henry Lawson Wyatt Monument:
  https://www.ncpedia.org/monument/henry-lawson-
  wyatt
- Civil War Meets Modern Archaeology, Ocracoke
  Preservation Society Museum:
  https://www.ocracokepreservationsociety.org/
- Cherokee In The Civil war, Museum of The Cherokee
  Indian https://mci.org/
- Smithfield Home Guard, Hastings House
  https://www.visitnc.com/listing/mVfJ/historic-hastings-
  house
- CSS Neuse, Civil War Interpretive Museum,
  https://cssneuse.org/museum/
- Harper House, Bentonville Battleground
  https://historicsites.nc.gov/all-sites/bentonville-
  battlefield
- NC Civil War Trails Tourism:
  https://www.civilwartrails.org/index.html
- Lion-Hearted Flusser, Museum of The New South:
  https://www.museumofthenewsouth.org/

- The Gibraltar of The South, Fort Fisher: https://www.ncparks.gov/state-parks/fort-fisher-state-recreation-area
- Port O' Plymouth Museum: https://portoplymouthmuseum.org/about-port-o-plymouth-museum/
- Museum of The Albemarle: https://www.museumofthealbemarle.com/
- Zebulon Vance Birth Home, https://historicsites.nc.gov/all-sites/vance-birthplace
- Network to Freedom, Ft. Raleigh NHS: https://www.nps.gov/fora/index.htm

Chapter 10

- The Greensboro Sit-Ins, Greensboro Historical Museum: https://greensborohistory.org/
- International Civil Rights Center & Museum: https://www.sitinmovement.org/
- Mattye Reed African Heritage Center: https://www.ncat.edu/cahss/gallery/index.php
- False Bottom to True Freedom, Medenhall Homeplace: https://www.mendenhallhomeplace.com/
- The Green Book Project, NC African American Heritage Commission: https://aahc.nc.gov/
- Charlotte Hawkins Brown, Palmer Memorial Institute: https://www.ncpedia.org/palmer-memorial-institute Charlotte Hawkins Brown Museum: https://historicsites.nc.gov/all-sites/charlotte-hawkins-brown-museum
- Museum of Princeville: https://princevilleheritagemuseum.com/

- Middle Passage Markers in NC:
  https://www.middlepassageproject.org/2020/06/03/afric
  an-presence-in-north-carolina/

Chapter 11

- Reed Gold Mine: https://historicsites.nc.gov/all-
  sites/reed-gold-mine
- NC Wine Festival: https://ncwinefestival.com/home/
- Hinnant Vineyards:
  https://hinnantvineyards.com/public-events/
- Castle McCulloch: https://castlemcculloch.com/
- Rub That Relieved Millions, Greensboro history
  Museum: https://greensborohistory.org/
- Birthplace of Pepsi, https://pepsistore.com/
- Queen Anne's Revenge, NC Maritime Museum :
  https://ncmaritimemuseumbeaufort.com/
- Duke Homestead: https://dukehomestead.org/
- Durham Tobacco Museum:
  https://dukehomestead.org/
- Museum in Yanceville:
  https://ncccha.org/memoranda/museum.html
- Tobacco Farm Life Museum:
  https://www.tobaccofarmlifemuseum.org/
- Winston-Salem Tobacco Museum: https://reynolda.org/
- Burt's Bees HQ:
  https://www.burtsbees.com/content/company-
  faqs/faqs-company.html
- Wild West in North Carolina, Love Valley:
  https://lovevalley.com/

Chapter 12

- Henry River Mill Village:
  https://henryrivermillvillage.com/
- John C. Campbell Folk School:
  https://www.folkschool.org/?gclid=CjwKCAiA2fmdBh
  BpEiwA4CcHzQvOQ_PcKQNdVHiBM63b59HJLl391K
  fDAVuea7VBOTPyUmoH0jM5txoCxxcQAvD_BwE
- Chanteymen, NC Maritime Museum:
  https://ncmaritimemuseumbeaufort.com/
- NC Tribute Festival to the King:
  https://www.nctributefestivaltotheking.com/
- John Coltrane Int'l Jazz Festival:
  https://coltranejazzfest.com/
- Music Maker Foundation: https://musicmaker.org/
- Wizard of Oz Theme Park:
  https://www.landofoznc.com/
- Waynesville-Folkmoot: https://www.folkmoot.org/

Chapter 13

- Carolina Tiger Rescue: https://carolinatigerrescue.org/
- Wild Horses, Currituck NWR:
  https://www.currituck.com/currituck-national-wildlife-refuge.html
- Ocracoke Banker Ponies:
  https://www.visitocracokenc.com/ocracoke-banker-ponies/
- Karen Beasley Sea Turtle Rescue and Rehabilitation
  Center: https://www.seaturtlehospital.org/
- Mattamuskeet NWR:
  https://www.fws.gov/refuge/mattamuskeet

- Great Smoky Mountain National Park: https://www.nps.gov/grsm/planyourvisit/nc-2-do.htm
- Monarch Butterflies in https://www.exploreasheville.com/stories/post/see-monarch-butterfly-migration-asheville
- Fayetteville Dogwood Festival: https://www.thedogwoodfestival.com/fayetteville-dogwood-festival
- Cradle of Forestry: https://gofindoutdoors.org/cradle-of-forestry/
- Azalea Festival: https://ncazaleafestival.org/
- North Carolina Aquariums: https://www.ncaquariums.com/ Discovery Place Science: https://www.discoveryplace.org/
- Mildred, The Mother Bear, Grandfather Mtn. Nature Museum, aka "Wilson Center for Nature Discovery": https://grandfather.com/wilson-center/
- Bear-Ology: https://bear-ology.com/

Chapter 14
- Museum of The Sea: https://www.nps.gov/caha/planyourvisit/visitor-centers.htm
- Chicamacomico Life-Saving Station: https://chicamacomico.org/
- "Beacons of Light" List of Lighthouses:
  - o Bald Head Lighthouse: https://www.oldbaldy.org/
  - o Roanoke River Lighthouse: http://www.roanokeriverlighthouse.com/

- Portsmouth Island:
  https://www.outerbanks.com/portsmouth-island.html
- Ocracoke Working Watermen's Association:
  http://www.ocracokewatermen.org/

Chapter 15
- NC Museum of Art: https://ncartmuseum.org/
- Ayden Collard Festival:
  https://www.aydencollardfestival.com/
- Cheerwine Festival: https://cheerwinefest.com/
- One of a kind Festivals:
  - Spring Hope Pumpkin Festival:
    https://www.visitspringhope.com/national-pumpkin-festival
  - Newport Pig Cooking Contest:
    https://newportpigcooking.com/
  - Banner Elk "Wooly Worm Festival":
    http://www.woollyworm.com/
  - Saluda Coon Dog Day:
    https://www.cityofsaludanc.com/community/calendar/30-fesitvals-and-events/2-coon-dog-day
  - Oriental-Croaker Queen Contest:
    https://croakerfestival.com/pageant/
  - Ocean Isle-North Carolina Oyster Festival:
    https://ncoysterfestival.com/
  - Winston Salem-Texas Pete Spirits of Summer:
    https://spiritsofsummer.com/details/
  - Mt. Olive- North Carolina Pickle Festival:
    https://ncpicklefest.org/
- Rivers Edge Restaurant: https://rivers-edge-restaurant-seafood-restaurant.business.site/

- Tryon Palace: https://www.tryonpalace.org/
- Morehead City NC Seafood Festival: https://www.ncseafoodfestival.org/
- Carolina Renaissance Festival : https://www.carolina.renfestinfo.com/
- Lexington Barbecue Festival: https://www.thebarbecuefestival.com/
- Smithfield Ham and Yam Festival: https://www.johnstoncountync.org/ham-and-yam-festival/
- Ocracoke Fig Festival: https://www.ocracokepreservationsociety.org/basic-01
- Gourd Museum: http://www.ncgourdsociety.org/Gourd_Museum.html
- Highest Swinging Footbridge, Grandfather Mountain: https://grandfather.com/swinging-bridge/
- Largest Unsupported Dome, St. Lawrence Basilica: https://saintlawrencebasilica.org/facilities
- Rockfish Capital, Weldon NC: https://www.historicweldonnc.com/departments/parks-recreation/rockfish-capital-of-the-world-weldon-nc.html
- Largest Open-Face Granite Quarry-Mt. Airy: https://www.nps.gov/places/granite-quarry-ol.htm
- Cultures- Lam Museum of Anthropology: https://lammuseum.wfu.edu/
- Highest Waterfall in The U.S.-Whitewater Falls: https://www.fs.usda.gov/detail/nfsnc/specialplaces/?cid=stelprdb5188436

- Largest Ammunitions Depot-Point Military Ocean Depot https://militarybases.com/north-carolina/motsp/
- Oldest Active Military Reservation-Fort Johnston: https://cityofsouthport.com/community-relations-department/#visitors-center--museum
- Worlds Largest Ten Commandments-Fields of The Wood: https://cogop.org/fow/
- Christmas Tree Capital-https://www.visitnc.com/story/9xnv/choose-cut-and-stay-in-the-christmas-tree-capital#:~:text=North%20Carolina%20Fraser%20firs%20have,of%20America's%20Christmas%20Tree%20Capital.
- First Nat. Military Park at Revolutionary War Site-Guilford County Courthouse National Military Park: https://www.nps.gov/guco/index.htm
- First Planetarium at a University-https://moreheadplanetarium.org/
- Only Rural Doctor Museum-The Country Doctor Museum: https://www.countrydoctormuseum.org/
- Largest Unincorporated U.S. City-City of Kannapolis: https://kannapolisnc.gov/
- Largest US University-related research park: Research Triangle Park: https://www.rtp.org/
- Second-oldest River In The World-New River State Park: https://www.ncparks.gov/state-parks/new-river-state-park
- Worlds Largest Frying Pan-https://www.townofrosehillnc.com/index.asp?SEC=F747AF1E-9E23-449E-B099-

4D7ECF15B278&DE=FB7FEBF0-FB5A-47CB-BA21-7773BE550A81&Type=B_LOC

- Largest Collection of Mugs-The Collettsville Cup House: https://www.atlasobscura.com/places/the-house-of-mugs-collettsville-north-carolina

Chapter 16

- Maplewood Cemetery: https://www.wilsonnc.org/Home/Components/Facility Directory/FacilityDirectory/138/34?npage=2
- Nell Cropsey, https://northcarolinaghosts.com/coast/ghost-nell-cropsey/
- Old Burying Ground in Beaufort, https://beauforthistoricsite.org/old-burying-ground/
- Ocracoke British Cemetery: https://www.nps.gov/places/000/ocracoke-british-cemetery.htm
- The Bodies Above the Tunnel, Great Smoky Mountains Railroad:
- Oakdale Cemetery: https://www.oakdalecemetery.org/
- Joyce Kilmer Memorial Forest: https://www.fs.usda.gov/recarea/nfsnc/recarea/?recid=48920
- Gimghoul Castle: https://historicchapelhill.org/tours/show/1
- Kituhwa https://www.allthingscherokee.com/kituwah-mound/

- St. James Church Wilmington:
  https://www.stjamesp.org/
- Jump Off Rock Visitor Center:
  https://visithendersonvillenc.org/businesses/jump-off-rock

AMAZING NORTH CAROLINA INDEX

N

T. Jensen Lacey

ABOUT THE AUTHOR

An award-winning author, novelist and freelance journalist, Lacey's work has been published for more than 50 years. Her published works thus far include six Native American history books, two young adult novels, a murder mystery, a children's bilingual picture book, four books in he Amazing series and more. She has been a frequent contributor to the New York Times Bestselling anthologies, CHICKEN SOUP FOR THE SOUL. Lacey's website is www.TJensenLacey.com and her email address is TJensenLacey@yahoo.com. Lacey is available for book signings, writers' workshops and speaking engagements.

Made in the USA
Middletown, DE
08 September 2023

37600322R00234